Why Walls Won't Work

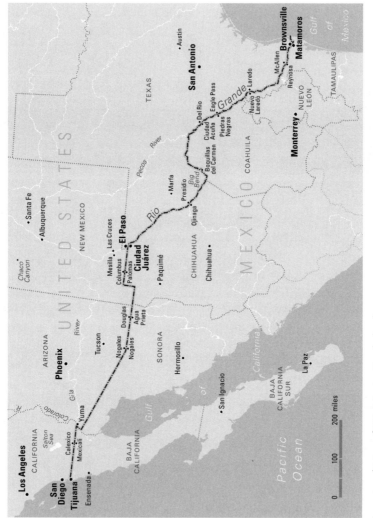

Locational Map of US–Mexico Borderlands
Artwork by Dreamline Cartography.

WHY WALLS WON'T WORK

Repairing the US–Mexico Divide

MICHAEL DEAR

OXFORD
UNIVERSITY PRESS

OXFORD
UNIVERSITY PRESS

Oxford University Press is a department of the University of Oxford.
It furthers the University's objective of excellence in research, scholarship,
and education by publishing worldwide.

Oxford   New York

Auckland   Cape Town   Dar es Salaam   Hong Kong   Karachi
Kuala Lumpur   Madrid   Melbourne   Mexico City   Nairobi
New Delhi   Shanghai   Taipei   Toronto

With offices in

Argentina   Austria   Brazil   Chile   Czech Republic   France   Greece
Guatemala   Hungary   Italy   Japan   Poland   Portugal   Singapore
South Korea   Switzerland   Thailand   Turkey   Ukraine   Vietnam

Oxford is a registered trademark of Oxford University Press in the UK and certain
other countries.

Published in the United States of America by
Oxford University Press
198 Madison Avenue, New York, NY 10016

CIP record is available with the Library of Congress
ISBN 978–0–19–989798–8

9 7 5 3 1 2 4 6 8
Printed in the United States of America
on acid-free paper

Contents

List of Figures

List of Tables

Preface

THE US–MEXICO borderlands are among the most misunderstood places on earth. The communities along the line are far distant from the centers of political power in each nation's capital. They are staunchly independent and composed of many cultures with hybrid loyalties. Historically, the eastern border counties were among the poorest regions in both countries; those in the center were sparsely populated agricultural and mining districts; and in the more affluent west, the upstart Baja California was always more closely connected to the State of California than to Mexico. Nowadays, border states are among the fastest-growing regions in both countries. They are places of teeming contradiction, extremes of wealth and poverty, and vibrant political and cultural change.

There are also enormous tensions along the borderlands, associated with undocumented immigration and drug wars. Neither of these problems originated in the borderlands. Instead, they came from outside, and borderland communities have limited capacity for self-determination in such matters. At the national level, the US and Mexico seek security and peace through the sacrifices of the small subset of their populations that resides in the border region. They are the people who must endure the exogenously-induced trials, often with scant assistance from their national and local governments beyond unpredictable military and police interventions. Border dwellers have made what adjustments they can, along the way demonstrating a remarkable durability and adaptability based in centuries of co-existence.

Mutual interdependence has always been the hallmark of cross-border lives. Over time, a series of binational "twin cities" sprang up along the line, with identities sufficiently distinct to warrant the collective title of a "third nation," snugly slotted in the space between the two host countries. The third nation does not divide Mexico and the US but instead acts as a connective membrane uniting them. This way of looking at the border substitutes

continuity and coexistence in place of concerns with sovereignty and difference. It is a view that runs directly counter to received wisdom in the US,
which regards the border as the last line of national defense against unfettered
immigration and runaway global terrorism.

The current fortifications along the border are without historical precedent, and threaten to suffocate the arteries supplying the third nation's oxygen.
Even after the 1848 Treaty of Guadalupe Hidalgo established the international boundary, the dividing line remained loosely marked, haphazardly
maintained, and casually observed. But in the 1990s, responding to increased
waves of undocumented crossings from Mexico, large fences sprouted on the
border edges of cities such as Tijuana and Ciudad Juárez. Then, following the
attacks of 9/11, the US unilaterally adopted an aggressive program of constructing fortifications along the entire line.

The new walls, fences, and checkpoints rudely interrupted the lives and
livelihoods of third nation dwellers. On the US side, the border became a
fortress containing an archipelago of law enforcement and justice agencies dedicated to apprehension, detention, prosecution and deportation of
undocumented migrants, all bolstered by a new industry of corporate security interests. On the Mexican side, tranquility was usurped from a different
source—the federal government's war against drug cartels. As the numbers
of dead catapulted into the tens of thousands, cartel power was consolidated
and Mexico seemingly drifted toward becoming a "failed state," incapable of
maintaining order or fulfilling its other obligations.

ON DECEMBER 17, 2002, I began traveling the entire length of the
US–Mexico border, on both sides, from Tijuana/San Diego on the Pacific
Ocean to Matamoros/Brownsville on the Gulf of Mexico, a journey of 4,000
miles. Assisted by a grant from the National Geographic Society, I voyaged in
the footsteps of giants: sixteenth-century Spanish explorers Cabeza de Vaca
and Francisco Vásquez de Coronado came this way; Generals Santa Anna and
Zachary Taylor fought important battles for these lands during the Mexican-
American War; and after the 1848 Treaty of Guadalupe Hidalgo ended the
War, William H. Emory and Jose Salazar Ylaguerri undertook the heroic surveys which marked the boundary between Mexico and the United States.

What began as an impulsive journey of discovery was rapidly overtaken
by events. I had the good (and bad) fortune to begin before the US undertook the fortification of its southern boundary, so I became an unintentional
witness to the border's closure, an experience that altered my understanding
of both countries. My border-long, binational exploration was completed on

March 16, 2005, but since then I have continued my visits, right up to the present, adding thousands more miles to my borderland travel log.

The borderlands have enormous significance as the place where immigration tensions and drug wars are enacted. Important as these are, I do not spend much time in this book addressing the nuances of US immigration policy, nor assembling yet another lurid account of Mexico's cartel-induced violence. As my travels unfolded, I became more focused on the well-being of the third nation and the lessons it was teaching; these insights are the focus of this book.

My story begins by outlining the origin and rise of the third nation from earliest times (chapters 1–6), then assesses how the US borderland fortifications and Mexican drug wars have impacted the third nation (chapters 7–9), and in the final chapter, explains precisely why walls won't work.

My experiences provide a powerful rejoinder to those who would abandon the Mexican border to the drug cartels, or those in the US who would use the borderlands as a surrogate battlefield against migrants. Despite these interruptions, the third nation endures. It reveals new ways of thinking about the joint future of the *Estados Unidos Mexicanos* and the United States of America.

Berkeley and Los Angeles, California, USA
Mexicali, Baja California, México

I

Monuments, Mexico, and Manifest Destiny

ON FEBRUARY 2, 1848, a "Treaty of Peace, Friendship, Limits and Settlement" was signed at Guadalupe Hidalgo, thus terminating the Mexican-American War that had commenced in 1846.[1] The war was ostensibly about securing the boundary of the recently annexed state of Texas, but it was clear from the outset that the US goal was territorial expansion.[2] Some decades earlier, the US had secured the Louisiana Purchase, and President Polk next saw it as America's "Manifest Destiny"—a term invented by John L. O'Sullivan—to capture the nation's desire to "overspread the continent allotted by Providence."[3] More prosaically, this meant the acquisition of lands all the way to the Pacific Ocean, incorporating what was then Nuevo México and the Californias (which included parts of the states of California, Nevada, Utah, and Colorado). In defeat, Mexico was ultimately obliged to cede Alta California, Nuevo México, and northern portions of the states of Sonora, Coahuila, and Tamaulipas. It is often said that hardly a day goes by without Mexico remembering this loss of territory, while those north of the border never think of their gain.

The Treaty of Guadalupe Hidalgo, as it came to be called, was the outcome of a protracted series of negotiations.[4] On the US side, Nicholas Trist proved to be an able and sympathetic negotiator, who courageously ignored a recall notice from an irate President Polk (who thought Trist was conceding too much) in order to complete negotiations and sign the Treaty. On the Mexican side, interim President Peña y Peña prevailed on Trist to stay on the job despite Polk's wrath; he also brought together warring factions at home to compromise with the US. Presented with a signed Treaty, an outraged Polk feared the political consequences of repudiating it, and the Treaty was eventually proclaimed on July 4, 1848. Mexico had gained peace and $15 million, but eventually lost one-half of its territory; and the US achieved the most important land grab in its history through a war that many (including

Ulysses S. Grant)[5] regarded as dishonorable. The dedicated Nicholas Trist returned to Washington, DC, only to be cruelly ignored by President Polk.[6]

The Treaty required the designation of a "boundary line with due precision, upon authoritative maps, and to establish upon the ground landmarks which shall show the limits of both republics."[7] The line would extend from the mouth of the deepest channel of the Rio Grande (known in Mexico as the Río Bravo del Norte); upriver to "the town called Paso" (present-day Ciudad Juárez); from thence overland to the Gila River, and down the channel of the Colorado River; after which it would follow the division between Upper (Alta) California and Lower (Baja) California to the Pacific Ocean.[8] (This division was established in the eighteenth century when the Spanish split the task of conversion into separate Franciscan and Dominican territories.)

The surveys took six years to complete, beginning in 1849 and ending in 1855. In a widely-respected, multivolume history of the American West, historian Carl Wheat refers disparagingly to the boundary survey as the stuff that "dime novels" are made of.[9] To justify this characterization, he invokes yarns about political intrigue, deaths from starvation and yellow fever, struggles for survival in the desert, and the constant threat of violent attacks by Indians and filibusters. He also complained that the US field surveys seem to have been plagued by acrimony and personal vendetta: "if ever a mapping enterprise in the American West was cursed by politics, interdepartmental rivalries, and personal jealousies, it was the Mexican Boundary Survey."[10] Certainly it's true that the letters, diaries, and official memoranda by individuals on the US team portray just about every American participant as a scoundrel or a self-promoter.[11] Yet to me the boundary survey is a story of heroism, skill, and endurance of epic proportions. It might lack the glamour of war, or the grandeur of Lewis and Clark's opening of the lands west of the Mississippi in the early 1800s, but the survey is one of the greatest episodes in US and Mexican political history. It remains deeply etched in the everyday lives of both nations. Dime novel it most certainly is not; it is more a narrative of nation-building centered in US President Polk's vision of grasping territory as far as the Pacific Ocean, with all its momentous consequences.[12]

The First Boundary Survey, 1849–1857

The postwar boundary survey commenced close to the Pacific Ocean on the low bluffs just north of Playas de Tijuana. In April 1852, US Boundary Commissioner John Russell Bartlett, who had spent most of his time on an extended tour of the American and Mexican West, happened across this monument. In his classic travelogue entitled *Personal Narrative of Explorations and Incidents in Texas, New Mexico, California, Sonora and Chihuahua, 1850–1853*, Bartlett described the majestic marker as: "an obelisk about twenty feet in height… seen from a great distance on land as well as by vessels at sea."[13]

Bartlett was a successful bookstore owner in New York City who seized the opportunity to become Boundary Commissioner as his ticket to adventure. He remains famous as author of *Bartlett's Familiar Quotations* as well as his *Narrative*, but also for shirking his obligations as Boundary Commissioner. Many on the survey teams thought Bartlett was only interested in writing a book, not advancing the survey. Of course, Bartlett had his defenders: had he not, for instance, rescued a local girl named Iñez Gonzales from Apaches and returned her tearfully to her parents? Was he not an honest gentleman and scholar? Did he not confront great dangers, and suffer through a bout of typhoid?[14] Well, yes, but he was also an inattentive commissioner who drove his anxious survey team wild with frustration.

The really hard work on the border survey was done by the man who would eventually succeed him as commissioner, William H. Emory, who had developed an intense animosity toward Bartlett,[15] and by Emory's Mexican counterpart, José Salazar Ylarregui. Very early in my travels in their footsteps, I came to regard Emory and Salazar as heroes. William Hemsley Emory was a seasoned surveyor and military man known as "Bold Emory" to his contemporaries. His Mexican counterpart, Commissioner José Salazar Ylarregui (described as "a charming person, active, intelligent and polite")[16] was an accomplished civil servant. Together they labored for many years to complete the boundary survey, enduring perils, physical hardships, and the trials imposed by their political masters (see Figure 1.1).

Salazar was appointed to the Mexican Commission when he was only 25 years old.[17] He had a prominent career in public affairs, including a position as Minister of Development in the administration of Emperor Maximilian (which much later led to his trial for treason and near-execution). Salazar had a patriotic dedication that led him to borrow money on his personal credit to keep the Mexican survey going, but such dedication seemed rarely to impress his superiors. After complaining on a couple of occasions about the lack of official support for the Mexican survey, Salazar was imprisoned for a month in Chihuahua by President Santa Anna on account of a disrespectful communication.[18]

Emory was already famous as an explorer before he joined the boundary survey. He had just completed (in 1846) a reconnaissance of the lands between Fort Leavenworth, Missouri, and San Diego, California, with the

FIGURE I.I   John Russell Bartlett. Fording a Stream, Packmules Sink in Quicksand, 1849(?)

From the sketchbook of Boundary Commissioner Bartlett. Courtesy of the John Carter Brown Library at Brown University

famous scout Kit Carson as one of his guides.[19] Emory was a dedicated professional but he also enjoyed his work, especially savoring California wines at the end of his travails (noting with admiration that "Many bottles were drunk leaving no headache or acidity on the stomach").[20] He also observed that Californians were excellent horsemen and enjoyed an unusual diet: "The fresh meat of a bullock is all that is required by the Californian for breakfast, dinner and supper." Bread, tea, and coffee they rarely used, he wrote, but their "white teeth" and the "blood tingling" in their cheeks suggested that they enjoyed a "very healthy diet." The military man in Emory also noted that the "advantages in the movement of troops with this kind of subsistence is very great, enabling them to move without wagons, and with no other care for the morrow than herding the animals intended for food."[21]

Emory was the perfect candidate for the job as boundary survey commissioner, but politics kept him out of a leadership role until people finally gave up on Commissioner Bartlett. A graduate of the US Military Academy at West Point, Emory later married the great-granddaughter of Benjamin Franklin, Matilda Watkins Bache. His three-volume account of the border survey, entitled *Report on the United States and Mexican Boundary Survey*, is today widely regarded as a masterwork of Western and American history.[22] Sadly, by comparison, Salazar's memoir provides only the briefest sketches of the Mexican surveyors' experience of the California section of the survey.[23]

In the field, relationships between the US and Mexican survey teams were reportedly harmonious. At the close of the survey, Commissioner Emory observed that: "the utmost harmony has existed on this Commission between the Officers of both governments, and that all questions likely to produce the least difference have been settled harmoniously."[24] Salazar's memoir recounted Emory's unfailing courtesy, how he communicated through a smile that said: "I am American, but without being treasonous I can, as brother of all men, love Mexicans and love the beautiful Mexican Republic."[25]

Such harmony was hard-won. Many difficulties hindered progress. Most problematic was the Treaty's specification that the land boundary from the Rio Grande was to strike west at a point eight miles north of Paso. Except that the Disturnell map (appended to the Treaty) showed Paso at a point 42 miles north of its true position. Disputes over the precise location for the land boundary after it parted from the river were not resolved until the Treaty of 1853, known as the Gadsden Purchase in the US and as the Treaty of Mesilla in Mexico. This agreement exchanged US cash for yet more Mexican land, providing the US with a much-coveted access for a rail link to the Pacific coast.[26]

The Mexican survey teams had their own trials. The Commission was anxious to prevent further loss of territory and was understandably suspicious of US motives, so the Mexicans had manufactured in London and Paris the most sophisticated instruments to undertake their surveys. These instruments had been certified as state-of-the-art. Unfortunately, they never arrived in Mexico City. The Commission discovered that someone had substituted inferior instruments, apparently before shipment. So the Mexican surveys were conducted using traditional instrumentation, accurate but much slower.[27]

THE ORIGINAL BOUNDARY survey maps prepared by the Mexican survey team are held in Mexico City at the Mapoteca Manuel Orozco y Berra, a slightly down-at-the-heels building with a colonial air that calls to mind some aging European museums. The Mapoteca was named after a famous Mexican scholar of the nineteenth century, Manuel Orozco y Berra, who was Director of the National Archives and a professor of geography and history. The survey maps do not disappoint. They are in excellent condition; the paper is clear and creamy and smells old, but it's a good old. The cartography and draftsmanship are superb. The maps are, in short, works of art, masterpieces of the pen as well as historical documents of the utmost significance (see Figure 1.2). They were executed by individual artists who stamped their own personalities into the cartographic representations. Mountains are inked as dramatic black clouds prohibiting passage. The deserts around present-day Mexicali are portrayed as a narrow strip of sand where the New River occasionally trickled; nothing else is noted except the boundary markers, because the surveyors saw nothing worth recording. On the Tijuana map, the arc of the coastal mountains and estuary is interrupted by a solitary name: "Rancho de la Tía Juana." These solitudes contrasted greatly with the map of Paso (present-day Ciudad Juárez), which explodes into a forensic detail portraying farmlands, properties, and roadways along the Rio Grande/Bravo.

The equivalent maps prepared by the US survey teams are deposited in the National Archives in Maryland (NARA). They are not identical to the Mexican maps.[28] Apart from the obvious linguistic differences, the two sets were drawn by different artists, plus some of the US maps have charming marginal sketches showing local scenes that the Mexican maps lack. What shocked me about the US maps was their state of disrepair. All but one map I saw had been painted over with some kind of varnish that was probably intended to preserve the object. By now, however, the varnish had itself become faded and cloudy, sometimes rendering the details almost illegible. It had also acquired a brittle quality that made me fearful of cracking the paper. I still worry about the deteriorating condition of the survey maps in the US archives. They are among the most important maps in our nation's history, and warrant proper care.

THE BOUNDARY SURVEY officially began on July 6, 1849, just south of San Diego. For the next six years, US and Mexican survey teams crisscrossed the borderlands, meeting regularly to check each others' work. The survey was undertaken in three sections, which were not done in orderly sequence but instead varied in location according to the exigencies of physical hardship, uncertain supplies, and political winds in the national capitals.[29]

Between 1849 and 1851, the California survey was the first to be completed, from San Diego to the Colorado River.[30] Attention was understandably lavished on fixing the initial points (*puntos iniciales*) of the boundary line. Emory and Salazar were charged with determining the very first *punto inicial* one marine league south of the port of San Diego, another at the

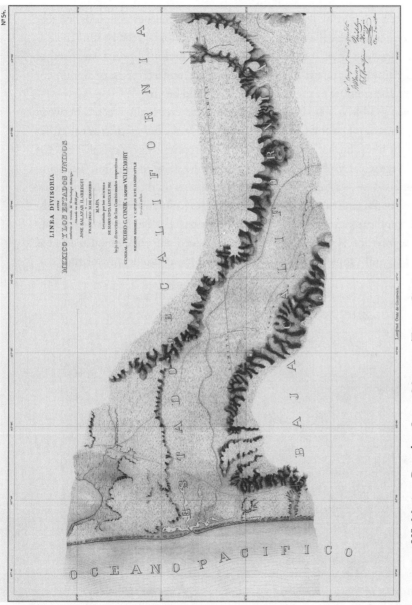

FIGURE 1.2 US–Mexican Boundary Survey Map, 1853, Tijuana Section.

LÍNEA DIVISORIA ENTRE MEXICO Y LOS ESTADOS UNIDOS, Colección Límites México–EEUU, Carpeta No. 4, Lámina No. 54; Autor: Salazar Ilárregui, José, Año 1853. Mapoteca 'Manuel Orozco y Berra', Servicio de Información Estadística Agroalimentaria y Pesquera, SARGAPA. Reproduced with permission. Digital restoration by Tyson Gaskill.

confluence of the Gila and Colorado Rivers, and then to connect and mark these points with a straight line. (Two more initial points for the survey were scheduled for El Paso and the mouth or *desembocadura* of the Rio Grande/ Bravo.) Disagreements arose immediately, since there was no standard measurement for a marine league. However, with a generous concordance that marked their entire collaboration, Salazar and Emory agreed to split the difference between their surveys. A location for the initial point was fixed at the shoreline near present-day Playas de Tijuana, and a temporary monument erected. The running of the California line could begin.[31]

Seven marble or cast-iron monuments were eventually erected between the Pacific coast and the Colorado River: two at the *puntos iniciales* at either end of the line; another at the New River (near present-day Mexicali); and the remaining two at visible points along the intervening mountains. The commissioners were satisfied that seven monuments would be sufficient because so much of the land between the Pacific and the Colorado was, in their words, "barren and can never be cultivated by either party."[32] But because such long expanses on the California line were left unmarked, the surveyors also decided to add several supplementary monuments of loose stones west of the New

FIGURE 1.3 Ancient boundary monument No. XVI was a simple pile of stones (early 1850s?).

Jacobo Blanco. Memoria de la Sección Mexicana de la Comisión Internacional de Límites entre México y los Estados Unidos que Restableció los Monumentos de El Paso al Pácifico. 1901.

River (see Figure 1.3). Today in these formerly barren regions you gaze out over the enormous agricultural empires of the Imperial and Mexicali Valleys, and the bustling state capital of Mexicali.

The survey work was difficult. One team leader, Captain Edmund Hardcastle, constantly complained to Emory about the weight of the principal monuments, saying in one letter:

> What a great mistake it was to have a marble monument of such dimensions—one piece alone weighs 5 tons and is so unwieldy that it will be difficult to get here and more difficult afterwards to put in position.[33]

The physical hardships of the survey were compounded by personality conflicts and ill-tempers. A memoir by Lieutenant Cave Johnson Couts, whose company of dragoons escorted the California boundary survey, is replete with snide comments about the survey team. Couts called its members "Washington dandies with white kid gloves." Impatient in the face of irresponsible behavior, Couts himself was a ramrod-straight, hard-driving, gregarious West Pointer. Yet he also revealed an ordinary humanity tucked beneath his military hide. Early in his memoir, as he departed Monterrey, Couts called to see a "particular friend and old flame," a Mrs. Susie Ann. He wrote: "In truth it was right hard to tear myself away from her, for... I never knew how much I loved her until after she was married."[34]

The second phase of the survey focused on the river boundary and proved to be more difficult because of the fractured terrain.[35] In 1851, the Rio Grande surveyors began trekking downstream from Paso del Norte, but they were halted by the mountains of Big Bend. This is a chaotic region of rocks, rapids, and canyons. Locals will tell you that it's where God reputedly dumped the leftovers when the task of making the world was completed. After this temporary halt, the river survey began again in 1853, but this time it proceeded upstream from the Gulf of Mexico, and was successfully completed later that same year. The eastern-most limit of the line, where the Rio Grande empties into the Gulf of Mexico, posed special problems for the survey teams. This was because the multiple shifting channels of the river made it difficult to follow the Treaty's specification that the boundary was defined by the deepest channel of the river. Moreover, unstable dunes on either side of the *desembocadura* at the Gulf of Mexico made it impossible for surveyors to identify stable sites for the marble monuments planned for either side of the river. Eventually, two high dunes at the same astronomical meridian were selected. The Mexican survey map of the *desembocadura* records both monuments, but, strangely, the US map shows neither. Today, at the mouth of the Río Bravo there are no visible monuments on either side of the river.

The third and final section of the survey was undertaken in 1855, between Paso and the Colorado River.[36] This was relatively swiftly completed once the initial point above Paso was settled following the Gadsden/Mesilla Treaty of 1853. This late in the game, the US Commission was a practiced, well-equipped unit under Emory's leadership, but the *Comisión de Límites Mexicana* remained chronically underfunded. (In a gesture of goodwill, "Bold" Emory had discreetly secured funding from the US in support of Salazar's team.)[37] Heading west, Emory's team often erected stone mounds as monuments, supplementing these with careful topographical sketches of the surrounding countryside. Despite Emory's objections, Salazar insisted on conducting his own survey west from Paso and discovered that many monuments that the US claimed to have established were missing. Salazar replaced the lost monuments and reconstructed several unsubstantial US monuments.[38] The last hurdle facing the survey teams as they headed west were the deserts of Arizona and Sonora. Potable water was scarce and the going was rough. First, a team worked east from the Colorado River but gave up when water ran out; so another team struck out westward from Paso to meet the line already marked in California.

Emory's *Report* on the monumental survey was published in 1857.[39] Even though much of it is a dry account of surveys, astronomical observations, and correspondence, it remains a thrilling narrative of the life and times of the nascent borderlands. There are scenes of indigenous peoples and costumes, of frontier towns and forts, as well as copious topographical drawings. Its three volumes also contain scientific studies devoted to cacti, plants, fish, mammals, birds, and reptiles.[40] Emory's *Report* takes some of the shine off his image, revealing a somewhat peevish, occasionally self-centered man, with a decidedly jingoistic view of the world. He was, for example, vocal about his suspicions concerning Indians, whom he referred to as "warlike savages who have devastated Sonora and Chihuahua," noting an expectation that they will remove many of the monuments. His narrative also gives credence to critics who accuse Emory of failing to credit the survey work of his Mexican counterparts, as in: "I looked for little or no aid from the Mexican commission, for although composed of well-educated and scientific men, their instruments were radically defective."[41] He goes on to explain how the US team did the hard work that was later received by the Mexicans "without correction." However, documents recently made available from Mexican archives demonstrate just how important were the original contributions of the Mexican surveyors.[42]

The Second Boundary Survey, 1892–1894

As the borderlands' population grew during the second half of the nineteenth century, disputes over the exact location of the boundary line became more frequent. The frontier region was lawless and in disarray. Many boundary monuments were missing or in a state of disrepair. After years of foot-dragging, a joint boundary commission was officially established in 1891 to undertake the resurvey task, led by Commissioners John Whitney Barlow and Jacobo Blanco, who met to begin work at El Paso in February 1892. Their instructions were to resurvey the line, locate and rebuild the old monuments, and install additional markers as necessary.[43]

The resurvey teams encountered predictable difficulties. Many of the original monuments were difficult to find, especially in mountainous terrain. Errors in the first survey meant that some monuments were incorrectly positioned. In total, these errors would have resulted in a net gain of territory to Mexico of over 300 square miles. But such mistakes were either quietly adjusted or left unchallenged so as to avoid the need for negotiating new treaties.[44] Further problems were the result of human interference: some monuments and stone mounds had been destroyed by Indians; others were dismantled for use as building materials, or as an expression of antipathy toward the US. Also to blame were ranchers and miners who destroyed or moved markers in order to gain control over nearby land, water, and mineral resources.[45]

More generally, many original monuments had simply been overtaken by the encroachment of human settlements. In Nogales, Arizona, for instance, an enterprising saloon proprietor had built his establishment around a post-1848 boundary marker that was by now little more than a jumble of stones propped up against the saloon wall.[46] (With one door opening to Mexico and another to the US, the saloon was much favored by itinerant smugglers.) Fearful for the integrity of the line, Commissioner Barlow recommended that a 60-foot easement be established along the entire land boundary to prevent further encroachment upon the line. President William McKinley later authorized a two-mile long, 60-foot-wide reserve along the Nogales boundary, and all US structures within that limit were removed.[47]

The second survey team faced nothing like the hardships of the first. Barlow and Blanco had the original survey maps and existing monuments as guides; they possessed superior instrumentation; and they enjoyed the convenience of telegraphic communication and the Southern Pacific railway, which ran just north of the border.[48] In addition, they were concerned only with the land boundary, which was less than half the length of the border. So in relatively quick time, by June 1894, the work of the resurvey commissions was completed and their final reports published in 1898.[49]

Barlow and Blanco increased the number of boundary monuments from 52 to 258. The new monuments are instantly recognizable: iron columns, six feet high, twelve inches square at the base, pyramidal in shape at the top, and set in concrete. They were acquired in El Paso at a cost of $150 apiece.[50] On either side, plaques in English and Spanish read: "Boundary of the United States [or Mexico], treaty of 1853, re-established by the treaties of 1882–1889." The original boundary monument number 1 at the Pacific Ocean was renumbered as 258, since the surveyors had worked west from El Paso. The original marble monument at the Pacific was defaced and damaged, so it was sent to San Diego for polishing and reengraving, and later reinstalled within iron fencing to prevent further vandalism (see Figure 1.4).[51]

The 18 maps produced by the resurvey commission are precise and workmanlike renderings of the land boundary. There is nothing of the artistry and panache of the scribes employed by Emory and Salazar, but fortunately the

FIGURE 1.4 Monument No. 258, 1851.

This was the first point (*punto inicial*) established by the boundary survey following the 1848 Treaty of Guadalupe Hidalgo. The photograph was taken during the last decade of the nineteenth century after the original marble monument had been renovated, and fenced to prevent further vandalism. Jacobo Blanco. Vistas de los Monumentos a lo Largo de la Línea Divisoria entre México y los Estados Unidos de El Paso al Pacífico.

maps are supplemented by a cornucopia of images contained in two volumes issued by the Mexican commission in 1910. The *Vistas* has photographs of all 258 monuments, and the *Memoria* has additional scenes and descriptions of land and life along the border as well as the survey work itself, both adding soul to the science of the maps. In one photograph, two workers have just dragged a new monument up a vertical mountain slope and planted it; together, they proudly display their handiwork, perhaps hoping to prolong the moment of respite before they would have to start hauling the next monument up the next damnable mountainside (see Figure 1.5). In another, there is evident pride in the faces of a relaxed but formally posed Mexican survey team alongside their tent outside Tijuana, in a kind of "Still Life with Tent and Instruments."

After the 1892–1894 resurvey, additions to the monument inventory were few. Around the turn of the century, 18 more were erected to "more perfectly mark" the line in congested towns, on new rail bridges, or to repair damage. For instance, in 1906 the International Boundary Commission (IBC) noted that the only visible indication of the border between the twin towns of Naco (in Arizona and the Mexican state of Sonora) was "a railroad spike driven into its head in the ground."[52] The Commission recommended that

FIGURE 1.5 Monument No. 185, c. 1895?

The monuments erected during the second boundary survey at the end of the nineteenth century were made from iron. Jacobo Blanco. Vistas de los Monumentos a lo Largo de la Línea Divisoria entre México y los Estados Unidos de El Paso al Pacífico.

three additional monuments be erected and a 60-foot setback of all building from the boundary line be instituted, since "much of the trouble between the citizens of the two countries last Spring would have been avoided had there been no buildings, canals or freight cars near the boundary to serve as places of concealment during the rioting and shooting."[53]

In another location, the IBC undertook the restoration of monument 221 and the erection of new monument 220-A to clarify the separation between the towns of Calexico and Mexicali. The restoration was necessary because of damage occasioned by the famous human-induced flood of 1905 when the Colorado River burst its banks at Yuma and flowed north for two years. The subsequent flooding created the Salton Sea, but also destroyed much of the town of Mexicali.[54] Finally, the Commission authorized monuments on new bridges under construction across the Rio Grande, including Brownsville–Matamoros (1910) and Laredo–Nuevo Laredo (1912). The markers were usually placed on the bridge at the center of the normal channel of the river, although by now many of them are off-center because the river channel has migrated.[55]

With the completion of 276 monuments, the IBC's official monumentation program was ended. Both countries agreed that any further delimitation would consist of smaller "markers" (*monojeras*) of concrete. By 1975, another 442 markers had been added, principally in and around the sprawling border towns; another 51 were added in 1984.

Fencing the Borderline after 1990

When I first saw the original boundary monument—a marble obelisk that still stands on a coastal bluff near Playas de Tijuana—the monument's cool whiteness was offset by adjacent rusty brown metal plates that comprised the fence at that time. The plates had originally been manufactured to construct temporary landing strips for aircraft during the war in Vietnam; they were of uniform size and could be quickly bolted together to allow for safe landing on inhospitable terrain. In the early 1990s, the border crossings in major border cities began to be fenced off, and someone had the bright idea that the Vietnam leftovers could be recycled as an international boundary by turning the panels upright on their edges and clipping them together to construct a fence. The corroded plates are ugly and crumbling, about ten feet high, and corrugated; anyone could easily get fingers and toes into their grooves and hoist themselves up and over the fence. It was common in the mid-1990s to see groups of people perched comfortably atop the fence, chatting while they waited for the right moment to cross.[56]

Outside the cities at this time, the boundary line remained a nondescript affair if it existed at all. Sometimes it consisted of low fences that resembled freeway traffic-lane separators, or a few strands of barbed wire fence occasionally bent wide to accommodate a passing human form. No obstacles prevented people from crossing freely to shop, attend school, or join in the weekend softball game on the other side.

Now all this has changed. Mexico has been walled off from the US.

In 2008, I returned to the borderline at Algodones Dunes not far from Yuma, where I had begun tracing the steps of Salazar and Emory six years earlier. The place was almost unrecognizable. In former days, you could walk out over the dunes unimpeded and cross the border at will (as many off-roaders, cyclists, and hikers were wont to do). There was scarcely a border patrol officer in sight. Nowadays, scores of mobile towers ceaselessly scan the horizon for perceived evildoers. It is against the law to approach within 100 feet of the fence in this place, and an afternoon hike can bring noisy swarms of dune buggy-riding Border Patrol officers rudely intent on ensuring observance of the law. Most of all, there is an enormous new fence, the so-called "floating fence," which snakes its way over the unstable, wind-whipped dunes. It stands out black against the blistering white sands, simultaneously threatening and beautiful. And, following the elementary physics of wind-blown sand, once the sand-saturated breezes strike the fence they lose energy and deposit the sand at the base of the fence, beginning the process of burying it. Similarly, tides and chemistry have battered and corroded all efforts to build a fence out into the Pacific Ocean in order to block the beach that is exposed at low tide.[57]

Much of the new "real estate" devoted to securing the border is attributable to the US War on Terror launched after 9/11. Since then, 700 miles of new fencing have been constructed along the land boundary at a cost of over $2 billion. The new fortifications are no longer confined to cities, but extend into suburbs and deserts throughout California, Arizona, and New Mexico, as well as parts of the Texas river boundary. A century or more after Salazar and Emory, and Barlow and Blanco, the US has walled off our neighbors to the south. Even my beloved monuments, now encased in steel or caged behind fences, are inaccessible and hidden from view on the US side.

Maps without Borders

CONTINUITY AND CONNECTION IN EARLY TIMES

THERE IS SOMETHING liberating about contemplating maps without borders. Our perceptions are freed from edges, political boundaries, and nationalistic taint; instead they become sensitized to a more universal human connectivity, and natural features recalibrate our internal compass to alternative geographies. For instance, on a map without borders the human presence in the Sonoran Desert flows organically from the Gila River in the north, through the Santa Cruz River Valley, and on to the Sonora River valley in the south. The settlements of Tucson, San Xavier del Bac, Tubac, San Ignacio, and Pitic form a natural progression of human occupation in a landscape dictated by the patterns of river, plain and mountain. But now superimpose the international boundary over the terrain. Tucson and its neighbors are transformed into distinctly "American" and "Mexican" places, the boundary line manufacturing divisions where none previously existed and altering the way we see places.

In beginning my exploration of the borderlands, I turned automatically to the 1848 Treaty of Guadalupe Hidalgo as the moment of creation. This turned out to be an elementary mistake—starting my account precisely at the moment of separation on the continent's map. Fortunately, through excursions into preborder eras, researching as far back as prehistoric times, I uncovered many moments of connection and continuity that were characteristic of borderlands' history before it became an international boundary line. Hence, my narrative begins by imagining a continent without borders.

First Immigrants

Our predecessors on this continent crossed the Bering Sea from Asia.[1] They followed rivers and traversed mountain tops in search of food and shelter.

They fought and slew Ice Age mammoths. And their descendants gave us some of the earliest and most spectacular urban civilizations the world has ever seen.[2]

Tradition has it that the earliest Americans were the Clovis people, who arrived in North America from Asia some 13,000 years ago, taking advantage of a narrow land corridor that had opened up between the two continents after the last Ice Age.[3] Some archeologists push back that arrival date to 16,000 years, believing that migrants skirted the ice barriers in boats. It did not take long for the new arrivals to fan out across North America seeking animals that provided their primary food source. Only later did they become more sedentary, creating (for example) large networks of mounds that extended from New York State to Nebraska, and from the Great Lakes to the Gulf of Mexico. The greatest concentrations of mounds were found in Ohio, Illinois, Indiana, and Missouri.[4] Ten thousand mounds existed in the Ohio River valley alone. Near St. Louis, close to the Mississippi River, a large settlement known as Cahokia had a population of about 5,000 people in 1150 A.D. It was home to Monk's Mound, which rose 100 feet above its surroundings; at 16 acres, it was the largest single earthwork built by prehistoric people in North America. The mounds had many purposes: some were built for burials, others for defensive or religious reasons. The cultural influence of the mound-builders of Cahokia spread widely but did not endure beyond the twelfth century. By the time Columbus arrived, large empires existed only to the south, in Mexico.

In Central America, the arrival date of the earliest humans is equally fuzzy.[5] Over 12,000 years ago, our forebears were drawn to the Lago de Texcoco, which covered much of the Valle de Mexico, where today's Mexico City is located. The largest ancient settlement in the Valle was Cuicuilco, which housed about 20,000 people during the period 600 to 200 B.C. before being buried by the eruption of the Xitle volcano.[6] However, all these developments were mere preludes to the emergence of Mesoamerican civilization, one of a small number of urban heartlands where the idea of towns and cities took hold and then spread around the globe. (The others included Mesopotamia, in the flood plains of the Euphrates and Tigris Rivers; China, in the valleys and alluvial fans of the Huang River; Egypt, along the Nile; and Pakistan, on the Indus River.)

Mesoamerica

The mere mention of Mexican prehistory conjures instant images of the fabulous cities of Mesoamerica.[7] They extended through most of present-day central, southern, and southwestern Mexico and the Yucatan, as well as Guatemala, Belize, and the western part of Honduras and El Salvador. Mesoamerica was home to the Olmec, Maya, Toltec and Aztec, (see Figure 2.1).[8] Today, pilgrims to the National Museum of Anthropology and History in Mexico City gaze in awe at their spectacular legacies. Yet for me, a small museum at Xalapa in the state of Veracruz provides a clearer sense of the great arc of millennial time in the region. There, in the Museo de Antropología, a long corridor with galleries on either side mimics a walk through time, each room displaying objects from various periods—from the earliest sculptural heads of the Olmecs to the pre-Spanish Aztecs. The massive Olmec heads have facial features that suggest African origins for the people.[9] The town of Xalapa is on the route from Veracruz to Mexico City that Cortés followed during his conquest of Mexico; centuries later, US General Taylor also passed this way to engage the climactic battle of the US–Mexico war in 1847. The Spanish changed the spelling of the city's name to Jalapa from the more ancient form of Xalapa, a linguistic variation intended to convey the changes in authority and tradition that followed the conquest. Even today, the way you spell the name, using an X or a J, is taken as an indication of your allegiances.

The chronological sequence of Mesoamerican history reveals an increasing sophistication in society and urban life. First were the Olmecs, who constructed an impressive urban culture between 2500 and 400 B.C. on the Gulf of Mexico near present-day Veracruz.[10] Next to rise in prominence were the Maya, who occupied the Yucatan and parts of today's Guatemala around 1800 B.C. to 925 A.D.[11] These two groups were subsequently overtaken by the aggressively militaristic states of the Toltecs (1000 B.C.E.–1200 A.D.), and the Aztecs[12] (from about 1200 A.D. until the Spanish arrival). Our knowledge of these distant times is hampered because the Spanish invaders systematically destroyed the architectural evidence and written codices that recorded Mesoamerica's history. Only recently have archeologists learned how to decipher the glyphs, or writing, on the historical fragments that escaped erasure. The history that is unfolding tells of advanced civilizations, unprecedented grandeur, warring communities, great cruelty, and the stunning calamities of the Spanish conquest.[13]

The cities of Mesoamerica extended throughout the Yucatan and central/southern Mexico into Central America.[14] The settlements were usually organized around a core of significant religious, political, and ceremonial structures, including the famous pyramids. Ordinary people lived in informal clusters around this core. A good deal of thought went into planning the formal buildings and their arrangement. In Guatemala's Tikal, for example, a long

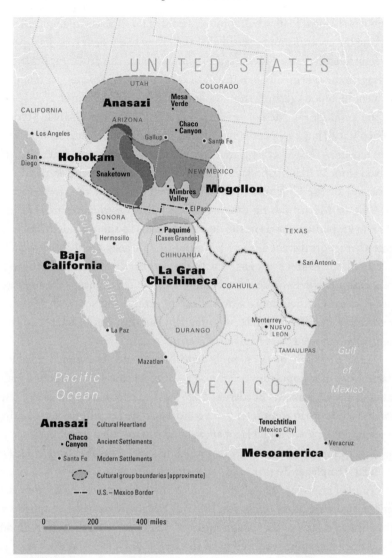

FIGURE 2.1 Major Cultural Traditions in Prehistoric US Southwest and Mexico. Artwork by Dreamline Cartography.

central avenue was covered with crushed limestone that gave the causeway a blinding, even unearthly glare in the tropical sunlight—a deliberate strategy intended to convey to ordinary mortals that they did not belong in this place. The beautiful architecture of the Toltec–Mayan Chichen Itza, not far from Mérida in the Yucatan Peninsula, contains a central plaza with many pyramidal structures. Adjacent features include a deep *cenote* (well), and one of the best surviving examples of a Mesoamerican ball court.[15] The game involved two teams who labored to hit a ball through a kind of hoop placed high on the wall flanking the court. Rumors persist that the losing team, or at least its captain, was slain after the game ended. As if to commemorate this gruesome practice, a carving on the side of Chichen Itza's ball court portrays serpents (representing spirits or lifeblood) gushing from the severed head of a ball player.

The pinnacle of Mesoamerican civilization was Tenochtitlan (today's Mexico City), built by people who called themselves the Mexica, who were later renamed the Aztecs by modern historians. The term Aztec is itself derived from "Aztlán" (or, Place of the White Heron), which was the desert homeland of the Chichimec tribes who migrated from the northwest to the Valle de Mexico during the early 1100s.[16] Exactly where Aztlán was, no one knows: perhaps it was in the near north close to the Valle de Mexico, or somewhere more distant in the US Southwest, or it may simply be a mythical ancestral homeland.[17] But by 1200 A.D. the peripatetic Mexica had arrived in the vicinity of the Lago de Texcoco and over the next century they systematically extended their control over much of central and southern Mexico.[18] Their capital city, Tenochtitlan, was officially founded in 1325, and the Mexica eventually bestowed their name on the entire nation.

By the time of Cortés's arrival, Tenochtitlan and its regional neighbor Tlatelolco had a population of over 200,000, with a million more inhabitants in the settlements bordering Lago de Texcoco, making it one of the world's largest urban complexes.[19] Tenochtitlan, together with its neighboring city-states of Texcoco and Tlacopan, formed the so-called Triple Alliance of the Aztec Empire.[20] Its political and religious center was the *Templo Mayor,* or Great Temple, at Tenochtitlan—a precinct with more than 75 individual structures of imposing architecture. The various urban clusters that composed Tenochitlan were connected across the lakes by causeways. Miles of aqueducts brought fresh water to the inhabitants, and dykes protected them from flood. The Aztec's hegemony endured until the arrival of Cortés. On the eve of its destruction, Tenochtitlan is said to have resembled, even surpassed, the Rome of the Caesars.[21] The Spanish subsequently demolished many structures in Tenochtitlan to use as raw materials for building their own city atop the ruins of the Aztec Empire.

Southwest

The first Asian migrants arrived in the US Southwest more than 12,000 years ago. They were hunters of large game that flourished in the region at a time when the climate was more tropical than it is today. As game resources declined and drought became common, the newcomers turned increasingly to plants for sustenance, although the cultures remained nomadic in their pursuit of food. However, by 1500 B.C., forms of agricultural settlements had emerged. Three main social groupings occupied relatively distinct territories in the present-day states of Utah, Colorado, New Mexico, and Arizona. They were: the Hohokam, a desert agricultural group in south Arizona; the Mogollon, hunters and gatherers in the more elevated mountain-and-valley ranges of New Mexico and Arizona, extending over the present-day border into the state of Chihuahua; and the Anasazi, famed cliff dwellers on the upland plateaus of northern Arizona and New Mexico (see Figure 2.1). Two smaller groups, the Sinagua and Salado, lived in the interstices among the three primary cultures and adopted many practices of their neighbors. The three cultures enjoyed varying degrees of prosperity for over a thousand years beginning about 200 A.D.[22]

Nothing in the US Southwest matched the splendor of the Aztec Empire. Nevertheless, the three Southwest regional hearths developed complicated settlement systems composed of hamlets, villages, and towns, achieving a pinnacle in the cultural brilliance of the late-ninth and early-tenth century.[23] By far the most advanced settlements were those of the Anasazi, including Chaco Canyon but also the urban networks of Mesa Verde. By 900 A.D., Chaco Canyon was the center of Anasazi culture, a cityscape of fine architecture, extensive road connections, and complex irrigation systems.[24] At its height, Chaco housed thousands of people, although occupation of the site may have remained seasonal in nature. The outer village of a typical settlement comprised simple structures suitable for family accommodation; the great houses were carefully planned and constructed around plazas and kivas (spiritual centers); and many town cores contained large residential structures up to five stories high.

Trade among Anasazi groups and other Southwest cultures was common, bringing with it the possibility of contact with the Mesoamerican south. The extent of this connectivity has long been the focus of controversy. Historian Robert Lister, while willing to concede the link, dismissed the whole Southwest Tradition in the US as merely a provincial, watered-down version of Mesoamerica cultures.[25] This judgment seems rather severe. It's true that there was no Southwestern equivalent of Tenochtitlan or the Aztec Triple Alliance, but the prehistoric Southwest was a long-lived, geographically extensive, and complex culture of impressive accomplishment. Other experts demur from Lister, stressing the independent, autonomous nature of the Chaco civilization.[26] The answer to this dispute as to whether or not the Southwest was peripheral to a Mesoamerican core seems to depend on what was happening in the space between the two cultures, in the land called Chichimeca.

Chichimeca

The history of the region between Mesoamerica and the Southwest, some-times called La Gran Chichimeca, is relatively unknown.[27] These vast lands extended northward from the edge of Mesoamerica, whose limits are placed around La Quemada and Alta Vista (in the present-day states of Durango, Sinaloa, and Zacatecas), and south from the present-day Southwest US and northern Chihuahua. The term "Chichimec" comes from an ancient Nahuatl word used to describe people who lived north of Mesoamerica. It has nega-tive connotations of "barbarian" or "sons of dogs," but also positive senses of "noble savage" and "ancestor." As in the case of Chaco, much has been written about whether Chichimeca was a vibrant independent culture, or simply a peripheral extension of Mesoamerica. One of the region's earliest archeologists, Charles di Peso, proposed that the Mesoamerican influx was so revolutionary in Chichimeca that it amounted to a cultural earthquake, completely transforming lives in the remote northern region.[28] Others regard the Chichimecan region as a sophisticated network of interrelated townships that developed independently from Mesoamerican influence. Only now are investigators beginning to entertain the notion that Chichimeca was a cul-tural bridge between the Southwest and Mesoamerica.[29]

Human occupation of the Gran Chichimeca began early, before 10,000 B.C. Small groups of nomadic hunters and gatherers roamed the landscape in search of food and water. A more sedentary settlement system based on for-mal agriculture practices appeared in many places between 2000 B.C. and 500 A.D. Not far from the present-day border in the Mexican state of Chihuahua, the town of Paquimé rose to dominate its hinterland from about 1200 to 1450 A.D.[30] Also known as Casas Grandes (the Big Houses), Paquimé is regarded as the largest and most complex prehistoric site in the Greater Southwest. At its peak, it housed 3,000 people and was a regional capital that controlled an extensive trading network extending south to Mesoamerica and north as far as Chaco Canyon.[31] From Mesoamerica, Paquimé absorbed ideas about archi-tecture, town planning, ceramics, and copper metallurgy.

Aside from Paquimé, Chichimeca was home to a number of loosely orga-nized settlement networks that exhibited a very mixed set of cultural tradi-tions. For instance, a separate Sonoran regional system was based in Cerro de Trincheras, a town of about 2,000 people that had trading ties west to Guaymas and east to Paquimé.[32] Both Cerro de Trincheras and Paquimé developed largely self-sufficient societies that were at the center of geographically-extensive regional trading systems. These systems were only loosely-affiliated politically,[33] and archeological evidence suggests that the Sonoran settlements almost certainly lacked a Mesoamerican connection.[34] Another local trading hierarchy in prehistoric times was found along coastal western Mexico, stretching from present-day Guadalajara, through Jalisco and Sinaloa, into Sonora and Chihuahua.[35] In 1932, geographer Carl Sauer was the first to refer to the "Aztatlán" tradition in connection with the northwestern coast. He also recognized the region's significance as a zone of cultural transfer with Mesoamerica and the US Southwest.[36]

Regional Integration

By now there is little doubt that the overlapping cultures of the US Southwest owe a great deal to Mesoamerican influences, principally via the Hohokam and Anasazi traders. An even stronger claim is that the US Southwest and the Mexican northwest (Chichimeca) add up to a single cultural identity connected to Mesoamerica along the Sierra Madre mountains.[37] In this scheme, Paquimé becomes the fulcrum of a Chichimecan bridge between the Southwest and the Mesoamerican heartland. Cultural borrowings in the southwest included ball courts, irrigation systems, pottery, and copper bells imported via Paquimé. However, not everything Mesoamerican was slavishly adopted by the north. Neither Chaco Canyon nor Paquimé developed a unified political authority similar to Mesoamerican monarchies. They remained a patchwork of independent communities, and their Great Houses are, for the most part, regarded as strictly local phenomena.[38]

One of the champions of a Paquimé-Chaco connection is archeologist Steve Lekson who regards the whole of Native North America as an interconnected society. Indigenous peoples, he claims, shared a common history on a subcontinental scale, and were not fragmented into a patchwork quilt of separate fiefdoms subordinate to any core, Mesoamerican or otherwise. His three-phase historical reconstruction of Chichimeca starts in the Hohokam culture between 750 A.D. and 900 A.D. This was succeeded by the hugely important Chaco Canyon network that was influential and widespread for over 100 years and peaked in 1020–1125 A.D. When the Chaco alliance finally fizzled around 1175 A.D., massive southward migrations began, placing entire peoples into motion. The Chaco settlements were some of the earliest to be

abandoned, and the southbound flows were instrumental in a third historical phase, which ultimately established Paquimé as the new regional hub. Its
dominance extended from 1250 until the settlement was sacked in 1340.[39]

There is as yet insufficient evidence in the archeological record to support
unequivocally the claim of a Mesoamerica-Chichimeca-Southwest cultural
link. But each new archeological discovery seems to require radical revisions
of prehistory that support the notion of a subcontinental linkage of considerable antiquity.[40] Early in 2009, for instance, archeologists announced that they
had discovered traces of cacao—a staple of a Mesoamerican chocolate drink—
in jar fragments dated to 1,000 A.D. in Chaco Canyon. Cacao was hitherto
believed to have been introduced into the Southwest *after* the Spanish invasion in the fifteenth century; just as importantly, the nearest known source for
cacao in Chaco was over 1,000 miles to the south in Mexico.[41]

Simple common sense also plays a role in revising the historical record.
For instance, it's been claimed that distances were too large to permit regular interaction on a subcontinental scale, and yet only 1,000 miles separate
Mexico City from Chaco Canyon via the Sierra Madre Mountains. South
from Paquimé lies the Barranca del Cobre and the isolated cliff-dwelling
Tarahumara Indians, who are also known as the Rarámuri, which translates
as "those who walk well." They were reputed to have run hundreds of miles
without rest, and their descendants are superb athletes. The distances separating Chichimeca from Mesoamerica and the Southwest seem inconsequential
when the Tarahumara could have covered the 450 miles between Paquimé
and Chaco Canyon in a matter of weeks.[42]

There is a perfectly good Nauha word to describe the place of Chichimeca
between Mesoamerica and the Southwest: *nepantla*.[43] Nauhatl was the language of the Aztec Empire. We know it today through such words as chocolate, cacao, chile and avocado. Nepantla describes the condition of being
"in-between." It connotes a bridging between cultures, a border zone or
hybrid place where interaction and learning occurs. There may be gaps in the
archeological record, empty spaces in our minds, and no agreement on the
extent of this bridging, but the north–south connectivity in the civilizations
of the ancient Americas is undeniable.

The Californias

The large amounts of time, money, and effort lavished on uncovering
Mesoamerican archeology have ensured that these are the societies we know
best. Virtually every discovery in Mexican archeology is inevitably filtered

through the Mesoamerican matrix. Much less attention has been focused elsewhere, even though there are many sites with long histories of human occupation. Mexico has more than 29,000 known archeological zones, but over 200,000 sites are thought to exist. The states of Baja California and Baja California Sur each have more than one thousand recorded sites, even though the two states are typically referred to as the "forgotten peninsula."[44]

Baja today is a land of coastal deserts.[45] Past climates were more benign and peninsular Baja was rich in flora and fauna, with relatively plentiful water. In a culture that depended on hunting, gathering, and fishing, shortages of food and water would have caused frequent migrations.[46] However, there is no reason to believe that Baja lagged behind other places in human settlement; on the contrary, the peninsula may have been one of the earliest parts of the continent reached from Alaska over 40,000 years ago.[47] Recent archeological investigations reveal strong connections among Baja settlements, reaching northward into the present-day US and across the Gulf of California to mainland Mexico. For now, the earliest accepted carbon date in the region comes from a piece of charcoal found at the Cueva Pintada, one of the largest caves in the Central Baja complex, which yielded a date of over 10,000 years antiquity.[48]

No settlements to match the grandeur of Chaco Canyon or Paquimé have yet been discovered in the Californias, but the Great Murals of Central Baja, near San Ignacio, indicate a civilization of some consequence.[49] The sites were first described in records of eighteenth century Jesuits. Then, in 1894 Frenchman León Diguet, an industrial chemist working at a copper mine near Santa Rosalia, carried out explorations in the Sierras of Guadalupe and San Francisco.[50] The famous novelist Erle Stanley Gardner was instrumental in drawing contemporary attention to the murals in the 1960s. (Gardner wrote the Perry Mason courtroom dramas, which became a hugely successful TV show starring Raymond Burr.) Gardner organized several expeditions into Baja, during one of which he was introduced to the cave paintings. He later published an article in *Life* magazine and followed up with a 1962 book called *The Hidden Heart of Baja*, which highlighted the murals and included some striking photographs.[51] Then in 1971, a determined southern Californian photographer named Harry Crosby began exploring Central Baja. Eventually he visited and documented over 200 different cave sites. Back then, Harry recalled to me, the locals were not terribly impressed by "their paintings," partly because murals were so common in the region.

The Mexican National Institute of Anthropology and History (INAH) restarted explorations in Central Baja after 1981.[52] Since then, two hundred separate sites have been identified in the Sierras de San Borja, San Juan, San Francisco, and Guadalupe.[53] The cave paintings in the Sierras have proven difficult to date accurately, because many have been overpainted and the paint itself is not susceptible to conventional dating techniques. The exact age of Great Murals remains in dispute, but the San Borjitas examples are considered to be 7,500 years old.[54] In 1993, the Great Murals of Central Baja were declared a UNESCO World Heritage site, and Harry Crosby told me that local residents now proudly regard "their paintings" as part of the region's patrimony.

North of Baja, in Alta California (now the US state of California) the archeological record reveals extensive human occupation that was sustained by the state's rich food resources.[55] A precise reconstruction of the historical record has been hampered by rising sea level (which has obliterated many coastal sites), and urban development (which has carpeted many inland sites). One exception occurs in the Channel Islands off Los Angeles, where some sites go back 8,500 years and reveal an active fishing culture. Skeletal remains found on the Islands may be as much as 13,000 years old, which would make them the oldest human remains discovered in the Western Hemisphere.[56] Settlements were established by the nomadic hunter/gatherer societies along the coastline and near inland lakes and streams.[57] Between 2500 B.C.E. and 1500 B.C.E., the acorn became a staple food source that supported permanent settlement, increased trade, and brought a more complex society to Alta California.[58] The acorn was not very tasty and had to be soaked for a long while before being ground into an edible paste. But acorns were plentiful at that time, were easily stored, and helped Indians get through a winter when game and other edibles were scarce. Alta California never attained Mesoamerica's grandeur, but in the words of archeologist Brian Fagan, by the sixteenth century A.D.:

> The inhabitants of California formed a dense network of groups, large and small, speaking over sixty languages, and numbering an estimated 310,000 people. They occupied about 256,000 square mile of varied terrain, with an average population density of about 1 person per square mile, a higher figure than average for the North America of five centuries ago.[59]

Once an effort was made to remember the Californias, a splendid new chapter in our prehistory was opened. Add this to what we already know from other regions, and the result is not a story of primitive ancestors eking out an existence from the inhospitable earth (even though things might have begun this way). Instead, the accumulation of regional histories adds up to a grand saga on a continental scale—of human occupation and civilization that included the emergence of one of the world's major urban heartlands as well as myriad other centers of astonishing sophistication. This cumulative synthesis points not only to north–south connections, but also east–west connections among ancient civilizations across Central America and the Southwest. The whole subcontinent was a hyperactive emporium of economic, political, and cultural connectivity.[60] To borrow a phrase, this truly was home to a 'cosmic race,' or *la raza cósmica*. Of course, it was on occasion disrupted by commonplace human habits such as war, which would play a role in the ultimate demise of magnificent Mesoamerica.

Collapse

The arrival of the Spanish in the Americas was an epochal event that irrevocably altered the entire hemisphere.[61] The present-day borderlands were visited, for example, by the peripatetic Cabeza de Vaca who roamed the Chihuahuan interior, crisscrossing the Rio Grande between 1534 and 1536.[62] Somewhat later, Hernando de Soto traveled from Cuba to Florida and around the Gulf Coast beginning in 1539, in 1540–42, Francisco Vásquez de Coronado swept through Aztatlán and the Pueblo cultures, and in 1542 Juan Rodrigo Cabrillo entered San Diego Bay. But by the time Balthazar de Obregón entered Paquimé in 1584, he encountered ruins that were already almost a century old.[63] Obregón wrote admiringly of Paquimé's former architectural elegance:

> There are many houses of great sizes, strength and height. They are of six and seven stories, with towers and wall[-]like fortresses for protection. The houses contained large and magnificent patios paved with enormous and beautiful stones resembling jasper.[64]

But the Spanish were too late. Apart from Tenochtitlan and the Aztecs, the fabulous Cities of Gold they had avariciously anticipated had already withered.

Exactly why the great settlements of Mesoamerica, Chichimeca, and the Southwest collapsed remains a mystery. The end of the Anasazi Pueblo culture of the Southwest has been attributed to many factors that were probably replicated (to varying degrees) in many places throughout Central America. In the early 1200s, indigenous peoples in the Southwest were widely distributed throughout mesa and valley in Utah and Colorado; but by the early 1400s the Pueblo peoples had retreated from the northern zones to settle principally in valleys where irrigated farming was possible. Prolonged drought coupled with falling groundwater levels seemingly caused this shift, but deforestation (leading to depleted stocks of fuelwood) and diminished game and plant resources have also been implicated in the collapse.[65] Social factors played an additional role. For example, in the Mesa Verde region, kinship networks were accustomed to exchanging maize, thus allowing the growing population to weather downturns in agricultural production. However, increasing population density and the geographical clustering of sharing households placed new demands on the already depleted landscape. As survival became more difficult, conflict inevitably erupted. Around Chaco Canyon in the early 1100s, a severe 45-year drought was marked by extreme violence; and by the mid-1200s, the population in Mesa Verde region had moved to more defensible sites such as the famous cliff dwellings of the Mesa Verde National Park. As survival became imperiled, the great southward migrations toward Paquimé began: some groups perished; others became absorbed into local populations.

DURING MY FIRST visit to the Yucatan over three decades ago, a local driver was conveying me around Chichen Itza and Uxmal, two of the greatest Mayan archeological sites near Mérida. At the end of our journey, perplexed by the miasma of a lost civilization, I asked : "Whatever happened to the Maya?" He looked at me with uncomprehending eyes: "What do you mean? I am Maya; the Maya are still here." I learned that day that presumptions about the past are hazardous. The Maya had simply outlived the ruins, right up to the present day.

By a similar reasoning, I understood that before the US seized the pretext for war in 1846 the borderlands had existed as something entirely different. In my search for borderland connections over time and space, I had passed through three centuries of Spanish colonialism and ended up steeped in evidence of prehistoric connectivity.

From the earliest times, this vast subcontinental region was interconnected by communications networks that linked distant and diverse civilizations from Chaco Canyon to Chichimeca and Mesoamerica. Looked at another way, a deep history that is prepared to ignore lines on maps revealed connecting tissues of a "third nation" that already existed in these lands long before the US–Mexico boundary line was so bloodily and laboriously inflicted.

3

From Frontier Settlements to Transborder Cities

THE SPANISH ARRIVED in Central America in 1521 and stayed 300 years.[1] The conquest spread outward from the Aztec heartland and on to the unruly edges. The conquerors lived mostly in a handful of cities, each of which was laid out according to a gridiron plan, and they carefully co-opted Aztec administrative structures in ways that accelerated their takeover. But further north among the splintered groups of the Gran Chichimeca—whom the Spanish regarded as the most ferocious savages—the colonizers gained little headway with permanent control or material wealth until silver was discovered a couple of decades later.[2] The Spanish conquest is noteworthy for the number of precedents it offers for the future borderlands, including belligerent resistance to external interference, regional power alliances independent of authoritarian centers, unique patterns of urbanization and economic development, and myriad cross-border alliances forged through commerce, custom, and war.

The Spanish Conquest in New Spain

The opening two centuries of colonial dominance in Nueva España, or New Spain, were overseen by Spain's Habsburg Empire. Habsburg strategies of conquest included military, material, spiritual, and political means. Military superiority was made easier by the drastic decline in indigenous population numbers after the Spanish *entrada,* mostly because of the new diseases introduced from Europe. Material transformation was achieved through the introduction of the *hacienda,* a new form of agricultural organization that focused on ranching and stock raising, as well as the *encomienda*, a system by which groups of Indians were assigned to Spanish conquistadors who were required to protect and convert them in return for labor and tribute. A privileged class of Indian *caciques* assisted the conquerors with the tasks of government, taxation, and justice. The wealth and power cornered by the colonial classes of *hacendados* and *encomenderos* would emerge to pose challenges to the authority of the Spanish crown, which saw in them the first stirrings of a local patriotism in New Spain.[3]

Another weapon in the conquerors' armament was the church. The mendicant orders—Franciscans, Dominicans, Augustinians, and later Jesuits—were the "shock troops" of the spiritual conquest.[4] They were highly successful, even though their claims regarding the number of conversions were likely exaggerated. As time passed and missionary zeal diminished, a hard authoritarianism and the Inquisition took over. The Habsburg King of Spain, Philip II, had trouble maintaining political control over the far-distant, sprawling colony, and the rise of a new colonial aristocracy (based in military and ranching) limited Spain's capacity to transfer revenues to the crown. So Philip imposed an increasingly centralized bureaucracy in which priests and lawyers dominated.[5]

No concerted challenge to Spanish authority emerged during two centuries of Habsburg rule. One reason for New Spain's relative calm was that colonial administrators adopted a pragmatic view of what was possible in the colony. Naturally enough, orders from Spain were accepted, but follow-through was a contingent matter, and reluctant officials frequently took refuge in the old saying "*Obedezco pero no cumplo*" (I obey but do not carry out).[6] Resources for policing and control were few and meager, and colonial officials frequently showed leniency and practiced diplomacy because they lacked a repressive apparatus to enforce their will.

In northern New Spain, things were more volatile.[7] Resistance and insurrection were commonplace in the Gran Chichimeca, and Philip II was obliged to abandon intentions to subordinate local officials to his authority. Northern economic development was based on silver mining at Zacatecas after 1546, and for the rest of the century silver constituted more than 50 percent of the colony's exports to Spain, peaking at 95 percent in 1595.[8] Silver production was a powerful stimulus to economic integration in the colony, linking Zacatecas with the south, generating demographic and urban growth that were instigated by mineral exploitation, commerce, and towns. Northern settlements and trade routes were prone to attack from ferocious Chichimecan tribes, and the necessity for self-defense bred, among northerners, a degree of independence and a quarrelsome self-reliance.[9]

In the half-century of resistance and insurrection that followed 1521, the peoples of the Gran Chichimeca defied pacification attempts. Spain conceded much of its power in the north to local oligarchs, and a fragile harmony was stitched together by the end of the sixteenth century. However, the border was never a restful place. New tensions erupted during the mid-seventeenth century, including recurrent uprisings by the Tarahumara Indians (the long-distance runners mentioned in the previous chapter), as well as the famous Pueblo Revolt of 1680, when over 300 Spaniards were massacred and 2,000 more fled south to El Paso.[10] The final decade of the seventeenth century witnessed the first major incursions of Apaches, who eventually occupied a land corridor from the Rio Grande to the Sierra Madre Occidental, further disrupting Spanish colonization of the northwest after 1700. The Habsburg era in New Spain ended with the northern territories in an uneven state of precarious peace with traces of an emerging sense of Mexican nationhood based in the erosion of old caste barriers.[11]

CHANGING POLITICAL FORTUNES in Europe brought about the end of the Habsburgs, who in 1700 were replaced by the Bourbons. This new, French-connected dynasty brought a single-minded rationality to its main goal, maximizing Spain's revenues from its colony. New Spain's relative autonomy was rescinded, and the Habsburg-inspired social contract was shredded; the seeds of the 1810 independence movement began to germinate as New Spain became an overtaxed and overgoverned society. It is said that the Bourbons set out on a "second conquest" of New Spain, but in so doing they "gained a revenue but lost an empire."[12]

Bourbon venality has been explained by Spain's economic difficulties and increasing threats posed by the colonial enterprises of Britain, France, and (after 1776) the US. The new regime set out to accomplish a revolution "from above," promoting an intense concentration of wealth and power but offering little beyond discipline for the impoverished masses. In a nutshell, the Bourbon project combined elements of: "rapid agrarian commercialization, hacienda expansion, mining boom, rising rents, falling wages, wild swings in the price of staples and increasingly oppressive labour systems."[13] However, once again pragmatism often overruled principle in Bourbon practices, partly because circumstances in the colony and in Europe were changing. For instance, New Spain's population was expanding rapidly as more immigrants arrived from Europe and the Indian population began to recover (but this time armed with guns and mounted on horseback), silver and other colonial products began to find a place in global markets beyond Spain, and the Spanish worried that other nations such as Britain and France were becoming too interested in the Americas.[14]

Early indications that things would not turn out well for the Bourbons surfaced predictably in the colony's northern territories, which had never been truly integrated into the empire. Economic and demographic growth stoked a strenuous opposition among indigenous peoples. A concerted rebellion led by Yaqui Indians erupted in 1740, and the always-contentious Tarahumara Indians simply melted into the landscape after the missions in their territory had been secularized according to Habsburg edict. In the north, militarization took precedence: mission gave way to *presidio* (fort), and where Habsburgs had used priests to cajole the natives, the Bourbons conscripted soldiers. In the case of the Apaches, the Bourbons abandoned all pretense of conversion or pacification and instead offered bribery and co-optation; guns and liquor replaced hymns and bibles.[15] In this practice, the Bourbon newcomers followed their predecessors by allowing pragmatism to supersede consistency.[16]

If the troublesome north was being cut loose, elsewhere in the colony the Bourbons of New Spain developed a knack for making choices that galvanized opposition. For instance, propelled by a vigorous anticlericalism, authorities expelled the Jesuits from the colony in 1767.[17] While this act was undoubtedly satisfying to ideologues, the expulsion terminated the most effective instrument of colonial authority in the north, thereby diminishing Spain's control of the region. But Bourbon anticlericalism was uneven in its application, and even into the late eighteenth century, clerics pioneered missionization and settlement in Alta California.[18] In the central-west cities of Bajío, the Jesuits' departure left gaps in charitable, religious, and educational life. Riots followed in Guanajuato and nearby towns, and the Bourbons' professional army and militia reacted with a stunning litany of hangings, floggings, and imprisonment.

A further push towards New Spain's independence came after 1793, when the mother country's communication with her colony was increasingly disrupted by wars in Europe. In a climactic moment, Napoleon invaded Spain in 1808, installing his brother Joseph on the Spanish throne. In New Spain, this change brought native Spaniards (*peninsulares*) into contention with American-born Spaniards (*criollo*, or creole) who saw no reason to offer fealty to France. In the vacuum opened up by Spain's defeat, the *peninsular* and *criollo* vied for leadership in the colony. The *peninsulares* eventually quashed the creole plot and reasserted some degree of control over the restless territory, but the lines of ethnic division exposed by this conflict were later to play a fateful role in the movement for independence from Spain.[19]

The march toward Mexican independence began in 1810 when Father Miguel del Hidalgo y Costilla issued his famous call to arms in the Bajío town of Dolores. This was the *grito*, now celebrated across Mexico every year on September 16. The call for liberty was a grassroots-inspired revolution that originated from an oppressed rural periphery, not from the urban core. Hidalgo and his allies rashly confronted the colony's military head-on, gained some victories but also suffered great losses, as preludes to ultimate defeat. Hidalgo himself was executed in 1811. At the Ahlóndiga de Granaditas (a corn exchange) in Guanajuato, you can still see the hook where the severed heads of rebels, including Hidalgo, were hung for a decade after their deaths.

Hidalgo's successors, notably José María Morelos, shifted to decentralized guerilla warfare. Shrewdly, Morelos also pressed for unification among diverse factions of the independence movement, convened an insurgent congress, declared independence, and drafted a constitution.[20] Yet once again the insurgency collapsed and Morelos was executed in 1815. A period of stalemate followed, but the colonial state had by now lost its legitimacy, and Spanish authority was maintained solely through force of arms. Spain's resolve was fatally weakened when Napoleon Bonaparte's wartime occupation weakened Spain's hold over her colonies. Then, in 1820 a military coup in Spain toppled the Bourbon dynasty and restored the liberal Spanish constitution of 1812. Within weeks the creole elite in New Spain had risen in revolt, supported by church and army, and this time the rebellion was brief and victorious. On September 24, 1821, Augustin de Iturbide's forces entered Mexico City, almost 300 years to the day after Cortés's conquest of Tenochtitlan.[21]

Town-Making in Nueva España

Town-making in New Spain was a very deliberate strategy of colonization based upon the Laws of Indies. Originally promulgated by Philip II in 1573 and based on Roman city-planning principles, the 148 ordinances dealt exhaustively with every aspect of site selection, construction, and political organization of the new towns. The ordinances "reinforced the unilateral objectives of conquest, emphasized the urban character of Spanish colonization, and specified clearly the physical and organizational arrangements that were to be developed in the new cities of America."[22] They also contained exhortations that conquerors should approach local populations in a friendly manner. By the end of the sixteenth century, municipal governments had been introduced throughout the provinces. And by 1585 Zacatecas, referred to as the *madre y civilizadora* of Northern Mexico and the first large mining settlement in New Spain, was large enough to earn the title of *ciudad*.[23]

The fulcrum of exploration and settlement along the borderlands was the valley of El Paso del Norte, which was traversed by Franciscan friars from Spain in 1581, en route to convert the Pueblo Indians of New Mexico.[24]

In 1598, Mexican-turned-conquistador Juan de Oñate led a party of settlers from Mexico to the upper reaches of the Rio Grande/Río Bravo River valley, establishing the first European settlement west of the Mississippi. He was fiercely dedicated to the colonizing mission, but also a cruel man. His legacy remains controversial, even though he is universally understood as a pivotal character in borderlands history.[25] One of his infamous exploits was to arrange for the destruction of the impregnable Acoma pueblo in 1599. The pueblo residents had been pressured by the demands of colonialists desperate for food and clothing and retaliated by killing twelve of them, including Oñate's nephew. In response, Oñate dispatched 72 soldiers who over the course of three days destroyed the pueblo, slaughtering 500 men and 300 women and children, and taking 80 men and 500 women and children captive. Oñate subjected the captives to a formal trial and all were found guilty of murder. Everyone between the ages of 12 and 25 was sentenced to 25 years of servitude; males over 25 had one foot severed; and children under 12 were removed from their parents and placed in the custody of the Franciscans.[26]

Don Oñate later wrote to the colonial viceroy about the Acoma incident: "As punishment for its crime and its treason against his Majesty, to whom it had already rendered submission by public instrument, and as a warning to the rest, I razed and burned it [the pueblo] completely."[27] There was no mention in his letter of those who died as a consequence of his brutality. Only much later was Oñate prosecuted in Mexico City for his regime of terror, found guilty, stripped of his titles, and exiled from New Mexico.[28] Reputable historians in the US refer to the Acoma campaign as a "miraculous" and "brilliant" victory,[29] but the sickening violence and terror used by the Spanish conquerors throughout the Americas had been well-known for over a half-century even at that time, and was a source of intense shame.[30]

The town of Paso del Norte gained importance as a connection between New Mexico and New Spain. In 1598 Don Oñate had claimed the locality for Spain, though it was not until 1656 that a mission was established at Paso del Norte, followed by a permanent settlement in 1659. In this isolated region, pacification of Indians was not easy. The 1680 Pueblo Indian revolt in the Santa Fe region shook Spanish authority to its core because never before had an indigenous people retaken a Spanish province in these territories. Spanish refugees from the revolt established new settlements close to San Elizario at Ysleta, Senecú, and Socorro, downriver from Paso del Norte. As a result of a shift in the channel of the Río Bravo, some of these formerly Mexican towns are today part of the US.

Emigrants from Paso del Norte encouraged further settlement along the Lower Rio Grande Valley, including a mission at Sonoita in 1701, and a presidio at Ojinaga in 1759. As settlers dispersed, towns were frequently located on riverbanks for defensive purposes, such as Camargo and Reynosa in 1749. Once established, these towns in turn spawned yet more settlements: Laredo was founded in 1755 at a river crossing on the route between Monterrey (Nuevo Léon) and San Antonio (Texas); Matamoros was established in 1774. Both were commercial enterprises, and neither was initially supported by mission or presidio.

At the other end of New Spain on the Pacific coast, San Diego had been claimed by Spain after Juan de Cabrillo's 1542 expedition.[31] Nothing much happened until Spanish interest in Alta California was rekindled when the British, French, and Russians cast covetous eyes in its direction. In San Diego, Gaspar de Portolá established a presidio in 1769, the same year that Franciscan Junípero Serra set up a mission. In a contemporary diary of the missionization of California, Father Crespi wrote of the first encounters with the Indians around present-day Los Angeles. He noted the advantages of the site, which had "all the requisites for a large settlement" including "an infinity of rose bushes in full bloom" and soil capable of producing "every kind of grain and fruit." Crespi went on to record that the Indians they met brought gifts to their visitors and some old men "puffed at us three mouthfuls of smoke." The Portolá party named the local river *Nuestra Señora la Reina de Los Angeles de Porciúncula*, and at this site twelve years later the Pueblo of Los Angeles was founded with a precise colonizer's eye attuned to the mandate of the Laws of the Indies.[32]

Another decision with far-reaching consequences was one of the first acts of boundary-making in the region. On August 19, 1773, Fray Francisco Palóu established an administrative division between Alta California and Baja California, authorizing the Franciscans to convert inhabitants of the former and Dominicans the people of the latter (see Figure 3.1).[33]

By the end of the eighteenth century, as the Bourbon empire was faltering, Spain possessed a discontinuous string of frontier towns extending along the Río Bravo, around Paso del Norte, and in the coastlands of the far west. Spanish colonization via fort, mission, and mine established a legacy of town-building that provided the enduring foundations of the present-day borderlands.[34] There was little east–west connection among the trading zones of Texas, New Mexico, or Alta and Baja California; the direction of connectivity along the frontier spaces was firmly north–south. For instance, by 1800 Santa Fe, the capital of New Mexico, was the largest settlement on

FIGURE 3.1 Georg Heinrich von Langsdorf Ein Tanz der Indianer in der Mision in St. José in Neu Californien / Dance of Indians at San Jose Mission, New California 1806.
Courtesy of the Bancroft Library, University of California, Berkeley.

the western frontier, with a population of about 5,000 people. Santa Fe trade reoriented the New Mexican and Chihuahuan economies toward Missouri and the United States; Spanish New Mexicans entered commerce and sent their children to learn English in St. Louis; and Anglo mountain men could get licenses from the Mexican government in Santa Fe to trap beaver on the upper reaches of the Río Bravo and Gila River.[35]

The advent of an independent Mexico in 1821 ushered in efforts to incorporate the northern peripheries into the new republic. Constitutional reform in Mexico in 1824 created a federal republic of states and territories but had the perverse effect of further marginalizing the northern jurisdictions by diminishing their local autonomy and representation. Foreign trade with the US, Britain, and France, which had been illegal (although tolerated) during Spanish rule, was legalized in the young republic, but the commerce that resulted reinforced the northward gaze. In addition, Anglo penetration into Mexico accelerated when immigration into the Texas borderlands from the US was encouraged by Guadalupe Victoria, first president of the Mexican Republic. In times of such rapid change, a prosperous Paso del Norte established ranching enterprises on the north bank of the Río Bravo. In bustling

Matamoros—the only fortified settlement along the border—population grew rapidly from 2,320 in 1820 to 16,372 by 1837; there, Anglo-Americans were joined by British, French, German, and Castilian emigrants who were often involved in the town's burgeoning manufacturing industries. In short, independence gave the northern border towns a fresh start, whose inhabitants directed their energies toward the US.

Following independence, a restless period of reform and adjustment presided in the northern territories. The presidios lost their imperial purpose of pacification and control, and by the 1830s, secularization had removed the missions' purpose in Texas, Arizona, California, and New Mexico. Widespread land reforms followed, often involving large grants of public lands to private entrepreneurs with the purpose of encouraging settlement. For example, enormous ranches were created at Tecate and Tía Juana (later Tijuana). Cultural and ethnic mixing became facts of life along the changing frontier. Through intermarriage and business arrangements many newcomers were absorbed into the new society, adopting food and clothing styles, merging languages, and serving in armies composed of mixed races.[36] A strong home rule sentiment became pervasive in the north, abetted by central government neglect. Deals with visiting Anglos were common, and many Mexican residents came to favor US sovereignty for the frontier.[37] Indeed, the integration of Mexico's northern territories into the US economy in the years leading up to the 1846–1848 war was the most pertinent factor in the lives of most ordinary people.[38]

After 1848: Twin Towns along the Border

After the 1848 Treaty of Guadalupe Hidalgo, the *frontier spaces* that the Spanish had struggled to conquer became *border places* that Mexico and the US sought to control, primarily in order to secure the fledgling territorial limits of their respective countries. Beyond the marking of the line, the task of occupation and control was principally achieved via urban and economic development, which together became the impetus for modernization on both sides of the line.[39] This was the time when matching settlements, or "twin towns," were founded on opposite sides of the international boundary.[40]

In the early nineteenth century, Spanish-speaking frontier dwellers, along with nomadic and sedentary Native Americans and recently arrived Anglo Americans, began to emerge as Mexicans, Tejanos, and Americans. The speed of such transformations is underscored by Andrés Reséndez: "Scores of Mexican-Texans went from Spanish subjects, to Mexican citizens, to Texans, and wound up as Americans, in the short span of a lifetime."[41] During this period, individual decisions regarding identity and allegiance were frequently opportunistic, responding to business opportunities, political convictions, or simply to survival needs. Such pragmatism, eminently commonsensical under the circumstances, clashed with the emerging Mexican national project. Although Mexico sought to bind its northern border to the new republic, secessionist movements were common on both sides of the border. Thus, far from being the struggle between two well-established nationalistic monoliths, the "nationalisms" of the post-1848 borderlands were being manufactured in places where none previously existed (with the possible exception of Texas). Having done nothing, frontier dwellers became border residents virtually overnight, finding themselves cast into an international milieu that only complicated daily dealings.

After the Treaty, the US moved systematically to occupy the northern bank of the Río Bravo in Texas, establishing new military bases for defensive purposes, including those at Fort Brown (in Brownsville), and Fort Ringgold (in Rio Grande City). The twin towns of Eagle Pass and Piedras Negras were both founded in 1850 at a river crossing near Fort Duncan. As border-town trade and commerce developed along the Río Bravo, Mexicans, including many from the Mexican interior, moved north of the river in search of economic opportunities. The principal exception to this northward drift was Laredo, which spun off Nuevo Laredo on the river's south bank, peopled by those who preferred to live under the Mexican flag.[42] Matamoros boomed following the establishment of a free trade zone in 1858. On the western edge of the continent, the postwar era coincided with the discovery of gold in northern California. Agriculture, trade, and industry sprang up in southern California to meet the demands of the miners. Long-distance migrations sparked by gold fever stimulated border-town growth, as at Franklin (soon to become El Paso, Texas), across from Paso del Norte. Roma, a lower Rio Grande valley town outside the economic mainstream, flourished as a center of illegal trade and smuggling.[43]

Later in the nineteenth century, national convulsions on both sides furthered the process of twin-town amalgamation. The US Civil War caused stagnation and loss at the western border, but war-related prosperity in the east. The Lower Rio Grande River valley acquired great strategic significance when a Union blockade closed most of the South's Atlantic ports. For a time, Brownsville–Matamoros became the South's principal port of entry. These twin towns were frequently occupied by warring armies, causing citizens to seek refuge on the other side. El Paso backed the South in the war but suffered when its civic leaders crossed over to Mexican Paso del Norte after Union forces had occupied Fort Bliss. Further west, the war's influence was less direct and was experienced mainly through the vagaries of commerce brought about by war. San Diego, for instance, witnessed the collapse of its trade and the prohibition of immigration.[44]

Mexican fortunes took a dramatic shift in 1876, when Porfirio Díaz came to power. His 34-year rule, known as the Porfiriato, with its mantra of "Order and Progress," offered the first Mexican-inspired borderland renaissance since 1848. Díaz brought rail connections to the northern frontier, irrevocably altering the region's history and ending its isolation. El Paso (Texas) and Paso del Norte (Chihuahua)—the latter subsequently renamed Ciudad Juárez— were the first to benefit, with transcontinental rail service to Mexico City in 1884 and to Los Angeles in 1888. These links enabled El Paso to become the most important metal smelting center in the Southwest. About the same time, Laredo became the rail hub between Texas and the emerging northern Mexico industrial giant of Monterrey, thus diverting traffic from Brownsville. San Diego's port boomed in connection with interior mining, especially after the opening of the Panama Canal in 1907.[45]

The railway boom in Mexico provoked a new round of twin-town urbanization along the international boundary. Nogales (Arizona) was founded in 1880 after it became clear that Mexican rail connections were imminent; Nogales (Sonora) followed in 1884. Agua Prieta in 1899 and Douglas in 1900 were based near the smelting industry. And the Naco twins were established in 1901 as gateway ports of entry between the states of Arizona and Sonora. On the Pacific, San Diego's post-Civil War recovery spilled over into the founding of Tijuana on June 11, 1889; a customs house had stood on the site since 1874, but growth was slow until the potential of the tourist dollar began to be realized. In 1901, the Southern Pacific Railway established Calexico and Mexicali after advances in irrigation technology opened up agricultural opportunities in the Imperial Valley of California and the Mexicali Valley in Baja. Tecate (California) was founded as another rail hub in 1907, followed by Tecate (Baja California) in 1918. Many border towns were ethnically mixed from their inception, as in Mexicali, where large numbers of Chinese immigrants were employed in railroad construction.[46]

Apart from infrastructure investment, another key characteristic of the Díaz regime was its openness toward foreign capital. By the time the Porfiriato drew to a close and revolution loomed, US citizens owned 17 of the 31 major mining companies operating in Mexico, controlling over 80 percent of the industry's total capital. Mineral wealth was primarily tied to gold, silver, lead, and copper in the Mexican states of Sonora and Chihuahua. British investors held another 15 percent of the capital investments, but investment capital in northern manufacturing tended to be of Mexican origin, including the flagship

Fundidora Monterrey, Latin America's first integrated steel plant, established in 1900.[47] Díaz's welcome mat for foreign investors also involved huge concessions of land that encouraged agriculture, mining, and town development. In the state of Baja California, for instance, the Colorado River Land Company—led by Harrison Gray Otis, owner and editor of the *Los Angeles Times*, and his son-in-law Harry Chandler—in 1904–1905 acquired colonization rights to most of the irrigable land in the Mexicali Valley. Another US company was granted over 10 million acres for the development of the town of Ensenada.[48] Such developments marked a new opening for US economic influence in the borderlands and in Mexico generally. By 1910, the six Mexican border states had a population of over 1.6 million (or 10.9 percent of the national total), and the four US states had 4.9 million inhabitants (7.3 percent).[49]

THE LOWER RIO GRANDE Valley has its own kind of beauty, but what I remember most is how many wars scar the landscape.[50] There are roadside markers everywhere commemorating past battles; the thick silence of glades reeks of earlier violence. Brownsville was one of the hot spots of fighting in many wars: the Texas War of Independence surged across the river there; and the first battles in the Mexican-American War of 1846–1848 war were fought at Palo Alto and Resaca de la Palma, near the place that would become Brownsville.[51] Across the river, the Casa Mata outpost of fortified Matamoros bombarded the troops of US General Zachary Taylor on the other side not long after the official outbreak of the Mexican-American war. And the final land battle of the US Civil War took place in 1865 at Palmito Hill, not far from Brownsville. During many encounters in too many wars, residents along the Rio Grande/Bravo frequently took refuge on the other side of the river to avoid the fighting.

A delightful sense of place in the twin towns at the end of the nineteenth century is provided by an almanac, assembled by US Army Lieutenant W. H. Chatfield, of life in Brownsville and Matamoros in 1893 (see Figure 3.2).[52] Chatfield evokes the rush to wealth during the US Civil War and its unifying effect on the two cities:

> In the close blockade of most of the southern ports, the Rio Grande was left free, and the Confederacy utilized it in exporting immense quantities of cotton and other accumulated products of the South, and in importing munitions of war and the food staples it was impossible to produce in the disorganized state of labor. Vast amounts of merchandise were stored in the warehouses of Brownsville and Matamoros, and the mutual interests then awakened were strengthened by friendly

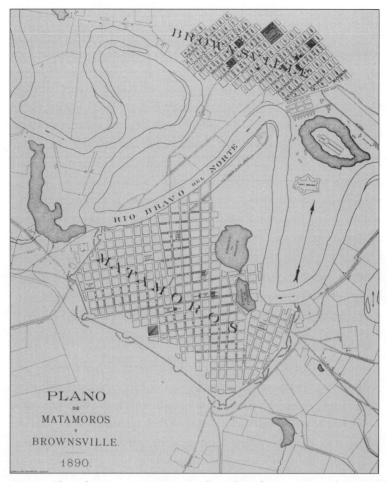

FIGURE 3.2 Plano de Matamoros y Brownsville / Plan of Matamoros and Brownsville 1890.

By the end of the nineteenth century, the twin towns of Matamoros (Tamaulipas) and Brownsville (Texas) were closely connected, even though they still bore traces of previous wars, such as Fort Brown on the north side of the Rio Grande/*Río Bravo del Norte*. Matamoros was the only fortified town on either side of the border, and this plan clearly indicates its defensive structures, including small forts (*fortín*). Clark & Courts, Lithographers.

intercourse, until these cities became in fact as well as in name, "The Twin Cities of the Border."[53]

Before the war the cross-border alliance of the two towns had been tested by ongoing strife. Brownsville was plagued by US filibusters who turned the city into a "citadel whence they sallied forth like buccaneers of ancient days, and made their onslaughts on the loyal and peaceful inhabitants of our neighboring city of Matamoros."[54] Needless to say, such bad manners seriously disturbed cross-border harmony, but goodwill prevailed even under the most trying of circumstances. When Mexican forces under General Juan Cortina (who later became mayor of Matamoros) raided Brownsville in 1859, the city was, for several hours, taken over by the raiders who murdered several citizens and were preparing to burn the city before Mexican authorities in Matamoros intervened.[55]

The twin towns' friendship became so "constant and familiar" that visitors to the region reported that it was hard to understand that they were "dependencies of separate republics."[56] Care was taken on both sides to observe cross-border courtesies, as when "national salutes are fired and acknowledged on the independence days of the two republics, each flying the other's flag for the nonce."[57] One reason for the mutual regard was demographic: the population of Brownsville at the century's end was about 7,000, one-half of whom were Mexicans who had largely adapted to the habits and customs of their American hosts.[58] Such was the level of acceptance that there were almost as many Spanish newspapers published in Brownsville as there were English-language periodicals.[59]

Chatfield's keen diagnostic eye recognized the region's geographic isolation as a factor in cooperation:

> The position of the city, on the farthest border of our territory and without the means of rapid transit to and from the great centers of population, combined with half its inhabitants being foreigners who clung to the traditions and customs of their native country, are facts which have heretofore retarded its growth and nurtured procrastination in developing its natural advantages.[60]

Yet the same factors that slowed development nurtured an almost idyllic vision of the valley:

> The sociology of this people for nearly half a century past is peculiarly remarkable and borders upon the romantic, replete as it is with incidents of pastoral ease and plenty; urban success and luxury; intermarriages and social seclusion; moral courage and freedom from crime.[61]

Chatfield provided a memorable pen portrait of diversity on the streets of the twin towns at this time:

> It is interesting to watch the tide of travel between the republics. Among the passengers there are representatives of every class in these

thoroughly cosmopolitan cities. The Mexican women, with their almost uniform dress of black and white, with heads bare and graceful "rebozos" draped about their shoulders; the "ranchero," with jingling spurs on his high-heeled boots, a gaudy sash, white shirt, and heavy, broad-brimmed "sombrero"; merchant and clerks, intent upon the business to be transacted at the Customhouse, the banks, or the market of the sister city; Spanish ladies tastefully and richly dressed, sparkling with jewels and shielding their bright eyes from the glare of the sun on the water with their proverbial weapon, the fan, which is also the only sunshade they ever carry; Englishmen, Frenchmen, American, Irishmen, and Africans; and they nearly all use the Spanish language or its Mexican "patois," in the affairs of daily life.[62]

An easy coexistence marked small transactions in personal lives across the border. For instance, excursions to Matamoros formed "no inconsiderable part of the amusements of the garrison."[63] Citizens of Matamoros made use of the Brownsville post office for receiving and sending mail.[64] The Mexican government tried to end this arrangement, but did not succeed because the Brownsville-based facility and services were superior.[65] Chatfield records the simple pleasure of strolling in each others' streets, noting that Matamoros had broad streets laid out with great regularity:[66]

> Matamoros was formerly a walled city, or at least, it was surrounded by a line of fortifications except on the side looking towards Brownsville, which has the river for the dividing line. The walls or fortifications were built by [General Tomás] Mejía during the imperial regime, but since the rule of President Diaz [sic] began, peace and quiet have reigned so long that the walls are nearly all leveled to the ground. Some are in use as levees against the overflow of the river.[67]

Chatfield was an unabashed booster of the Lower Rio Grande, occasionally letting his rhetoric off-leash, as in his vision for Cameron County, in which Brownsville is located:

> This modest satellite of the Lone Star [state of Texas] has not yet been charted as of the first magnitude, owing to the nebula of underdeveloped wealth which has obstructed the field of vision; but the powerful instruments of this age of progress are now directed upon her and the gauzy cloud is being rapidly resolved into clusters of golden stars… promising ample reward to the patient explorer.[68]

Chatfield reassured readers that this prognostication was imminent because: "Capital, keen scented and sagacious, is spying out the goodly land."[69] Ironically, his optimism was misplaced because in the early 1880s, wise Capital had already sniffed out a superior US–Mexico railroad connection through upstream Laredo, thereby bypassing Cameron County.[70]

Today, Brownsville has a population of around 170,000, but it retains a small-town feeling. The renovated Southern Pacific railroad station, which opened in 1928 and operated as a passenger terminal until 1952, is now the Historic Brownsville Museum, perhaps the town's most evocative link with its fabled past. There are new residential subdivisions on Brownsville's east side, and the road and rail bridges into Mexico are busy. In prosperous Matamoros (population 460,000), it's a bit difficult to find Casa Mata these days. The fort has been renovated as a museum, and it's smaller, more hidden than you'd expect. The two towns remain sutured by the meanders of the Río Bravo, and you can still walk along the high earthen embankments that once served as Matamoros' defenses. A "Hands Across the Border" ceremony every year celebrates the Brownsville–Matamoros concord.

THE 1910 MEXICAN Revolution brought an end to the dictatorship of Porfirio Díaz. The borderlands were home to several leaders of the Mexican Revolution. Conflict erupted on the western border soon after the outbreak of hostilities, including efforts led by Ricardo Flores Magón from his base in Los Angeles. Ciudad Juárez played a pivotal role in the Revolution, and revolutionary leader Francisco Madero established a camp at boundary monument number 1 between Juárez and El Paso. The Baja towns of Mexicali, Tijuana, and Tecate were also directly involved in conflict. One skirmish in Tijuana was led by Welshman Carl Rhys Price, and was watched by curious onlookers on the San Diego side.[71] It was not unusual for people to cross into Mexico during this turbulent era. In the Andreas Brown Postcard Collection at the Getty Research Institute in Los Angeles, there is a picture postcard addressed to a Miss Birtha de Goot of Lynden, Washington, signed by "Ted" and dated January 22, 1913. In his message, Ted relates how he saw soldiers on the street when he went over the line into Mexico; they wore straw hats because of the heat, "but it is all right if you minde you one bisnis [mind your own business]."

As the Revolution spread eastward, economic disruption and depopulation became more widespread, especially around Matamoros, which acted as the main port of munitions imported from the US. Many Mexican border towns (Matamoros, Ciudad Juárez, and especially Tijuana) offset the war's losses by turning to "sin" industries, such as prostitution.[72] On the US side, local economies boomed in service to the Revolution; mining and agriculture, especially cotton, flourished. Nevertheless, political instability was prevalent in many Texas locations, especially El Paso and Brownsville, which had become staging posts for incursions into Mexico. The military economy of El Paso benefited from the arrival of thousands of US troops at Fort Bliss as well as the influx of prosperous refugees from Chihuahua. Sometimes, in the heat of battle, whole towns would cross over from Mexico into the US in search of sanctuary. For instance, in October 1913, eight thousand people fled Piedras Negras for Eagle Pass. Many Mexicans sought more permanent residence in the US, and the numbers of legal and undocumented migrants and refugees grew.[73]

Dictator Díaz was gone, but he had put in place the fundamental urban and economic infrastructure of the borderlands. This was manifest as a series of twin towns strung along the boundary line, linked by rail, commerce, and society. Throughout the twentieth century, these towns were to become increasingly synchronized in a series of "boom and bust" cycles that determined their joint futures.[74]

Twentieth-Century Modernization and Integration

The pace of economic modernization and borderland integration began to pick up after the Revolution. Between 1910 and 1930, as much as 10 percent of Mexico's population moved to the US. The 1919 Volstead Act brought Prohibition to the US, and Mexican border towns were transformed overnight into tourist destinations providing liquor and entertainment that could not be obtained legally on the other side. In a ten-year period, Ciudad Juárez added two new international bridges to cope with increased traffic in border-jumping sinners. This form of cross-border tourism came to an end in 1933, when Mexican President Lázaro Cárdenas abolished many "sin" industries.

The Great Depression was hard on border cities.[75] Large job losses on the US side caused the rise of anti-Mexican sentiments that led to the repatriation of Mexican workers in the 1930s, many of whom remained in border towns.[76] The slump in border economies lingered on both sides until World War II (1939–1945) when, under the stimulus of wartime shortages in the US, Mexico's agricultural economy flourished, especially the cotton industries of Matamoros, Reynosa, Ciudad Juárez, and Mexicali.[77] Oil and gas production boosted Reynosa, while Nuevo Laredo became Mexico's top export conduit to the US. The tourist industry flourished in Ciudad Juárez and Tijuana; the latter was home to 16,000 people in 1940, rising to almost 60,000 a decade later. El Paso grew to over one-quarter million people by 1960, while in San Diego, military bases helped stimulate growth.[78]

As a consequence of World War II, a shortage of labor in the US led to the 1942 "Bracero" program which issued identity cards to Mexican nationals wishing to work in *El Norte*. By 1960, over 4 million workers had participated in the program. But the post-war need to absorb returning troops led to a backlash against bracero workers, culminating in "Operation Wetback" in 1953–1954, when thousands of workers were returned to Mexico. For a while, the Bracero and Operation Wetback programs in the US simultaneously worked at cross purposes—one promoting immigration, the other casting out migrants. When the Bracero program was officially terminated in 1964, Mexican border towns were once again clogged with returning workers, who tended (as in earlier repatriations) to remain at the border instead of returning to more-distant home towns.[79] The crisis provoked by this massive influx of returning nationals caused an unprecedented response by the Mexican government.

In 1961, Mexico launched a program aimed at local industrial development, boosting tourism, and upgrading living standards in towns along the line. The program was only partially successful, primarily benefiting Tijuana and Nuevo Laredo. A much more radical transformation followed with the introduction of the Border Industrialization Program (BIP) in 1965, with the goals of developing the border towns' manufacturing industries and giving employment to returning workers. Out of this, the Mexican *maquiladora* (assembly plant) industry was born.[80] Located just across the border in Mexico where labor costs were relatively low, *maquilas* imported raw materials and components from the US, assembled them into finished products, and returned the finished goods to the US for distribution and sale. Although slow to start, by 1979 *maquila* production accounted for one-quarter of Mexican manufacturing exports. In subsequent decades, two-thirds of all Mexican *maquilas* were established in just three border towns: Tijuana, Mexicali, and Ciudad Juárez. Tijuana became the television assembly capital of the world. Smaller clusters of *maquilas* at Matamoros–Brownsville, Reynosa–McAllen, Nuevo Laredo–Laredo, and Ambos Nogales later joined the boom. In 1965, there were 12 *maquilas* along the border, and 1,500 by 1996. By 2000, as the industries spread to other states, *maquilas* employed over one million Mexican

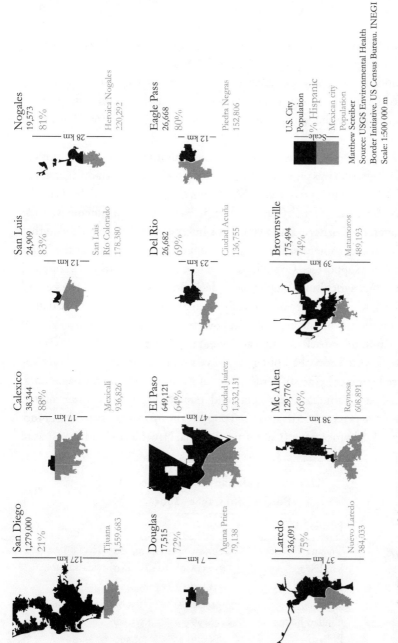

Nogales
19,573
81%

Heroica Nogales
220,292

⊢—— 28 km ——⊣

Eagle Pass
26,668
80%

Piedra Negras
152,806

⊢— 12 km —⊣

San Luis
24,909
83%

San Luis
Río Colorado
178,380

⊢— 12 km —⊣

Del Rio
26,682
69%

Ciudad Acuña
136,755

⊢—— 23 km ——⊣

Brownsville
175,494
74%

Matamoros
489,193

⊢——— 39 km ———⊣

Calexico
38,344
88%

Mexicali
936,826

⊢—— 17 km ——⊣

El Paso
649,121
64%

Ciudad Juárez
1,332,131

⊢——— 47 km ———⊣

Mc Allen
129,776
66%

Reynosa
608,891

⊢——— 38 km ———⊣

San Diego
1,279,000
21%

Tijuana
1,559,683

⊢———— 127 km ————⊣

Douglas
17,515
72%

Aguna Prieta
79,138

⊢— 7 km —⊣

Laredo
236,091
75%

Nuevo Laredo
384,033

⊢— 37 km —⊣

U.S. City
Population
% Hispanic

Mexican city
Population

Scale

Matthew Screiber
Source: USGS Environmental Health
Border Initiative. US Census Bureau. INEGI
Scale: 1:500 000 m

FIGURE 3.3 Twin Cities of the US-Mexico border at the end of the twentieth century, showing relative city sizes and the percent Hispanic population of US cities north of the international boundary.

Matthew Schreiber with amendments by Tomás Janusas, 2012, used with permission.

workers. Women formed the majority of *maquila* workers until about 2006, when the gender share was about equal.[81]

Modernization along the borderlands was facilitated by political agreements between the two countries. Chief among these was the 1889 establishment of the International Boundary Commission/*La Comisión Internacional de Límites* and its 1944 successor, the International Boundary and Water Commission/*La Comisión Internacional de Límites y Aguas*. Their actions ushered in an era of long-term cross-border collaboration, including irrigation schemes and the construction of dams for hydroelectric power and flood control.[82]

Toward the end of the twentieth century, another push toward international integration was provided by the North American Free Trade Agreement (NAFTA), or the *Tratado de Libre Comercio* (TLC) signed by Canada, Mexico, and the US in 1994. To date, it has had mixed outcomes.[83] Ten years after, the Carnegie Endowment for International Peace concluded that NAFTA had been neither the disaster its opponents predicted nor the savior hailed by its supporters. Overall, employment in manufacturing increased in Mexico, but agricultural employment declined precipitously in the central heartland, which was very bad news for rural households.[84] NAFTA had little effect on the rate of job creation, and poverty had in fact increased as a result of the stunning setback in wages attributed to the peso crisis of 1994–1995.[85]

By the year 2000, the border region was home to about 22 million people (see Figure 3.3). The six border states of Mexico (Baja California, Sonora, Chihuahua, Coahuila, Nuevo León, and Tamaulipas) contained 18.2 million people or 16 percent of Mexico's total population, up from 10 percent in 1900. The four US border states (California, Arizona, New Mexico and Texas) were

Table 3.1 Population Growth, Selected Border Cities, 1980–2005

POPULATION	1980	2005
Tijuana	429,500	1,410,700
San Diego	875,538	1,255,340
Mexicali	341,559	855,902
Calexico	14,412	36,005
Ciudad Juárez	544,496	1,313,338
El Paso	425,259	598,590
Matamoros	188,745	462,157
Brownsville	88,997	167,493

home to 66.9 million or 21 percent of the US population, up from 6 percent in 1900.[86] The rough-and-tumble twin towns had become transborder cities with rapidly growing populations, especially on the Mexican side (see Table 3.1).

Writing in 1995, two Brownsville professors, Milo Kearney and Anthony Knopp, boldly predicted that NAFTA/TLC would open up an era of integration not seen since Spanish times, and that the twin towns foreshadowed a "bilingual and bicultural Englanish-speaking Spanglo society which could spread through most of North America."[87] Though their phrasing may have been inelegant, the future they imagined is upon us.

4

Law and Order at the Border

THE BORDERLANDS HAVE always been a place of strife. In a masterpiece of understatement, the informal dean of border studies, Oscar Martínez, referred to the region as a "troublesome border."[1] Between 1848 and 1920, many low-intensity transborder conflicts came close to rekindling war between the US and Mexico. The irritants derived from many sources, including repeated infringement of territorial boundaries, ultrasensitive nationalistic sentiments, and spillovers from internal disputes (especially the US Civil War and the Mexican Revolution). The persistent depredations caused by the "Indian problem" fueled an atmosphere of anarchic violence on both sides of the line. Only after the Mexican Revolution did political diplomacy substitute for the reflexive military actions that characterized cross-border relations prior to 1920.

There was blame enough to go round for the carnage.[2] The Anglos were incontestably interlopers, brandishing manifestos proclaiming religious and political freedoms, together with self-defined notions of natural rights and their nation's Manifest Destiny. Indigenous Indian groups had long battled one another, but soon transferred their attention (often in unison) to the newcomers. The Spanish and (later) Mexican governments already had ongoing conflicts with Indians, but a newly independent Mexico was promptly confronted by a belligerent northern neighbor intent on a land grab of continental proportions.

After the 1848 Treaty, Indian raids continued on both sides of the border for many decades. Northern Mexico was also bludgeoned by an epidemic of postwar filibustering expeditions by illegal US mercenaries intent on enriching themselves. Most notorious among these was William Walker, who landed in La Paz (Baja California) in 1853 and declared himself president of the "Republic of Lower California." The US was unable to restrain the banditry of the filibusters, but lack of government support was one reason these aggressions ultimately failed.[3]

Thus it was that in the second half of the nineteenth century and early decades of the twentieth, borderland peoples were thrown together without knowledge of one another's languages, history, culture, or true intent. Their agitated interactions were frequently based on mistrust, racism, even hatred. Yet, temporary alliances of convenience were also common in matters of trade and collective defense. In a paradoxical way, a combination of antagonism and alliance fashioned connections that, over time and space, fostered borderland integration.[4]

The Indian Problem and the Rise of Borderland Policing

The persistent stereotype of North American Indian as savage has long obscured understanding of the orchestrated symphony of lives that was being composed during the nineteenth century. Historian Gary Clayton Anderson concisely articulates the diversity and utility of Indian contributions in the history of Texas:

> Comanches became excellent breeders of horses, building a political economy that benefited Anglos, especially those on the high plains and in New Mexico, but one that was based, to some degree, on raiding. Caddos and Wichitas were fine farmers…and often served as scouts for rangers and the army. Cherokees built towns, farms, and even schools in Texas.…Tejanos often taught Anglos how to be cowboys and wanted to become respectable ranchers themselves, exporting their mutton and beef to the United States. All of these [Indian] groups made contributions to Texas history; they can no longer be dismissed as simple murderers and rapists.[5]

More generally, Brian DeLay makes a convincing case that Indian peoples "fundamentally reshaped the ground upon which Mexico and the United States would compete in the mid-nineteenth century."[6] This astonishing narrative brought a powerful Comanche empire into contact with the Spanish, Mexicans and upstart Anglos during a period of rapid modernization and geopolitical change.[7]

The distant origins of the powerful Comanche are hazy, although many experts believe they are part of the Uto-Aztecan-speaking people, who by the early sixteenth century had come to occupy a large swath of land in the northern Great Plains and southern Plateau regions of the US. Migrations had sent one Uto-Aztec group to the Valley of Mexico, where they established the legendary Aztec empire; a second stream (the Numic people) ventured into the Great Basin and Rocky Mountains. The Numic expansion was led by the Shoshones, the parent group of the Comanche who eventually occupied much of the Great Basin up to the edge of the Great Plains.[8]

By the early 1700s, the Comanches were still a small tribe of hunter-gatherers along the northern edge of Spanish New Mexico. They appear in Spanish records of the early eighteenth century, with a minor reputation for belligerence. After further migrations, they entered the home territory of the Utes, also a Numic-speaking peoples, and founded a political and military alliance that formed the basis for Comanche power. The Utes ushered the Comanche into a new era of horses, guns, metal tools, commerce, trade networks, and slave raiding. The Comanche soon gained a reputation as fierce and elusive fighters, highly mobile and with impressive geographical range. They fought a half-century-long war with the Apaches that did not end until 1723 when the last Apache village disappeared from the contested territories. The Apaches petitioned for Spanish assistance against Comanche aggression, but Spain instead turned its back on the Plains, thereby leaving the territory open to Comanche takeover. Within a generation, Comanches would command the southern plains along the entire length of Spain's northern frontier from New Mexico to Central Texas (see Figures 4.1 and 4.2).[9]

Not only did the Comanche confront other Indian tribes, they also assertively blocked the colonial expansion of Europeans, obliging them to conform with Comanche ways. The Comanche sought not to conquer and colonize, but to coexist and control.[10] Their empire was not a single centralized authority, but its regional core (the Comanchería) was linked with adjacent tribes whose fortunes were tied to Comanche hegemony. Historian Pekka Hämäläinen is unambiguous in her assessment of the significance of this empire:

> In character and logic, the eighteenth and early nineteenth-century Southwest was unequivocally a Comanche creation, an indigenous world where intercolonial rivalries were often mere surface disturbances on the deeper, stronger current of Comanche imperialism.[11]

SINCE THE CONQUEST, Spain had been only intermittently successful in pacifying indigenous peoples.[12] In order to regain some measure of control, the conquerors often returned to a tried-and-tested system of 'soft' subjugation.[13]

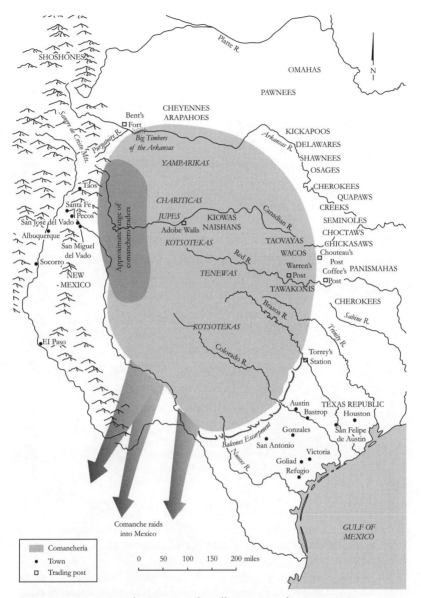

FIGURE 4.1 The Comanche Empire and its alliance network, 1830s–1840s.

Comanche commerce and kinship extended over a vast mid-continental region during the first half of the nineteenth century. Its alliances helped curtail inter-tribal warfare. Comanche control of the horse trade was an important factor in its regional hegemony, but so were cultural influences such as the diffusion of language and religious practices. Map by Bill Nelson. From: Hämäläinen, P. *The Comanche Empire*, Yale University Press. Copyright © 2008 by Yale University.

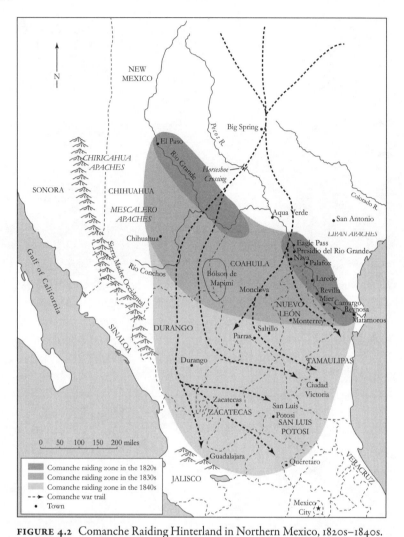

FIGURE 4.2 Comanche Raiding Hinterland in Northern Mexico, 1820s–1840s.

In the late-eighteenth and early-nineteenth centuries, the Comanche moved aggressively out of their Plains homeland and into Northen Mexico, intent on weakening their Apache rivals, extending their tribute area, and acquiring horses, mules, guns and food. At the height of their power, Comanche raiding extended from Chihuahua to the Gulf coast, and south almost to Mexico City. Map by Bill Nelson. From Hämäläinen , P. *The Comanche Empire*, Yale University Press. Copyright © 2008 by Yale University.

By introducing new populations from outside, Spain anticipated that self-interested settlers would work to her advantage by diluting local unrest. In 1818, Moses Austin proposed to the Spanish government that Catholic Americans be allowed to settle in Texas as loyal Spanish citizens. Spain agreed, but Austin's death and Mexico's independence prevented the proposal's realization.

After Independence, the Mexican government regarded all Indians as implacable foes of a settled society.[14] However, the responsibility for everyday security usually fell to border dwellers themselves. For instance, the state of Sonora expanded its militia system and offered a cash bounty on all Apache scalps, a practice that endured to the end of the nineteenth century.[15] Mexico also adopted the Spanish practice of introducing new settlers into troublesome districts. Moses Austin's son, Stephen, followed his father's example by securing an agreement with the Mexican government that fatefully opened the doors to thousands of Anglo settlers, both legal and illegal.[16] In 1835, Austin was sent by Anglo-Texans on a tour of the US to drum up sympathy for their cause. At meetings from New York to New Orleans, Austin made the case:

> … a few years back, Texas was a wilderness, the home of the uncivilized and wandering Comanche and other tribes of Indians, who waged constant battle against Spanish settlements…In order to restrain the savages and bring them into subjection, the government opened Texas for settlement…American enterprise accepted the invitation and promptly responded to the call.[17]

Nearly 30,000 Anglo-Americans arrived in the decades of the 1820s and 1830s. By 1845, their population had grown to 160,000.[18] When Anglos, including the US military, arrived in northern Mexico during the early years of Independence, they developed more pragmatic relationships with Indians.[19] For instance, Anglo-Apache trade in goods stolen by the Apache from Mexicans was commonplace, but so were Anglo bounty hunters seeking Apache scalps.

By the early 1830s many Indian tribes, including Apache and Comanche, abandoned the working arrangements they formerly held, and the region descended into a fearsome violence. Historian DeLay suggests that declining Mexican power and Anglo expansion caused old allegiances to unravel and contributed to heightened levels of instability and violence. He refers to these pulverizing times as the "War of a Thousand Deserts:"

> The raids and counter-raids escalated throughout the 1830s and 1840s, reducing thriving villages into ghostly deserts…By the eve of the U.S. invasion, the violence spanned nine states and had claimed thousands of Mexican and Indian lives, ruined much of northern Mexico's economy, stalled its demographic growth, depopulated a vast countryside and turned Mexicans…against each other in the struggle for scarce resources.[20]

This devastation worked in favor of the US in its conquest of the Mexican north during the 1846–1848 war. The US invaders encountered broken, abandoned landscapes and enemy combatants already exhausted by years of struggle against Indians.[21]

The "Indian problem" persisted for many decades after the Treaty of Guadalupe Hidalgo, ending only after the surrender of Geronimo and his Chiricahua Apache in 1886. Even so, many contemporary settlers attested to the peaceful relations that some newcomers enjoyed with Indians, as one nineteenth-century homesteader recorded:

> We succeeded in purchasing several mules, which cost us between ten and twenty dollars' worth of goods apiece. In Comanche trade the main trouble consists in fixing the price of the first animal. This being settled by the chiefs, it often happens that mule after mule is led up and the price received without further cavil. The Santa Fé caravans have generally avoided every manner of trade with the wild Indians, for fear of being treacherously dealt with in the familiar discourse which necessarily ensues. This I am convinced is an erroneous impression; for I have always found that savages are much less hostile to those [with] whom they trade, than to any other people. They are emphatically fond of traffic and being anxious to encourage the whites to come among them, instead of committing depredations upon those with whom they trade, they are generally ready to defend them against any enemy.[22]

The Treaty of Guadalupe Hidalgo placed most Indians on the northern side of the new boundary line, and Mexican–Indian conflict intensified because Indian raiders simply retreated over the line after their attacks. This was an enormous political headache for the US which, under Article 11 of the Treaty, had committed to preventing Indian incursions into Mexico.[23] The magnitude of this policing task was totally underestimated by the US Government, which faced claims amounting to millions of dollars from victimized Mexicans. Legal relief from Article 11 was only achieved in 1854 as part of the Gadsden Treaty, but such laws made little impression on the Indians who continued their cross-border skirmishes until the 1880s. Mexicans increasingly sought alliances with Anglos against Apache, and even engaged the assistance of Indians hostile to the Apache.[24] The relationship between Apache and their enemies dissolved into an uncontainable vortex of raid and counter-raid.[25]

IN 1823, JUST two years after he began bringing colonists to the region, Stephen Austin hired ten experienced frontiersmen as "rangers" to ride punitive expeditions against Indians and other hostile elements. A decade later, delegates to the Texas revolutionary convention in 1835 approved formation of an organization known as the Texas Rangers, consisting of a force of 56 men divided into three companies.[26] The Rangers were mainly local men, a motley crew drawn from "brave defenders of the republic, rather harmless stay-at-home show-offs, or (more often than not) brutal murderers."[27] They were encouraged to attack Indian villages, rob, rape, and spread terror so that Indians would leave. Texans supported the Rangers; they would likely have accepted any form of police authority that quelled the violence in their favor.

The Texas Rangers dispensed their own kind of brutal justice. In early 1848, for instance, one company led by Captain Samuel Highsmith stumbled onto a hunting party of 26 Wichita and Caddo Indians, men and boys who had camped south of the Brazos River. Highsmith's troops crept to within one hundred yards and then charged, firing their pistols indiscriminately. The startled Indians had scarce opportunity for self-defense. When the guns were quiet again, 25 Indians were dead. Highsmith and his men gathered up the hides, meat, horses, and scalps and rode back to a heroes' welcome in San Antonio.[28] Such vigilantism was not universally popular. General Zachary Taylor at one point dismissed the Rangers, but it didn't last.[29] People wanted the Rangers; they were already a legend.

Gary Clayton Anderson takes an opposite view, charging that the Rangers were on a mission of "ethnic cleansing" to remove Indians from the territory.[30] Western novelist Larry McMurtry rejects this viewpoint, claiming that it's pretty much impossible to tarnish the Rangers image, at least in Texas.[31] McMurtry demonstrates how easy it is to shift blame, writing of the

> terror, carnage, and widespread desolation suffered by the *citizens* of northwest Mexico and the American Southwest, mainly in the second and third quarters of the nineteenth century. This *terror was wrought* for the most part by Apaches, Comanches, and other raiding tribes of the plains and deserts.[32]

I've added the two emphases here to underscore the McMurtry view that good "citizens" were at the receiving end of "terror" wrought by Indians, overlooking the fact that it was the invasion by stateless citizens that caused indigenous peoples to rise up in the first place to protect their life, liberty, and happiness in their nations.

Different interpretations of history do not detract from the fact that the border during the nineteenth century was an extraordinarily violent place, lacking formal law enforcement agencies and institutions.[33] In another notorious example, during the early dawn of April 30, 1871, a combined party of Anglos, Mexicans, and Tohono O'odham Indians gathered outside an Apache camp in Aravaipa Canyon in the Arizona Territory.[34] When the combined party attacked the camp, many Apache were killed in their sleep, mostly women and children. A few succeeded in scaling the canyon walls only to be shot by men waiting above. In less than 30 minutes, almost 150 Apache were dead and 29 captured. All this despite the fact that the Apache had established a private treaty for use of the canyon land with the nearby local military at Camp Grant, which subsequently lent its name to the massacre. The cruel slaughter attracted national attention. President Ulysses S. Grant called it "murder, purely."[35] Arizona settlers countered that a distant US government had failed to provide proper protection so they were entitled to act in their own defense (a complaint used today by protagonists in Arizona's immigration battles). A trial of about 100 defendants was held in Pima County courthouse in December, 1871; it was the first time in Arizona's territorial history that the killing of an Apache by a non-Apache had led to prosecution of the alleged perpetrators. In Tucson that day it took the jury only 19 minutes to acquit the accused.[36] The Camp Grant Massacre is notable not only for its ferocity and planning, but also for the alliance of convenience among three groups infamously regarded as enemies: Anglo, Mexican, and Tohono O'odham Indian.[37]

The success of the Texas Rangers was not lost on adjacent territories. In 1901, Arizona Territorial Governor Nathan Oakes Murphy referred to their inspiration: "What we need is a hardriding, sure shooting outfit something like the Texas Rangers or the Mexican Rurales."[38] That same year, the Arizona Rangers was officially established by the Legislative Assembly, and was followed a few years later by a New Mexico Mounted Police Force.[39] Previous incarnations of the Arizona Rangers had existed in the early 1860s, but the force was disbanded and absorbed into the Confederate Army at the onset of the Civil War. The new Arizona Rangers established between 1901 and 1909 was a result of cattle industry concerns over rustling and of pressure for Arizonan statehood. These Arizona Rangers were every bit as rough-and-ready as their Texas counterparts; indeed, many of them were Texans by birth. Many Arizonan cities such as Phoenix, Tucson, and Prescott were modernizing, but the majority of the Arizona Territory remained a wide-open territory of more than 114,000 square miles. With prosperity and statehood at stake, Arizonans felt that their Rangers could provide the rule of law needed to secure the future.[40]

The Arizona–Mexico line was a two-way path to freedom for outlaws. As a former ranger in Douglas, Arizona, explained: "If peace officers appeared in town, lawbreakers could slip over to Agua Prieta, where sordid pleasures awaited among the cantinas and cribs of the ranchita on Calle Cinco. Likewise, men wanted by the law in Mexico found Douglas a ready haven."[41] Although laws technically forbade the Arizona Rangers from going to Mexico in any official capacity, the pursuit of fugitives often took them over the line.[42] They observed the technicalities of Mexican law and protected their jobs by requesting a leave of absence from the company before crossing. Forces in Arizona and Mexico could then collaborate to patrol the border for rustlers, smugglers, or gun runners; one famous ally was Colonel Emilio Kosterlitsky of the Mexican *Rurales*.[43] Cross-border interaction was so common that as early as 1903, the Arizona Rangers required proficiency in Spanish.[44] Some attempt was made in 1907 to curb their riotous behavior, when six General Orders for Rangers were issued. They advised against congregating in saloons or bawdy houses; prohibited entering Mexico in any official capacity whatsoever, armed or unarmed; insisted on the humane treatment of prisoners; and required that reports should be made out on the first day of each new month and sent to Headquarters.[45]

In 1853, the Los Angeles Rangers was founded in response to the proliferation of Mexican bandits and incursions by desert Indians into Southern California. The LA lawmen were mostly known for the pursuit of the Mexican Joaquin Murietta, viewed by some as "an outlaw and enemy to the human race," but by others as a revolutionary patriot and "champion of his countrymen."[46] In 1881, Major Horace Bell published an entertaining memoir of the LA Rangers, unusual for being short on violence and long on social commentary. Mindful of his readers' expectations, Bell set out early to establish LA's lawlessness:

> I have no hesitation in saying that in the years of 1851, '52, and '53, there were more desperadoes in Los Angeles than in any place on the Pacific coast, San Francisco with its great population not excepted. It was a fact, that all of the…cut-throats of California and Mexico naturally met at Los Angeles, and at Los Angeles they fought. Knives and revolvers settled all differences, either real or imaginary. The slightest misunderstandings were settled on the spot with knife or bullet, the Mexican preferring the former at close quarter and the American the latter.[47]

Bell then proceeded to relate tales of legal battles over a mule, splendid society balls, and of meeting "Major Emery [sic]" of boundary survey fame.[48]

LA's ethnic diversity was already well-established by the mid-nineteenth century, a characteristic that led Arthur Ellis, in an introduction to Bell's book, to disqualify it as "an American community."[49] As was typical of the fractious times in Arizona and Texas, Los Angeles was not a tolerant community; in fact, the whole state of California was regarded as an "ultra white man's government."[50]

THE CLOSEST MEXICAN equivalent to the Texas Rangers was the *Rurales*, or *Guardia Rural*, an armed constabulary established by President Benito Juárez in 1861. The *Rurales* came into existence just as the Indian problem was ending, and their jurisdiction was more oriented toward the capital region rather than the borderlands. Nevertheless, they played a part in the border story largely because their absence allowed the incursion of other law enforcement agencies (including US-based rangers) into the north.

Various forms of *rurales* had existed before 1861 and the term had been applied to many rural police forces.[51] Following Mexican Independence, widespread concern for public security along the roadways led to the establishment of the first detachment of Juárez's *Rurales*, which patrolled the busy road between Mexico City and Veracruz.[52] The *Rurales* grew slowly, becoming a major presence only during the long dictatorship of President Porfirio Díaz (1876–1911). Díaz expanded the *Rurales* from a few hundred officers to 2,700 by the end of his dictatorship. At its peak, the *Rurales* numbered about 4,000. They were spread unevenly across the country, mostly in and around Mexico City. Detachments were moved around with some regularity, which might have contributed to impressions of their ubiquity.[53]

Much speculation has been devoted to assessing the effectiveness and reputation of the *Rurales*.[54] As in the case of the Texas Rangers, legends have served only to obscure a balanced assessment. On one hand, in the early 1900s, Ethel Brilliana Tweedie had this to say:

> No braver, more trustworthy, or finer horsemen exist. These Rurales are most courteous and polite, always thinking of little things for the comfort of anyone they are escorting, and the mere remembrance of my association with them is a pleasure.[55]

On the other hand, Carelston Beals offered this bitter denunciation:

> In the country districts stern order was maintained by the mounted cossacks, the *rurales*, comprising the highest paid military corps in the

world, who massacred first and inquired afterwards—if they inquired at all.[56]

In fact, the volunteer *Rurales* were poor and illiterate with an ill-formed sense of duty. Desertions, drunkenness, and disobedience were endemic problems throughout the force. Their reputation for excellent horsemanship and marksmanship was illusory, since prerequisites on paper were routinely ignored by recruiters.[57] But on public parades in Mexico and at international events such as the 1901 World Exposition in Buffalo, New York, only the very best performed. Clad in flamboyant uniforms and mounted on fine horses, the *rurales* recalled a Spanish past of gentlemen *hacendados* (ranchers).[58] Mexican poet Amado Nervo witnessed a parade of *Rurales* in 1891 and was moved to exclaim: "*¡Es la patria que pasa!*" (It's our country passing by!)[59]

The murderous reputation of the *Rurales* was deliberately cultivated by Porfirio Díaz once he came to power. Just as President Juárez before him, Díaz was concerned to secure public security, but he also wanted to reduce the size of the army and give work to discharged soldiers so that they would not become a threat to his regime. Díaz set up the army and *Rurales* as counterweights, though in times of national crisis, the two branches joined forces.[60] He also used the *Rurales* to promote national identity and consciousness, a symbol of unity in his push for "order and progress."[61] For this reason, he did not use *Rurales* (overtly at least) to crush his political opponents, nor involve them in his harshest repressions. Instead, the force was generally occupied in a wide variety of routine ways: patrolling, guarding shipments from mines, supporting local police, escorting prisoners, and protecting public payrolls and buildings. Not all localities welcomed the presence of a federal police, and when Díaz received complaints, he sometimes curtailed the reach of his *Rurales*.[62]

The *Rurales* helped Díaz in one of his most important public relations efforts—calming the concerns of foreign investors.[63] By curbing labor unrest, eliminating brigandage, and pacifying the countryside, Díaz was able to attract the foreign capital he so ardently desired. The mere suggestion that *Rurales* were being dispatched to areas of unrest was often enough to satisfy queasy mineowners. However, skepticism regarding this cozy picture of an elegant, patriotic, and skillful police is fully justified. In 1907, a textile strike at Río Blanco (in the state of Veracruz) was brutally suppressed when *Rurales* and federal troops fired into crowds on two separate occasions, killing over 100 people. In another 1873 incident, *Rurales* murdered about 100 Indians who had rebelled in the State of México.[64] But when a detachment of *Rurales* was

sent to Cananea (Sonora) in 1906 to quell the rioting of striking copper miners, they arrived only after the turbulence had been settled by the army and
a force of visiting Arizona Rangers. Like the Texas Rangers, the *Rurales* were
violent and abusive in pursuit of their goals. US writer Doug Meed concluded
that the Rurales was an elite force of cutthroats, a hard-riding, fast-shooting,
and utterly ruthless constabulary.[65] The rural poor in Mexico endured the
Rurales with a mixture of fear and respect.

The Mexican Revolution brought an end to the *Rurales*.[66] Most of them
supported President Díaz in his campaign against the rebels, and contin-
gents of the *Rurales* occupied northern border states during the uncertain
years leading up to the Revolution.[67] However, when the time came for
battle, the army—not the *Rurales*—was dispatched north to contain the
rebellion.[68] The Revolution also ended Díaz's dictatorship, though for a
while the *Rurales* continued to function during the presidencies of Francisco
Madero and Victoriano Huerta.[69] Indeed, Huerta used the *Rurales* to assas-
sinate Madero during the lawless and vengeful "Ten Tragic Days" of 1913.
The *Rurales* were officially disbanded in 1914 after Huerta himself fled into
exile.

THE US COULD not refrain from meddling in the conduct of the Mexican
Revolution. One extravagant day in 1916 Francisco "Pancho" Villa invaded
Columbus, New Mexico, which rests in the middle of the New Mexico "boot
heel." In the early morning of March 9, Villa and a large contingent of his
followers crossed the border to attack Camp Furlong, home of the US 13th
Cavalry. Rebuffed by its occupants, Villa retreated to nearby Columbus,
setting fire to buildings, killing 18 people and wounding another 12 before
returning to Mexico. The next day, an outraged US Congress authorized a
punitive expedition into Mexico to capture Villa and disband his troops.[70]

Villa's attack on Columbus is recounted first-hand by Elías L. Torres, who
acted as an intermediary between Villa and the government of Adolfo de la
Huerta.[71] Torres wrote that Villa was neither a "genius of warfare to whom is
owed the triumph of the Revolution," nor a "monster who fills all Mexicans
with shame." He was, more precisely "one of the most prominent figures of
the [Revolution]…who will, in spite of everything, go down in history."[72]
According to Torres, Villa's invasion of Columbus was not one of his shrewd-
est moves. Villa was angry because his former ally-turned-enemy, Venustiano
Carranza, had received permission from the US government to move troops
through US territory to defend Sonora against Villa's attack. When Sonora
was saved, Villa was furious and planned to invade US territory. On the eve

of the Columbus attack, Torres reported that Villa goaded his troops: "We're going to kill gringos, boys."[73]

Contemporary US reports of Villa's invasion ranged from bombastic to hysterical. A small museum in present-day Columbus—run by a man who claims that his grandfather was in Columbus when Villa crossed the line—sells facsimile front pages of the *Santa Fe New Mexican*. Under the banner headline of the issue of March 9, "Villa Invades the U.S.: Bandits Burn and Kill in Columbus," the *New Mexican* ran several accounts of atrocities with lurid headlines:

DEATH TO AMERICANS, PANCHO'S CRY:
WANTS TO CHOKE HATED GRINGO.

AMERICAN TORN FROM WIFE'S ARMS,
SHOT LIKE A DOG AND ROASTED.

AMERICAN CITIZENS ON AMERICAN SOIL ENTICED
FROM HOMES
BY BLOOD-MAD TORCH-SQUAD OF MEXICAN BRUTES
AND SHOT DOWN.[74]

A few days later, the newspaper argued that an army of 150,000 men was needed to deal with Villa;[75] and on March 15, less than one week after the invasion, the *New Mexican* proclaimed: "American Army Crosses into Mexico." Despite efforts led by General John Pershing, Villa was not captured, though he dispersed his followers for their own safety.[76]

Founded in 1891, turn-of-the-century Columbus was a thriving town a couple of miles north of the border, supported by nearby Camp Furlong and standing across from its twin town, Palomas, in the Mexican state of Chihuahua. After the Camp closed, Columbus declined. Today, the tiny town commemorates the 1916 invasion in a 99-acre Pancho Villa State Park and two small museums. There isn't much to see beyond a rail station and a few splashes of homes. A residual bitterness still clouds some conversations about the invasion, but locals understand that Villa's incursion is the only thing that people remember about Columbus. Except until now.

On March 10, 2011, the citizens of Columbus awoke to the sound of helicopters and people with guns in the street. Ninety-five years and a day after Villa's raid, federal agents stormed into town, arresting the town's mayor, police chief, and other officials on charges of smuggling guns, ammunition, and body armor across the border to Mexican drug traffickers.[77]

Birth of the US Border Patrol

After 1917, legal migrants to the US were required to undergo a personal inspection (including health and literacy tests) and pay a head tax and visa fees before entering the country. In those days, if you were a Mexican crossing the border from Ciudad Juárez to El Paso, you would enter a disinfection area where your clothes would be steam cleaned and fumigated. If lice were found, your head and body hair would be shaved and you would be scrubbed with kerosene and vinegar. Other cleaning agents included gasoline, sulfuric acid, DDT and Zyklon-B (later used to exterminate people in Nazi death camps). In 1921, over 127,000 Mexicans were bathed and deloused at the Santa Fe Bridge crossing alone. If for some reason you were detained, your clothes were routinely soaked in a mix of gasoline, creosote, and formaldehyde; and detainees were themselves obliged to step into baths of gasoline. In one notorious episode at El Paso jail in 1916, a misplaced match ignited the explosive vapors and 27 people died. The routine bathing and fumigating of migrants continued until the 1950s along the Texas–Mexico border.[78]

By the 1920s, the numbers of crossings made by Mexican nationals increased. Cross-border smuggling became a serious problem, and smuggled goods from the US were so pervasive that some Mexican officials even contemplated building fences around their towns. Faced with an increasingly chaotic border situation and pressure from US agriculturalists to ensure their labor supply, Congress passed the National Origins Act on May 28, 1924. The Act tightened immigration laws and set aside $1 million to establish a "land border patrol" which became known as the United States Border Patrol (USBP). No longer a frontier or a border, the division had been transformed into a line on the ground, commonly known as *la línea* in Spanish. For the first time, the US possessed a separate police force dedicated solely to enforcing its national boundaries.[79] Early recruitment advertisements for the Border Patrol were emphatically "Ranger" in their orientation, accepting only those who were "big, strong and fearless;" experienced in cowboy work and horseback riding; and of good moral character.[80]

The 1924 Act transformed the issue of labor migration into a problem of criminal behavior. Mexico's "migrant" became the US's "illegal immigrant," leading to an entirely predictable upsurge in recorded illegal crossings as well as the birth of a lucrative business of migrant smuggling.[81] Mexican views on migration and border policing at this time were supportive of greater control. Mexican law protected the right of citizens to free entry and exit from Mexico, but authorities were worried as much by the loss of its citizens as by their reclassification as criminals. So Mexico elected to police emigration through a variety of means, including checkpoint, passport confiscation, and fine.[82] The Mexican Department of Migration, established in 1926, worked with the US Border Patrol to curtail unauthorized border crossings. The Department's efforts were largely ineffective, but set a precedent for cross-border cooperation. Mexico from this time forward became an enduring partner in migration control and border enforcement, albeit frequently in response to US-led initiatives.[83]

The USBP was set up with three regional districts: Los Angeles, El Paso, and San Antonio. The decentralized system allowed much local autonomy and discretion. Within months agents were on duty at the Canadian and Mexican borders. Officers were given broad powers to interrogate, detain, and arrest any person suspected of illegal entry. The geographical extent of their authority extended from the moment when migrants entered the US until they reached their final destination, giving agents a nationwide reach. The force doubled in size to 916 officers between 1925 and 1939.[84]

The work of Border Patrol agents took the form of *line watches*, i.e., observing the boundary line to intercept migrants in the act of crossing, which was not very effective; *apprehensions*, which mainly occurred along back roads and traffic stops rather than at the line itself; and tracking people after they had crossed, also known as *sign cutting*.[85] Some agents appeared to possess uncanny forensic powers, capable of recognizing that "A Mexican always walks heavy on the outside of his feet. When he walks, he puts his foot down on the heel first and then rolls it off—Indians will do that too. Whites and blacks ordinarily put their feet down flat."[86]

Border Patrol work was dangerous. By 1933, 21 officers had been killed, and each death led to vengeance-seeking by aggrieved officers.[87] A frontier ethos akin to the Texas Rangers permeated the USBP, and personal vendettas were as strong a motivation as defense of national interests. The 1937 opening of the Border Patrol Training School brought some standardization to on-the-ground practices. That year, the agency had 325 officers in place on the Canadian border compared with 234 along the line with Mexico.[88]

A massive repatriation of Mexican workers during the Great Depression was followed by an equally enormous labor shortage during the Second World War. The US entered the war in 1941, and Mexico in 1942, joining the nations in mutual concern for national security and economic development. The numbers of border patrol personnel grew substantially, and their responsibilities shifted as resources multiplied. The agency responded to national needs, becoming a de facto branch of federal law enforcement. For example, agents were deployed to guard the coastline against enemy incursions; they transported inmates to internment camps; and served as guards at the camps. Funding for the agency doubled between 1939 and 1941 to $3.8M; and the number of border patrol officers doubled between 1939 and 1941, to just over 1,500. War also intensified bilateral cooperation. For instance, the first collaborative deportations began in 1945, including train and plane removals to the Mexican interior. [89]

World War II increased demand for agricultural production in support of the war effort. On August 4, 1942, the US and Mexico signed an agreement called the "Bracero Program," under which the US government contracted with Mexican laborers to work in agriculture. Mexico supported the Bracero Program as a way of managing unsanctioned emigration, and only healthy males from areas in Mexico not experiencing labor shortages were eligible.[90] The two countries jointly upgraded their rail and road connections, and Mexican agriculture was reorganized in favor of war-needed goods (such as cotton) to the detriment of corn production. The consequent domestic food shortages in Mexico stimulated yet more northbound migration. Mexican growers pressured their government to prohibit illegal exit by their workers, who were by now essentially crossing unopposed. They pressed for army patrols in the Mexicali and Matamoros cotton-growing districts and urged the US to become more aggressive in preventing crossings. Disputes between the two countries about their respective responsibilities in policing the border became so intense that at one point Mexico temporarily suspended its participation in the Bracero Program.[91]

During the war years, an important shift in the geography of USBP policing occurred. In response to the growing volume of undocumented migration, a majority of new USBP personnel was assigned to the southern border, which henceforward became its principal locus of operations. In 1944 the so-called "Mexican Deportation Parties"—short-term assignments of agents to immigrant hot-spots—doubled the number of apprehensions in a single year.[92] Increased numbers of undocumented crossings in California caused a chain-link fence to be erected for over five miles on either side of the All-American Canal at Calexico in 1945, using materials that had been recycled from a former World War II internment camp. Mexican soldiers were dispatched to patrol and protect the fence during its construction.[93] Yet migrants remained undeterred. They cut holes in the Calexico fence, and began crossing in desert and mountain regions; as nowadays, the numbers of deaths and disappearances escalated in these more remote regions.

Migrants also became bolder. In one notorious case, 4,000 migrants stormed the El Paso border in October 1948, using their large numbers to overwhelm Border Patrol officers.[94] Mexican authorities became increasingly nervous about a situation that appeared to be spinning out of control, deploying military forces along the border in order to prevent crowds from charging the crossings. In 1949 a national emergency was declared when the Reynosa–Matamoros area lacked sufficient numbers of cotton workers; fines and prison sentences were imposed on anyone taking a Mexican worker out of the country. Five thousand Mexican troops policed the border in the early 1950s, and in 1953 Mexico created its own border agency, the Mexican Border Patrol, to regulate migration to the South Texas region.[95]

By now, the principal concern of the USBP had become removing Mexicans from the US. One of its most successful tactics was to deploy mobile field units near workplaces and transportation corridors. The success of these mobile units became the foundation for the well-funded "Operation Wetback" program.[96] On June 10, 1954, a small army of USBP officers set up roadblocks in California and western Arizona. Over the next seven days, they apprehended almost one thousand migrants, and six months later claimed that over one million migrants had been removed from the US. Mexican-American leaders in the US supported the crackdown; so did Mexican-American workers who saw their wages and livelihood threatened by a flood of newcomers. At one point members of the US National Farm Labor Union patrolled the border line and turned back intercepted migrants.[97]

The ripple effect of Operation Wetback was widespread.[98] The hundreds of thousands of detained migrants exceeded the USBP's capacity to house them. Two new detention centers were rapidly constructed, but county jails were also rented—a financially lucrative arrangement for many localities, then as now. Many public spaces were converted into temporary holding stations. Although Mexican authorities collaborated in returning detainees to the Mexican interior, the receiving localities could not cope with the sheer numbers arriving at border towns. (In a two-week period in June 1954, for instance, Nogales, Arizona, received over 23,000 migrants for deportation.) The sweeps prompted more workers to seek official status before entering the US; following accelerated apprehensions in the Lower Rio Grande Valley, the number of Texas Bracero contracts grew from 168 to almost 42,000 over a one-year period in 1954.[99]

Things calmed down along the line after Operation Wetback. The number of apprehensions plummeted as the agency entered another period of adjustment. Agents found themselves involved at the Canadian border; in Florida, after Fidel Castro's takeover of Cuba; and policing civil rights disturbances in the south, school integration in Mississippi, and Native American unrest at Wounded Knee. The agents' evolving workloads placed more emphasis on crime control and police work, including the routine fingerprinting of those taken into custody. The annual budget of the USBP grew from $7 million in 1954 to $12 million by 1956.[100]

Border patrol officers were cross-designated as customs inspectors in 1955, thus acquiring a larger role in illicit drug interdiction. Before the Second World War, most of the opium and heroin consumed in the US came from Italy, France, and the Middle East. The war disrupted these supply routes and Mexico took over as supplier, encouraged by the US, which needed medical morphine and hemp for fibers and ropes in the war effort. As a consequence, by the mid-1940s some Mexican states (e.g., Sinaloa) were growing opium as a primary cash crop. Later, Mexico became the primary supply route for South American drugs with US destinations. Border Patrol officers complained that it was getting harder to distinguish migrants from drug smugglers.[101]

Another pivotal moment in USBP history was the passage of the 1965 Immigration Reform Act, which placed the first numerical limits on legal immigration from Mexico into the US, capping it at 120,000 persons annually.[102] This was insufficient to meet the demands of the US labor market, and stringent rationing of legal immigration slots coupled with hard times in Mexico boosted unsanctioned crossings. Border apprehensions once again escalated (from 100,000 in 1968, to half a million by 1973). The situation deteriorated further as the Mexican economy weakened; by 1975, the country was experiencing zero growth, unemployment rates as high as 45 percent, and declining real wages—all coinciding with a baby boom. Ten years after the 1965 Act, the incoming commissioner of the US Immigration and Naturalization Service (INS) confessed that the flood of illegal entries across the southern border had returned, and that the crisis of control was worse than ever.[103]

Over the next two decades, the USBP and INS waged a losing battle against undocumented migration from Mexico. The Border Patrol mandate during these times was little more than "catch-and-release"—i.e., rounding up migrants without papers and returning them directly to Mexico. Then, in the mid-1990s the first border fences began to appear in major crossing zones such as Tijuana where the program was known as Operation Gatekeeper, and in Ciudad Juárez's Operation Hold-the-Line.[104] The metal fences were constructed from panels used to provide temporary landing strips for aircraft and had been recycled from the Vietnam War (see Figure 4.3).

A VISIT TO the United States Border Patrol Museum in El Paso, Texas, conveys the enormity of transformation in border policing after the Gatekeeper era. Opened in 1994 at its present site along Transmountain Road on the

FIGURE 4.3 Border fencing during 1990s Operation Gatekeeper era, near Campo, California.

The first modern-day attempts to fortify the boundary line began in the mid-1990s with Operation 'Hold-the-Line' in El Paso, and Operation Gatekeeper in San Diego. The fencing was constructed from left-over aircraft landing mats from the War in Vietnam. Copyright © 2002 by Michael Dear.

northeast side of the city, the museum is a bit isolated but urban sprawl is creeping up the nearby freeway and road improvements are in the offing. The building itself is less than welcoming since its severe walls lack windows, and its main entrance resembles a security barrier.

Inside, there is a cornucopia. Some of the exhibits are unexpected—there are real trucks, real aircraft hung from the ceiling, and a real boat is out back. A souped-up USBP Firebird automobile rests in prominent retirement on the Museum floor, a nearby caption promising that it could chase down migrants faster than any standard four-door sedan. There are guns, flags, and artwork on display, as well as instructions on how to wear a gun holster while seated in a vehicle. Most moving is the Honor Roll of those who died in the line of duty. This includes a canine section, where police-dog lives are recorded in a series of trading cards that feature a dog's picture, age, weight, and record of drug seizures. K-9 Harry uncovered drugs with a street value of over $8 million; K-9 Duco pulled in over $5 million. (This explains why drug runners offered bounties on dogs they wanted killed.)

Nostalgia takes over with a collection of long-playing vinyl records for learning Spanish (French for the Canadian border). A collection of models of USBP vehicles includes a spectacular two-door 1960 Plymouth Fury with fins. The display cabinet on "sign-cutting," or the art of tracking in the landscape, contains a mini-diorama of the border line. In it, an innocuous border fence bisects the sandy terrain, which is scattered with clues officers use in tracking migrants, including a few tortillas (made from white paper the size of cutouts from a hole-puncher). There are knots of tires that are dragged behind vehicles in order to smooth sand and make it easier to spot migrant tracks, and there is ranching equipment for mounted horse patrols along the line. Nearby, books written by retired agents are replete with expressions of patriotism, camaraderie, and dedication to a job that demanded physical and mental toughness.[105]

Since Gatekeeper, the USBP workforce swelled to 20,000 agents and things have changed a lot along the line. Once upon a time, the job consisted of line-watching, apprehensions, sign cutting, and perhaps a little horse and canine care. Now line-watching is done remotely by surveillance camera, sign cutting is done from drones in the sky, and glittery all-terrain vehicles require servicing but no grooming or feeding. At night, agents can watch exaggerated reality-TV versions of their daily routines (though I'm told that the shows edit out the tedium and paperwork that the job entails).

By and large, I've met the friendlier kind of USBP agent along the line. Early on, I received a warm welcome at Marfa station, near Big Bend in Texas. My interview was initially mediated by a communications officer whose job included protecting line officers from visitors. But one lifelong agent later took me aside and began talking openly about life on the line: the camaraderie and traditions, the challenge and thrills of sign cutting, the beauty of the desert, and new worries about transportation upgrades in the neighboring state of Chihuahua that could propel more people closer to the border. In contrast, during a postfortification visit near Yuma, Arizona, I was deafened by clusters of angry agents mounted on noisy all-terrain vehicles, totally uninterested in why I was near the fence but uncommonly determined that I should not encroach within 100 feet of it. Then again, on my most recent visit, a California officer volunteered to climb atop the fence to help me obtain a photograph of a monument that was hidden behind it.

In today's altered landscapes of borderland homeland security, it is far tougher out on the line than when I began my travels. I believe that the fence itself has contributed to an atmosphere of mistrust, and elevated levels of fear and hostility along its length. The fence has created a mean place, slicing though what is still a troublesome border zone that is paradoxically being united by the actions of binational law enforcement agencies. The miracle is how much civility still lingers along the line.

5

Third Nation before the Wall

THE BOUNDARIES SEPARATING nation–states are usually regarded as robust, established features of the human condition, but they are not.[1] The map of present-day European nation–states, for example, is largely a consequence of two twentieth-century world wars; and the principal impetus for this book is an adjustment in the boundary of the Mexican nation–state that is only a century-and-a-half old. Moreover, since the 1848 Treaty, the line separating the US and Mexico has been constantly renegotiated and adjusted as a consequence of geopolitics and daily life among border-dwellers. Exigencies of place and practice have often trumped the rigid imperatives of international law, as national histories become subordinated to pragmatism, convenience, local memory, and informal tradition. It is the ascendancy of such local practices and traditions that gave birth to "alternative" spaces such as a third nation.

A "third nation" is a community carved out of the territories between two existing nation–states. The idea encompasses notions of a people, identity, territory, and practice. We speak of a *nation* when referring to a group of people whose members voluntarily identify with one another on the basis of a shared history and geography, including (for example) ethnic traits, cultural traditions, and joint alliances against external threats. The sentiment that unites its members is commonly called *nationalism*. Because many of the characteristics underlying nationalism are nebulous and even transitory, Benedict Anderson famously referred to nations as "imagined communities."[2] Attachment to the land is one important feature of identity, and when a people acquires the sovereign right to govern a territory—and that right is recognized by others—the territory is deemed to be a *nation–state*.[3]

A *third nation* is an "in-between" space, transcending the geopolitical boundary that divides the constitutive nation–states and creates from them a new identity distinct from the nationalisms of the host countries.

The third nation at the US–Mexican border is not yet a nation–state, but we have encountered many of the characteristics of previous nations in the borderlands. These include the ancient Chichimecans, the Spanish colonialists, and the Comanche and Apache imperiums; their vestiges stand as palimpsests of the present-day third nation. The Tohono O'Odham Indian Nation already exists as a third nation on both sides of the US–Mexican boundary between Arizona and Sonora. It possesses a long-standing, strongly-developed sense of nationalism, autonomous tribal institutions and laws, and formal territorial jurisdiction (albeit subject to consent from Mexico and the US).[4]

Third nationhood and third nationalism are complicated phenomena, whose existence may be difficult to measure and hard to prove. Third-nation sentiments are likely to vary over time and space, and rise or recede in prominence according to contingencies of the hour. A single action can have multiple, contradictory outcomes: for instance, migration may increase tolerance in receiving nations but simultaneously cause dislocation in the migrants' communities of origin, as well as stressful alienation among migrants themselves. Also, not everything that goes into making a third nation is good. For example, the flow of drugs north from Mexico and the traffic in guns south from the US are both indicative of a perverse kind of transborder integration.

The idea of a third nation is not without precedent. In the mid-1990s, artist and border philosopher Guillermo Gómez-Peña described the situation between Mexico and the US with characteristic forthrightness:

> It is time to face facts: Anglos won't go back to Europe, and Mexicans and Latinos (legal or illegal) won't go back to Latin America. We are all here to stay. For better or worse, our destinies and aspirations are in one another's hands.[5]

Gazing out at San Diego and Tijuana, Gómez-Peña foresaw a "new world border" emerging in the "gap between two worlds."[6] This is not an outlandish claim. The world is full of in-between peoples, making the production of cosmopolitan hybrid cultures (or *culturas híbridas*) emblematic of the human condition. The spaces of material transformation and cultural mixing by now extend along the entire length of the Mexico–US border, even deep into the heartland of both nations.[7] The evidence considered in this chapter presages a kind of "postborder condition" that enabled and promoted the emergence of a borderland third nation long before the new fortifications were erected.

Crossings

At the most elementary level, binational integration may be measured in the number of crossings between two countries, including those crossing for work, family, tourism, and related purposes.[8] In the early 2000s, approximately 286 million people legally crossed the border every year between Mexico and the US, along with almost 100 million vehicles (see Figure 5.1). The busiest crossings were San Ysidro (San Diego)–Tijuana, Calexico–Mexicali, El Paso–Ciudad Juárez, Laredo–Nuevo Laredo, and Hidalgo (McAllen)–Reynosa. The US Customs Service collected over US$20 billion in duties and fees each year.[9] Tourism was Mexico's third most important source of foreign currency earnings, drawing tourists to a *gringolandia* with the promise of sunshine, history, and hedonism in an atmosphere where they could feel comfortably at home while tasting the exotic.[10]

The flow of people was not simply one way, nor limited to border towns. Baja California witnessed a land and property boom fueled by US consumers and investors, especially after 1997 when foreign ownership of Mexican coastal property was made possible through locally-administered land trusts. About 100,000 US citizens lived in Baja at that time, plus an unknown number of undocumented residents. One-quarter of the inhabitants of the coastal town of Rosarito were of US origin, and many new residential and commercial development plans were marketed directly to consumers north of the border.[11]

No one knows exactly how many undocumented immigrants were coming to the US in prefortification days. By the early 2000s, official estimates put the number of crossings from Mexico at around 350,000 people per year, although informal estimates suggested a number as high as 500,000. In 2002, agents in the Tucson sector of the USBP apprehended undocumented migrants from 51 different countries, though only 1 percent of those arrested were from outside Latin America.[12] Some of the most important non-Mexican migrants—known as OTMs, or Other-than-Mexicans—were from Brazil, China, Ecuador, El Salvador, and Honduras.[13] In those days, most migrants were picked up around four major urban ports of entry: San Diego–Tijuana, the Nogales twins, El Paso–Ciudad Juárez, and Brownsville–Matamoros. But fence-building by the US government in the 1990s closed off these urban crossing points, and apprehensions in their vicinity declined.[14] Migrant waves moved away from the cities toward more remote regions such as the deserts of Arizona. As a consequence, the number of deaths from exposure and drowning increased from 57 in 1994 to 422 by 2003;[15] migrants were less likely to

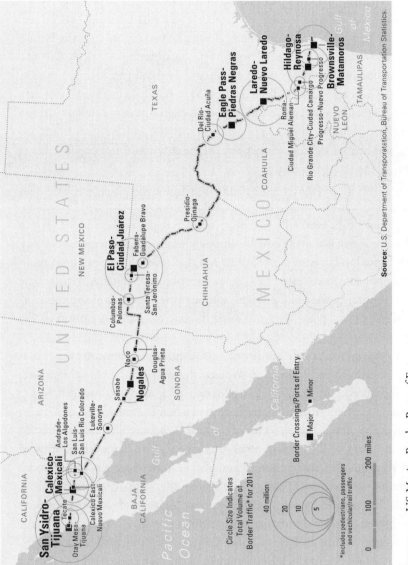

FIGURE 5.1 US-Mexico Border Ports of Entry, 2011.

Growth in the number and capacity of the official Ports of Entry between the US and Mexico (including rail, truck, private vehicle and pedestrian traffic) is testimony to the increasing integration of the two countries. Artwork by Dreamline Cartography, with assistance from Connery Cepeda.

Source: U.S. Department of Transportation, Bureau of Transportation Statistics.

return to Mexico because of difficulties in crossing;[16] and organized migrant smuggling became a big business (see Figure 5.2).[17]

Border policing extended beyond the boundary line in efforts to curtail crossings. In 2004 a "deep-repatriation program" began voluntary deportations by air, returning border-crossers to hometowns across Mexico instead of simply depositing them just over the line in border towns.[18] In addition, interior checkpoint programs began arresting suspected illegal immigrants farther north in Southern California. Such roving patrols had been in operation for many years throughout the US southwest, especially in Texas.[19] However, their reintroduction in 2004 caused much alarm, disrupting everyday activities such as shopping, school attendance, and medical visits.[20]

Border crossings are not solely about large questions of migration and security; they are also about people's everyday lives. After 9/11, many informal

FIGURE 5.2 The Casa del Túnel, Tijuana, Baja California, 2007.

The Casa del Túnel (top left) once contained a tunnel that people used to cross over from Tijuana into the US. Migrants would arrive at the nearby Hotel de Londres (top right) and proceed to the Casa where they would descend by ladder. The original ladder is displayed by Carmelo Alvarez who was Executive Director at the Casa after the tunnel was sealed and the building was converted to a community arts center (bottom left). In the final panel, the Casa wall (facing the US) displays a sign proclaiming: *'¡El arte tumbará este muro!* / Art will knock this wall down!' The fence separating the two countries is visible at center right in this final panel. Copyright © 2007 by Michael Dear.

river crossings fording the Río Bravo were closed for security reasons. Yet at Texas's Big Bend National Park just opposite Boquillas del Carmen, in Chihuahua, signs still give directions to the informal cross-river ferry and promise good food and shopping on the other side. The signs are not temporary or amateurish. Instead they are mounted in concrete, with directions engraved on stainless steel plates. In earlier times, this ferry had bristled with day-trippers, and business in Boquillas was good. These days, the signs and path to the river are neglected and overgrown; you are more likely to encounter an aggressive javelina than a human being. Many Mexican villages like Boquillas were devastated by the loss of tourist income that followed the sealing of the border. However, it was not long before folks in Terlingua (Texas) were collecting fabric for Boquillas neighbors to sew into quilts for sale back in Terlingua. The money earned from these sales was turned over to the residents of Boquillas to help them weather their economic misfortune.

Economy

The cause of much migration is economic opportunity. The passage of the North American Free Trade Act (NAFTA, or TLC) provoked many collaborations among its cosignatories.[21] At the state level, California's trade with Mexico and Canada boomed, jumping from US$12 billion in 1993 to US$26 billion ten years later.[22] Around 2000, Mexico overtook Japan as California's leading export market, accounting for more than 17 percent of the state's exports.[23] The growing integration of the two economies was revealed in many ways, such as the volume of remittances sent back to Mexico by migrant workers. In the first six months of 2004, Mexican emigrants (many in California) sent nearly US$8 billion to Mexico, a 26 percent increase from the previous year. The average transaction was about US$400 and was destined for household budgets across Mexico for spending on personal consumption items.[24] Remittances became second only to oil as Mexico's largest source of foreign exchange.[25] Roberto Suro described remittances as a new kind of integration among nations, with migrant workers being "players in the era of globalization," part of transnational networks operating beyond traditional markets and institutions.[26] In Suro's view, the two-way channel—with people flowing north and money going south—had become central to the social stability of the hemisphere.[27]

Small-scale local adjustments in economic integration were equally revealing. When, in 2002, US residents began to drive across the line to purchase cheaper gasoline, the Mexican oil authority, Petróleos Mexicanos (PEMEX) announced that Tijuana gas prices would be set at the same rate as Chula Vista across the line in California, and Ciudad Juárez prices were set at the same level as El Paso. Through such actions, PEMEX hoped to retrieve some of the US$54 million in revenue that it lost that year.[28] The market in mailbox addresses is another example of how local lives are threaded between the two countries. In 2001, San Ysidro, California, was a community of 30,000 people opposite Tijuana, with more than 26,000 private postal boxes that mostly catered to Mexican customers.[29] Demand was fueled principally by the unreliability of Mexican postal services, as it was in nineteenth-century Matamoros (described in chapter 3).[30]

In McAllen (Texas), 80 percent of businesses were Mexican-owned by the mid-2000s, a reversal of the proportion from a decade earlier. McAllen was drawing a greater share of Mexican spending than any other US city, affecting everything from retail sales to home purchases and vacation destinations. Most of the money came from the major industrial metropolis of Monterrey (in the state of Nuevo Léon), only two hours away by freeway. So common was the trip from Monterrey to McAllen that a new Spanish verb was coined—*macalenear*, literally "to do McAllen."[31]

The effects of economic integration were not always positive. The American Hospital Association estimated that in 2000 the 24 southernmost counties from Texas to California accrued US$832 million in unpaid medical bills, a quarter of which was directly attributed to undocumented migrants.[32] Integration was also extended via transnational crime, including trafficking in drugs and human beings, although the scale of these problems in the early 2000s was small by comparison with the present day. And after 9/11, several small settlements on both sides along the Río Bravo saw their economic livelihoods wither. The new restrictions sparked protests and unity rallies on both sides of the border, as well as spontaneous efforts at cross-border assistance.[33]

Environment

According to Enrique Martínez, former governor of the state of Chihuahua, struggles over water and the environment will be the "gravest problem" in Mexico's future.[34] For the longest time, water resources have been the principal source of environmental tension between Mexico and the US, especially the sharing of the waters of the Colorado River and the Rio Grande/Río Bravo. Three-quarters of a century after a 1944 treaty on water sharing, Mexico owed 465 billion gallons to the US (enough to satisfy the needs of New York City for one year). Repaying this debt became evermore difficult as population grew in the lower Río Bravo Valley (200,000 people in 1944, now over 20 million), dramatically increasing local water demand. The situation was aggravated during years of drought that caused reservoirs to shrink to below one-tenth of capacities.

A closely-linked environmental problem requiring international coopera-tion is pollution from industrial and residential sources, involving issues of water contamination, air quality, and exposure to pesticides. Raul Arriaga, undersecretary of the Mexican environmental protection agency, stated the problem succinctly: "The environment does not know boundaries. On the contrary, the geography and resources that we share are the element that validates our friendship and binds our destinies."[35] In 2003, Mexico and the United States signed the *Border 2012* agreement, intended to ensure security and address problems of pollutants and contaminated water supply. Critics complained that the agreement came without a financial commitment from either country. The Bush presidency subsequently shied away from interna-tional and domestic regulation of environmental pollutants, casting further doubt on the future of the agreement.

Yet there is some history of successful federal and local collaboration, most notably the long-standing efforts of the joint US International Boundary and Water Commission (IWBC) and its Mexican partner, *La Comision de Límites y Aguas* (CILA). These have included protections for the Tijuana Estuary though cleaning the river-borne pollution that crosses over from the city of Tijuana into San Diego County,[36] and successes in the conservation of environmentally-sensitive desert regions between Texas and Chihuahua.[37] Actions at the state and local levels are urgently needed but seemingly harder to realize. In California, cleanup efforts have been slow along the Río Nuevo/ New River—generally regarded as the most polluted river along the border— before it crosses from Mexicali en route to the Salton Sea. In addition, unilateral actions by one country can create practical problems and erode cross-border good relations. No longer does water seep from a formerly-unlined canal into the aquifers of the Mexicali Valley, whose enormously productive farmlands depend on these aquifers to raise their crops; a few years ago the channel of the All-American Canal between Calexico and Mexicali was lined with concrete. In addition, local activists for years have been unable to persuade the Imperial County Irrigation District to construct safety lines across the canal to prevent border crossers from drowning in its swiftly moving waters.[38]

Law and Politics

Political relations between Mexico and the US are dominated by the big-ticket items of free trade and immigration. But beyond these hot-button issues lie a host of other unresolved tensions, as well as innovative solutions. Following 9/11, the lines at the San Diego–Tijuana border crossing were endless. One enterprising individual began a thriving bicycle rental program that would enable pedal-pushers to avoid pedestrian and vehicle lines by riding rented bicycles to the front of the queues, crossing, and then dropping off the rental. The trouble was, in so doing, they inadvertently broke local bylaws on the US side, which required cyclists to wear helmets. The crisis was solved in less than 48 hours, when local laws were amended to permit cycling without a helmet within a short distance of the border crossing.[39]

Cross-border integration stimulated a host of other legal and political adjustments, small and large. For instance, Mexican law prohibits the extradition to the United States of criminals facing death sentences or life-without-parole prison terms. As a consequence, there were as many as 3,000 US murder suspects who had fled to Mexico to escape prosecution, causing many in the US to call for changes in Mexican statutes. Others lobbied for the end of the death penalty in the US.[40] Such cases starkly illustrated how current disputes in international law rapidly exceeded the capacities of the two nation–states to protect cross-border lives. Perhaps most poignant were child custody battles caused when Mexican parents in the US illegally sought to be reunited with children they left behind with relatives in Mexico, but the relatives no longer wished to relinquish the child. Legal and emotional difficulties were exacerbated when parents without papers could not risk returning to Mexico to confront antagonistic relatives.[41]

One of the most intriguing of burgeoning trends in cross-border political relations was increasing participation in Mexican elections by US-based Mexican nationals. In 1996, Mexico amended its constitution to allow citizens to cast ballots from outside their voting precincts. Four years later, then-President Vicente Fox promised to extend the franchise to the approximately 11 million Mexican nationals in the US, an absentee-voting provision that was approved by the Mexican congress in June 2005.[42] The desire of US-based Mexicans to participate in the politics of their homeland grew strongly, at least at the local level. Migrants reported that they had learned a lot about politics in the US, and desired to make "real change" in Mexico, and "give something back" to their country.[43] In 2003, under pressure from migrants who were sending US$2 million per day in remittances to Zacatecas, state governor Ricardo Monreal signed a constitutional reform ending residency requirements for elected office in the case of US-based Mexicans born of Zacatecan parents. Two seats in the legislature were set aside for migrants only.[44] A California university professor was subsequently elected to the state government of Michoacan.

The web of border crime inevitably drew US and Mexican law enforcement agencies into a spiraling sequence of response and counterresponse. As border crossings tightened, gangs linked to the *narcotraficantes* became involved in the lucrative business of human smuggling.[45] Border-crossers risked being assaulted and forcibly sequestered at "safe houses" in large cities, such as Los Angeles and Phoenix, until hefty ransoms were obtained for their release.[46] Police in Phoenix estimated that two-thirds of the city's crime was related to smuggling and kidnapping.[47] The smugglers' cargo included young children seeking reunification with parents who lacked legal standing in the US. Over 10,000 unaccompanied minors were intercepted at the border in 2003 and repatriated by the Mexican foreign ministry,[48] prompting the Mexican government to seek legal reform.[49]

Gangs were another outlaw phenomenon that reached across borders at this time. The Los Angeles-based Mara Salvatrucha (MS-13), a street gang organized by Salvadoran immigrants, had 10,000 members in the US, although their international enrollment was five times greater. MS-13's influence was prominent along the border, where members operated human smuggling rings and victimized migrants.[50] Once again, international law enforcement agencies in North and Central America became engaged in cooperative efforts to curb such activities.

Culture

The growing complexity in transborder lives is perhaps most visible in the cultural sphere. As the number of Latinos grew to more than 35 million, or one-seventh of the US population, integration and hybridization in personal lives became more pervasive. For instance, celebrations for the Mexican *quinceañera*, or coming of age for young girls, became commercialized and mainstream. Wal-Mart stocked *quinceañera* gowns in 200 stores in thirty US states, and the celebrations spread outside the Catholic Latino community with guest lists that increasingly were composed of multiethnic celebrants.[51]

Even more ubiquitous was the rise of "*el espanglés*/Spanglish," a mongrel language somewhere between Spanish and English. On my long drives through south Texas, I heard radio stations with announcers who spoke three languages concurrently, often starting a sentence in English, switching midsentence to Spanish, and ending with Spanglish. Their patter was endlessly inventive, bouncing the listener among languages and diverse cultural worlds. To be sure, some form of Spanglish existed from the first moment

English speakers arrived in Nueva España. But *espanglés* had now become dominant in many agricultural areas, had moved into the streets of Los Angeles and Chicago, and now into small-town America. Part of the reason for Spanglish's rise was the need to communicate, but it was also practiced for the sheer pleasure of playing with language. As the hybrid moved out of Latino neighborhoods it even became a marketing device for cross-over consumer products.[52] Professor Ilan Stavans marked the transition by suggesting that Spanglish might become a fully fledged language that would in time replace Spanish.[53]

Other rich veins of postborder sensitivities were found in the art world. A "postborder" aesthetic was directly implicated in the explosion of cultural activities in Tijuana.[54] For many years in Tijuana and San Diego, the InSite collaborations expanded to become an international art festival (though the scale of informal, local collaborations was far more pervasive and persuasive).[55] The imbrication of cultural spheres was also evident in film, television, music, and video productions; for instance, Los Angeles became the production and distribution capital of the Mexican *corrido* music industry.[56]

Such burgeoning cultural hybridities inevitably began to filter beyond border communities, affecting many aspects of everyday life from food to faith. Ten years of NAFTA changed Mexican supermarkets.[57] Mexican brands now competed for shelf space with US brands such as Gatorade, Hershey bars, and Dove soap; and US supermarkets stocked more products bearing the label *Hecho en México* (Made in Mexico). Salsa reportedly replaced tomato ketchup as the favorite family condiment in the US. I can buy Mexican-made Coca-Cola in many Berkeley stores, which is much more flavorful than its US counterpart because it uses cane sugar instead of corn syrup.

In the fluid traditions of religious belief, Mexico's popular *Virgen de Guadalupe* was adopted as a universal symbol of faith everywhere in the US, sometimes only tangentially related to organized religion. The adoption of other national icons contradicted standard precepts of faith. For example, the reverence accorded to *La Santa Muerta* ("Saint Death")—the patron saint of the very poor and criminals—spread from tough neighborhoods of Mexico City to Tijuana and other border settlements, and made her way to Texas, Chicago, and Los Angeles.[58] Such cultural mixing was not always welcomed. In the southern Mexican city of Oaxaca, for instance, the opening of a McDonald's fast-food restaurant in the city's *zócalo* (central square) was vigorously opposed by residents who claimed a preference for slow food, *mole* sauces, and *chapulines* (crispy fried grasshoppers) over "McTacos."[59]

Identity

The most profoundly consequential changes affecting borderland mentalities may be related to shifting identities. In 2001, for the first time since the 1850s, a majority of California newborns were of Hispanic heritage, and more than two-thirds of those were born in Southern California. (In 1975, Hispanic births accounted for only one-quarter of the state's total.) A new hybrid California identity, not based in Anglo origins, is being foreseen as inevitable.[60] In some US cities, people of Mexican origin reached a plurality in terms of demographic numbers. And in the bellwether state of California, Hispanic population growth is now principally driven by natural increase, and not by immigration. Nationwide, two Spanish surnames entered the list of Top Ten most common surnames for children born in the US. These were García and Ramírez. The four other fastest-rising names on the Top Ten were Hernández, Martínez, Gonzalez, and... Nguyen, which is Vietnamese. And when Mexican scholar Luis de la Calle examined the top 50 Mexican baby names in 2008, he found that for girls the list included: Elizabeth, Evelyn, Abigail, Karen, Marilyn and Jacqueline; and for boys: Alexander, Jonathan, Kevin, Christian and Bryan.[61]

As might be expected, not everyone contemplated this future with equanimity.[62] Some in the US regarded the Mexicanization of the borderland as a reoccupation of territories that once belonged to Mexico—a kind of peaceful *reconquista* (reconquest).[63] Although they represented only 47 percent of California's population, Anglos were still more than 70 percent of the registered voters. Late in the century, a series of hostile state ballot initiatives sought (among other things) to deny public education to children of the undocumented, and to end programs for affirmative action and bilingual education. US states along the border sprouted anti-immigrant vigilante groups composed of private citizens who volunteered their services to support the US Border Patrol.[64] Opponents of continuing immigration (especially by the undocumented) were often themselves former immigrants fearful of a widening backlash, and some of the greatest foes of bilingual education in New York were Spanish-speaking immigrants who shunned bilingualism because they regarded fluency in English as the best way for their children to advance.[65]

On the national scene, immigration remained one of the hottest political issues in US politics. Yet by most standards, Mexican immigrants did exactly what was expected from them by the host nation. They assimilated rapidly, often within one generation; learned to speak English; worked hard and paid taxes; progressed up the economic ladder; became geographically dispersed instead of remaining ghettoized; adopted local consumption habits (for better or worse); became homeowners; and volunteered for military service.[66] In Mexico, where the pace of immigration was slower, demographic diversification was less of an issue. Attitudes to migrants who entered Mexico from Central America were not welcoming, reflecting an undertow of racism toward indigenous peoples that has a long history in Mexico. An intensification of overt prejudice was also noticed, as in the rise of neo-Nazi groups who targeted gang members and *cholos* (indigenous and *mestizo* persons who adopt western habits) in their hate messages.[67] Meanwhile, domestic migration within Mexico transferred enormous numbers of migrants to the Mexican border, intent not on crossing but on getting jobs in the booming border economies, and thereby becoming part of the third nation.

In the Space between Two Nations

At the time new border walls were being contemplated, cross-border integration was already a fact of life in the spaces between Mexico and the US. These material connections were evident in myriad large and small ways, ranging from international collaborations to casual ferry-boat rides across the Rio Grande/Río Bravo (see Figure 5.3).[68] Even negative forms of interconnection cemented lives and stimulated integration across the line.

FIGURE 5.3 A manhole cover in the City of Los Angeles, California, 2006.

An ironic reminder for passers-by of the link between Los Angeles and Mexico. Copyright © 2006 by Michael Dear.

Such material connections were only one dimension in the creation of a
third nation. A second element is mental (or cognitive) and relates to people's
perceptions, emotions, attitudes, and behavior with respect to their material
world. Even among the native-born, a complicated nationalism may emerge
from the intersection of personal background, prejudice, and life experience; thereafter, it remains constantly buffeted by the exigencies of altered
history and geography. On days of national celebration, Mexican children in
Matamoros still sing the popular song, *México, creo en tí* ("Mexico, I believe
in you") even though many attend school in the US, have relatives there, and
feel intense longings to be on the other side. This hybridization of sentiments
is not such a contradiction as may first appear; joint loyalties may in fact be
the norm among most border people.

6

Third Nation of the Mind

NO MATTER HOW integrated cross-border material lives become, a third nation is only as strong as the cognitive ties that undergird residents' lives. Such "mental maps" or "psychogeographies" of belonging and attachment are intensely personal and highly variable. They can give rise to "imagined" communities that possess deep roots in the past, but are also actively recalibrated by the present.[1]

Origin Myths and Nationhood

Mexico's foundational stories stretch back many millennia to mystical accounts of a people's birth, a cosmic race, and fatalistic narratives of conquest. One of the most famous Mesoamerican written legacies is the *Popol Vuh*, a product of the Mayan postclassic period (1200–1521 A.D.), which recorded the beginning of human history this way:

> This is an account of how all was in suspense, all calm, in silence; all is motionless, still, and the expanse of sky was empty.
>
> This is the first account, the first narrative. There was neither man, nor animal, birds, fishes, crabs, trees, stones, caves, ravines, grasses, nor forests; there was only the sky....Nothing existed.
>
> There was only immobility and silence in the darkness of the night. Only the Creator, the Maker, Tepeu, Gucumatz, the Forefathers, were in the water surrounded with light....
>
> Then while they meditated, it became clear to them that when dawn would break, man must appear. Then they planned the creation, and the growth of trees and the thickets and the birth of life and the creation of man.[2]

Later peoples evolved their own origin myths.[3] For example, the fifteenth century Aztec ruler Moctezuma sought the legendary source of his ancestors, called "Aztlán," which was believed to lie somewhere in the present-day US

Southwest. The power of this legend remained so great that the Spanish conquerors sent out expeditions in search of Aztlán, though their motivation was more pecuniary than spiritual.[4]

The Spanish brought their own myths and obsessions to the New World. The Bourbon-era colonists, for instance, feared the consequences of social mixing in Nueva España, and its effect on racial purity. The *Casta* paintings that emerged during the early 1700s (and remained popular for the rest of the century) encapsulated their concerns. The paintings represented an attempt to codify the consequences of race mixing and create order out of increasingly confused social rankings.[5] The paintings served a didactic purpose, confirming the desirability of a Spanish norm while revealing the consequences of interracial dalliance. Castes were ranked according to the percentage of white, Indian, or black blood, and the paintings conveyed how certain racial mixings were more desirable than others. Native Indians were a special category because they were considered as "new Christians," and thus potentially the equals of Spaniards; if Indians continued intermarrying with Spaniards, their offspring would become Spanish by the third generation. Other ethnic categories were denied an opportunity to improve their social status. For example, the combinations of Spaniard with African, or Indian with African, would never result in becoming "white" since Africans were associated with slavery and regarded as inferior. This whole system was intimately tied to Spanish laws concerning the *limpieza de sangre*, or purity of blood.[6]

The paintings themselves usually took the form of family portraits—mother, father, and child—carefully conjugating the outcomes of various racial permutations that led to regression or progression. Here is an example of how it was possible to recover the coveted Spanish whiteness:

De Español e India, Nace Mestizo (From Spaniard and Indian, a Mestiza is born);
De Español y Mestiza, Nace Castizo (From Spaniard and Mestiza, a Castizo is born); and
De Castizo y Española, Nace Española (From Castizo and Spaniard, a Spaniard is born).

Unions that increased distance from Spanish ancestry were explicitly identified, as in *De Español y Negra, Nace Mulata* (From Spaniard and Black, a Mulatto is born). The labels could be quite blunt, noting some offspring as *torna atrás* or "return-backwards." At other times, the taxonomist appeared at a loss for words, as in *De Cambujo e India, Nace Tente en el Aire* (From

Cambujo and Indian, a "Hold-yourself-in-mid-air" is born). Viewed as a rational response by a social elite intent on preserving its status, the system had enormous practical significance in the colonial mentality, especially in Mexico City, where the survival of Spanish nobility was regarded as being under threat (see Figure 6.1). However, the *casta* classification was only loosely applied beyond the capital. In Northern Mexico—the present-day borderlands—the *casta* system was much more flexible and informal.[7]

The US has no universal narrative to match Mexico's in terms of longevity. Accounts of origins based in Judeo-Christian religious traditions find adherents principally within the faiths; efforts to proselytize beyond them are often

FIGURE 6.1 Miguel Cabrera, *De Mestizo y de India, Coyote* (From Mestizo and Indian, Coyote), 1763.

Cabrera was one of the most important painters in eighteenth-century Mexico City, but only a single set of casta paintings by him is known to exist. He used clothing to distinguish racial and social distinctions in his paintings, reflecting broad concerns over the erasure of social boundaries in New Spain. Courtesy of Elisabeth Waldo-Dentzel Studios, Northridge, California.

roundly rejected. The country does not lack a prehistory that could be mined for myth and meaning on a secular or spiritual basis, including the adventure of human occupation on the continent and the spectacular indigenous civilizations that developed throughout the land. Anglo-Americans simply prefer to start their story in 1776.[8] Narratives of nation-building in the US tend to emphasize revolutionary struggle, the quest for liberty and equality, and rugged self-sufficiency. Such tales are frequently embellished by explosions of geopolitical ambition, as in the quest to realize a Manifest Destiny. The nation's other principal universal narrative, and a source of justifiable pride, is the saga of immigration and its promise of E Pluribus Unum (One Out Of Many). However, this has today become the topic of partisan political bickering of the basest kind.

The absence of a foundational creed was one reason that nineteenth-century US explorers and archeologists became obsessed with Central American ruins; their fragile sense of self *required* a legitimizing legend.[9] Prior to Mexican independence in 1821, the very existence of most pre-Columbian sites was generally unknown outside the closeted archives of Spain. The lack of any certifiable history about the ancients allowed nineteenth-century archaeologists freely to mythologize about the Mesoamerican past, since no conclusive evidence was available to challenge even the most bizarre ideas about the ruins' provenance.[10] Consequently, nineteenth-century adventurers freely exercised their imaginations. Many of their drawings from life were distorted to the point of falsification in an effort to forge links with classical times.

Thus it was that between 1839 and 1843 American writer and amateur archaeologist John Lloyd Stephens and British architect Frederick Catherwood collaborated on producing four volumes devoted to ancient Maya architecture.[11] Their publications were at that time the most complete record of pre-Columbian sites ever produced. Stephens concluded that the architectural wonders were evidence of a superior race whom he claimed as forebears of Americans, thereby establishing a cultural inheritance that owed no allegiance to Europe. So enamored was Stephens of his conjectures that he even planned to pack up the ruins and ship them to a kind of nineteenth-century "theme park" in the US. Gathered under one roof, the exhibits would present a seamless evolution from Mesoamerica to the present day. Stephens' contemporary Joseph Smith, founder of the Church of Jesus Christ of Latter-day Saints, also nurtured a desire to co-opt the archaeological past of Central America. He claimed that the Americas had been settled in ancient times by wandering members of the lost tribes of Israel.

The Maya grip on contemporary imaginations remained undiminished for several decades. During the period 1870–1880, it was the turn of French émigré photographer Augustus Le Plongeon and his wife Alice to suffer over-heated imaginations while journeying in the Yucatan. Le Plongeon made a variety of important archeological finds but ended up doctoring photographs of Mesoamerican sites in order to prove their remote origins as well as their significance in the foundation of Freemasonry. He asserted that world culture had originated from the American continent, and nominated himself and his wife as reincarnated monarchs of the so-called former "Kingdom of Móo" which had supposedly flourished over 1,000 years before their arrival.[12]

Anglo Arrival and Hybrid Cultures

The looming prospect of war between Mexico and the US curdled the latent hostilities among peoples of the increasingly comingled territories. For most of the early nineteenth-century, Texas was ground zero for volatile shifts in interethnic attitudes. Waves of Anglo settlers streamed into the territory after 1821, when the Mexican government granted colonization rights in the province to Missouri entrepreneur Moses Austin.[13] The newcomers came to regard Mexicans as primitive beings who were "religious pagans, purpose-lessly indolent and carefree, sexually remiss, degenerate, depraved, and ques-tionably human."[14] Stephen F. Austin, who followed his father Moses into the settler business, expressed an almost predatory desire to populate Texas with what he regarded as intelligent, honorable, and enterprising people. Austin believed that redemption would come about by "whitening" Texas, and baldly announced his intention "to *Americanize Texas.*"[15] In an echo of the *casta* prej-udices, Anglo newcomers viewed the colonial Spaniards as the embodiment of impurity as a consequence of earlier racial mixing on the Iberian peninsula, and lumped everyone else in the category of inferior colored peoples.[16]

Not to be outdone, Mexicans in Texas were equally dismissive of their new Anglo neighbors. José María Sánchez was a Mexican military man sent in 1828 to investigate the troubles in that province. Like other educated Mexicans liv-ing on the frontier, Sánchez deplored the backwardness of frontier people. He wrote complainingly about the Tejanos of east Texas: "The character of the people is care-free, they are enthusiastic dancers, very fond of luxury, and the worst punishment that can be inflicted upon them is work."[17] The stereotype of the "Lazy Mexican" gained wide currency, but Sánchez reserved his most cutting remarks for the upstart Anglos:

> The Americans from the north have taken possession of practically all
> the authorities. They immigrate constantly, finding no one to prevent

them, and take possession of the *sitio* (location) that best suits them without either asking leave or going through any formality other than that of building their homes.[18]

The Tejanos themselves, longtime border residents, maintained a more pragmatic outlook on the Anglo newcomers. The *ayuntamiento* (town council) of San Antonio in 1832 complained about the neglect of Texas by Mexican authorities, and argued that continued Anglo immigration would provide a pipeline for goods needed by native inhabitants, develop roads and commerce, encourage good government, and protect the town from Indian attacks.[19] This prescient opinion prefigured what was to become reality in the borderlands.

Meanwhile, on the Pacific coast, a less belligerent but no less turbulent Alta California was adjusting to its newcomers.[20] The impact of the Spanish arrival on indigenous populations had been as devastating as elsewhere in Nueva España.[21] Yet settlers from colonial Mexico who arrived on the California frontier at this time soon formed a prosperous ranching class, calling themselves *gente de razón* (people of reason) as distinct from *gente sin razón*, (or, people without reason, meaning Indians).[22] They came to be known as "Californios," who enjoyed generally congenial relations with Anglo newcomers, including intermarriage.[23] But in his personal narrative of a life at sea, Yankee Richard Henry Dana, Jr., referred to them as "an idle, thriftless people,…[who] can make nothing for themselves."[24] His 1840 book, *Two Years Before the Mast*, was one of a handful of books influencing US public opinion in the prewar years. In it, Dana delivered the ultimate put-down of the Californios: "What a country this could be in the hands of an enterprising people!"[25]

On the eve of war in 1846, anti-Mexican sentiments raged. In a dyspeptic frame of mind, former US newspaperman Rufus B. Sage reported on his visits to Taos and nearby Nuevo México: "There are no people on the continent of America, whether civilized or uncivilized, with one or two exceptions, more miserable in condition or despicable in morals than the mongrel race inhabiting New Mexico."[26] Matters improved little after the war. Emblematic of the postwar legacy of mistrust were early Mexican *corridos*, or ballad songs, that were inevitably tainted by the bitter legacy of the conflict. One chastised the Yankee invader:[27]

> *The evil Yankees*
> *Never cease to speak*
> *Of what they will do to destroy*
> *Our nation.*

The crusading Texas Rangers did little to assuage bitterness. Officially established to fight Indians, the Rangers became local heroes by adding Tejanos to their hit list.[28] The force was disbanded during the Civil War, then reestablished in 1874 to continue its own brand of riotous peacekeeping. A small group known as the Special Force was sent to the Mexican border to stamp out cattle theft and outlaw behavior. Ranger Jennings described the work carried out by the Special Force in 1875 at Brownsville, Texas:

> We paid frequent visits to Matamoras after nightfall. We went there for two reasons: to have fun, and to carry out a set policy of terrorizing the Mexicans at every opportunity. Captain McNelly assumed that the more we were feared, the easier would be our work of subduing the Mexican raiders.[29]

The early 1900s were particularly brutal as the Rangers carried out campaigns of persecution against the Tejanos of south Texas on the pretext of putting an end to Mexican revolutionary raids in the region.

By the beginning of the twentieth century, the numbers of Mexican immigrant laborers in the US had increased, and stubborn stereotypes took hold. Writing from Stanford University in 1912, Samuel Bryan conceded that Mexican immigration was a necessary evil, but lamented that the newcomers lacked education, were slow to learn English, harbored criminals, and lived together in a clannish manner.[30] He offered a summation that embraced the universe of Anglo complaints against Mexican migrants:

> Their low standards of living and of morals, their illiteracy, their utter lack of proper political interest, the retarding effect of their employment upon the wage scale of the more progressive races, and finally their tendency to colonize in urban centers, with evil results, combine to stamp them as a rather undesirable class of residents.[31]

Twentieth-Century Integration

Mexican attitudes to the US after the Revolution typically invoked two contradictory sentiments: a belief that binational economic integration was the answer to Mexico's perennial problems of poverty and uneven development; but also a fear that too close a relationship with the US was dangerous because of her power and aggression. Mexicans worried about being assimilated by a culture they regarded as guided by excessive and unrestrained materialism. Stay-at-home Mexicans bristled angrily when prosperous former neighbors returned from the US laden with ostentatious trappings of material success.[32]

For most of the twentieth century, binational attitudes began cycling through consecutive periods of hostility and reconciliation. Attitudes expressed through *corridos* only began to change during and after World War II. In 1942, Mexico entered the war as an ally of the US, prompting many lyrics recognizing common cause between the nations:[33]

> *I am a Mexican bracero,*
> *I came to work*
> *For our sister Nation*
> *Which has issued the call.*
> *They ask for workers from my Country*
> *To substitute for*
> *Those who fight*
> *Without fear of death.*

When US President Franklin D. Roosevelt died in 1945, Mexico mourned; and when Presidents Miguel Alemán and Harry S. Truman met in 1947, Mexican goodwill toward the US was reputedly at the highest point in history. This did not mean that "anti-gringo" sentiments disappeared, but expressions of traditional animosity became muted and subject to public disapproval.

Since that high point, the ebb and flow of cross-border attitudes quickened as the two nations converged in their everyday dealings. Typical of the ensuing contradictions was the mid-century Bracero program that welcomed Mexican workers into the US but was interrupted by Operation Wetback, which simultaneously required their repatriation. Later, a rise in undocumented migration from Mexico darkened the public mood north of the border, which in turn prompted an anti-US backlash in Mexican media, school books, and political writings.[34] And so it went.

As the century drew to a close, the elite, intellectual, and business leaderships in Mexico had muted anti-US rhetoric in an effort to signal Mexico's openness to the modern world.[35] Yet both countries still evinced a readiness to take offense at the smallest slight. The US was portrayed as a clumsy bear constantly treading on its neighbor's sense of sovereignty, while Mexico was accorded the role of a hypersensitive porcupine attuned to any insults, real or imagined, from its northern neighbor.[36] The US simply could not shake off a stereotype of the "Ugly American:" power-hungry, hypocritical, and anti-Mexican.[37]

Present-Day Binational Attitudes

In a changing world, national and local myths of origin and affiliation are never static monoliths. Nevertheless, some ancient legends have considerable staying power.[38] In Mexico, anthropologist Guillermo Bonfil Batalla drew attention to the continuing relevance of two opposing legacies: a *México profundo*, referring to the Mexico of indigenous peoples and their Mesoamerican heritage; and a *México imaginario*, the Mexico of the Spanish colonialists with European sensibilities. According to Bonfil Batalla:

> The recent history of Mexico…is the story of permanent confrontation between those attempting to direct the country toward the path of Western civilization and those, rooted in Mesoamerican ways of life, who resist [39]

Present-day *mexicanidad*, or "Mexicanness," results from the fusion of a glorious prehistory and the legacy of conquest, and Bonfil Batalla surmised that Mexico's future depended upon recovering the traditions of *México profundo*. It may already be too late for this because both traditions are being overlain by a third—a radical opening of Mexican society to globalization that could be called a *México global*, or global Mexico, which is transforming the nation through awareness of and engagement with the world of nations.[40]

The US, too, is witnessing a fracturing of two foundation myths: the melting pot, and Manifest Destiny. As immigration continues unabated and the diversity of national origins expands—both prefigured by immigration reforms in 1965 and 1986—the prospect that newcomers will adopt a universal nationalism seems slim. By now, the melting pot and E Pluribus Unum fade like quaint memories of a distant time. After the demise of the Soviet Union, the US's reign as the world's single superpower was quickly overshadowed by an increasingly multipolar world. Internationally, the attacks of 9/11 and subsequent wars in Afghanistan and Iraq drained the nation's resources and damaged its global reputation. At home, unease over vulnerability and diminished capacity was fueled by economic recession and unemployment, only intensified by environmental crises such as Hurricane Katrina and the Gulf of Mexico oil spill. What emerges is a fractured polity, consisting of individual and regional interests, that turns inward for more personal framings of belonging.

There may be an important paradox here. Just as a globalizing Mexico gazes beyond its boundaries and thereby loosens the tenacious grip of its center, a splintering US witnesses the rise of myriad local autonomies, each claiming space for self-determination. There are many different forces behind these shifts, but the net consequence may be the same on both sides: a fragmentation that enables space for a third nation.

In this changing context, attitudes toward Mexicans in the US today are worse than any time during the past 50 years, according to border expert Professor Douglas Massey. Negative feelings about Mexico and Mexicans may even have morphed into a generalized "Latino Threat" based in concerns about large-scale immigration, the numbers of undocumented migrants, the diaspora of peoples of Mexican origin, and fear of a *reconquista*—a future in which Mexico "recovers" the lands lost after the 1846–1948 war not by aggression but simply by becoming a demographic majority.[41]

Media expert Roberto Suro forthrightly blamed the US media for the rising tensions. Debates about migration, he pointed out, have hardly changed over the past 30 years. They have focused on how to improve border controls and halt employment of undocumented workers, develop appropriate entry programs for temporary workers, and open up paths to citizenship for undocumented people already in the country. What has changed dramatically, Suro claimed, is US media, notably the decline in newspaper readership and revenues, and the advent of cable TV and the Internet. The new media's clamor for attention has provoked an "advocacy journalism" that exaggerates and distorts difficult issues, making it easier to mobilize opposition but harder to gain consensus for political action.[42] For instance, when a Mexican child was reported to be the first death from swine flu in the US, one radio commentator seized an opportunity: "Make no mistake about it," he bellowed, "illegal aliens are the carriers of the new strain of human-swine avian flu from Mexico."[43]

Not all media coverage is bad.[44] In the recent past, public opinion in the US has been exposed to a proliferation of academic and popular accounts that gave credence to the Latino immigrant experience. These encompassed poignant accounts of the hardships of crossing,[45] the heartbreak of becoming American,[46] and the longer-term outcomes of crossing.[47] Such narratives were leavened by rigorous research on the impacts of migration into the US,[48] as well as subversive satires on the emerging social order.[49]

Polls in the US consistently report that a majority of US citizens favor a comprehensive approach to immigration that encompasses secure borders, equal protection under law, pathways to citizenship, and guest worker programs adequate to meet employer needs. Mexico began the twenty-first century with a generally favorable view of the US and its people, but remained divided over whether or not to trust the US.[50] The pull of *el norte* remained great even though economic recession and increased border enforcement had slowed migration from Mexico.[51] Meantime, the Mexican government continued supporting efforts to help migrants in transitioning to life in the US through an array of health, education, and financial services.[52]

As usual, business communities on both sides took a more practical view of cross-border relations. A 2009 report in *Business Week* heralded that US business is "standing its ground" in Mexico, anticipating a market turnaround when "Nobody…wants to be caught without capacity." Major global companies remained optimistic about investing in border communities.[53] For its part, Mexican border commerce was overtly concerned with the decline in tourism from the north. A similar pragmatism characterized the political arena. For example, pro-immigrant demonstrations in many major US cities[54] were led by Latino groups who were highly cognizant of the rhetoric of earlier civil rights' movements, but at the same time they also strove for specific legislative reforms.[55]

The US bear and the Mexican porcupine still live. Recent cross-border debates were more akin to the ill-tempered foot-stamping of family quarrels than great matters of state. One of the silliest spats in this minor key concerned a colorful advertisement for Absolut vodka that appeared in Mexico in 2008. The advertisement was a sight gag depicting what a map of North America might look like "In an Absolut world," that is, an ideal world. On the map, the Mexican border stretched northward to its position *before* the Mexican–US War of 1846. Many people in the US professed outrage and called for a boycott of Absolut, whose makers soon apologized for their transgression. It was a measure of hypersensitivity that Absolut's witty ad could stir such bile and provoke swift capitulation from the manufacturer.

In another situation whose logic quickly eluded reasonable minds, five postage stamps were issued in Mexico to commemorate Memin Pinguin, a beloved cartoon character. Memin has a black skin color and exaggerated African features (see Figure 6.2). Some people in the US were offended by what they perceived as the racist nature of the portrayals. They complained and the controversy escalated. The Bush White House even got into the act, lecturing Mexico about racism and ethnic insensitivity. These interventions incensed Mexicans who countered that the US, with its shameful history of slavery and discrimination, was unqualified to lecture Mexico about racism. (Some Mexicans were pleased that the binational brawl had prompted a long-overdue national conversation about racism in Mexico.) Ultimately,

FIGURE 6.2 Memin Pinguin Postage Stamps, Mexico 2005.

the stamps became collector's items on both sides of the border, and quickly sold out.[56]

Border Mentalities Are Different

The daily rigors of coexistence along the borderline make a mockery of national grandstanding. The depth of the divide separating Washington DC-based politicians and border residents was evident to me during an April 2008 meeting in Brownsville, Texas. Then-US Representative Tom Tancredo (a Republican, far from his political home in Colorado) dismissed local residents' concerns that the pending border fortifications would damage the environment and destroy a centuries-old bond between residents on both sides of the Rio Grande. Betty Perez, a rancher and local activist, responded: "It really isn't a border to most of us who live down here." Tancredo sharply rejected Perez's concerns, calling her a "multiculturalist" (intended as an insult), and added that perhaps the boundary fence should be built north of Brownsville so that the city could become part of Mexico

To be sure, border states have moments of madness too. California's major cities have become accustomed to diversity but the state also has a history of anti-immigrant legislation, even though such laws have usually been voided after court challenge. Extreme nativist views warned of an emerging "Mexifornia." Fraudulent Mexifornian driving licenses once circulated with ID photos that portrayed a sombrero-wearing Mexican; in place of a signature on the license was a scrawled "X" indicative of an illiterate person.

EVENTS IN THE post-9/11 era undoubtedly aggravated cross-border community relations. In 2004 a high-profile anti-immigrant project surfaced in the third nation. This was the "Minutemen," a loosely-organized, high-profile vigilante group of volunteers anxious to transform the border into an impassable barrier. The organization's members took it upon themselves to patrol the border and report to authorities any suspicious border crossers. Their spokespersons employed some of the strongest racist language allowed on the airwaves up to that point,[57] encouraging vigilantes to draw firm and uncompromising lines about who is worthy of inclusion in US society.[58] Membership in the Minutemen was small but vocal; its leaders were masters of the media; and their events got fulsome coverage in print, television, and radio.

Perhaps the high point of the Minutemen's short history was an April 2005 blockade of the Arizona–Sonora border.[59] Responding to what they described as an "illegal invasion," about 1,300 volunteers were expected to attend the blockade, but only 200 showed up on the day, about the same number of media representatives who came along to observe the blockade. It was quite a spectacle, with SUVs tearing along the dirt roads adjacent to the fence, their occupants often dressed in military fatigues and carrying an eclectic assortment of two-way radios, binoculars, and maybe a few weapons. They were closely pursued by hot-rodding members of the press corps. The event was splashed across the media and a Minutemen organizer, Jim Gilchrist, declared victory before disbanding the border monitoring project.

After the heady days of the short-lived blockade, the Minutemen project faded from view. Other vigilante groups sprang up in Texas, New Mexico, and California, and further from the line in the states of Idaho and Michigan. A separate organization, the "Civil Homeland Defense" founded by Chris Simcox, continued the border monitoring project. Internal squabbles over leadership between Gilchrist and Simcox caused the organizations to fracture. In 2007, Gilchrist was removed from the Minutemen Project's board of directors because of alleged accounting irregularities.[60]

Do "sleeper cells" of Minutemen survive, ready to respond at the first trace of new proposals for immigration reform? In 2008, I visited the "Mountain Minutemen" encampment on a prominent hilltop called Patriot Point, on the US side of the border near Campo, California, just east of Tecate. The site had a commanding view of the fence in both directions. Frequent flash floods had carved deep channels under the fence so that you could easily crawl under it, or else flooding had piled up enough debris so you could stroll up to the fence and jump over it. At one point, a small doorway had been blow-torched through the fence, with hinges and a lock on the Mexican side to allow the key-holder easy passage. Nearby, on the steepest hillsides, the fence petered out altogether. In the clear desert morning, flashes of sunlight illuminated small aluminum plates fixed to an informal fence that impatient Minutemen volunteers had constructed to protest the long delays in government action to defend the border. The plates had been sponsored by supporters from across the country, and each was engraved with messages directed toward migrants (see Figure 6.3). Among the milder salutations was: "God save America. Bless all those who guard and protect her borders." Other plates recommended "Drop dead;" or curtly advised "You are not welcome in the USA. Stay out or die."

Captain Robert "Lil' Dog" Brooks was a former military man and retired offshore fisherman who'd been at Patriot Point for three years. The day of my visit, he shared duties with an African-American Vietnam War veteran. Brooks's business card announced that Patriot Point Posse is "In A Canyon Near You." He held unambiguous opinions; the only thing that would stop the inflow of migrants from Mexico was to bring in troops and arrange for "line of sight" patrols, where one patrol unit had direct visual contact with its nearest neighbors. He called the idea of a virtual fence (involving high-tech surveillance operations) a "virtual folly" doomed to failure. He was against all politicians, referring to the unholy trio of "Obama, his Mama, and McAmnesty," meaning the future president, Hillary Clinton, and then-presidential-candidate John McCain. Wearing a black baseball hat with the motto "Mountain Minutemen, Patriot Point Posse" on its visor, Brooks directed his gaze to the horizon: "What a place! If you were going to give America an enema, this is where you'd insert the tube."[61]

FIGURE 6.3 "Come Legally and Be Welcome."

Aluminum tag on a Minutemen-constructed fence at the US side of the international boundary line near Campo. California. The barbed wire fence extends for about 200 meters and carries about 50 such signs conveying messages with varying degrees of hostility toward border-crossers. Copyright © 2006 by Michael Dear.

A year later, demonstrations were occurring across the US in support of immigration reform, and Lil' Dog was gone from Patriot Point. The only trace was a small plaque set into a boulder, commemorating the Mountain Minutemen. I was told that he'd tired of his years of solitary vigil and gone back to ocean fishing, but another Border Patrol officer could not suppress a smile when he hinted that Brooks was in jail in Arizona, arrested for running illegal immigrants across the border.

PEOPLE SOUTH OF the border line also have distinct personality quirks. A national poll in December 2010 revealed some dimensions of the Mexican character and northern differences.[62] Pollsters discerned five temperaments across the nation:

> *Nostalgic traditionalists* who believed Mexico was on the wrong path but still revered their nation (an opinion held by 30 percent of the respondents, the majority);
> *Dreamers without a country* who considered that their personal lives were on track but the country was not (25 percent);
> *Unyielding Pessimists* (20 percent);
> *Optimists* (16 percent); and
> *Non-conformist nationalists* who blamed the country's institutions for the nation's misfortunes (9 percent).

In northern Mexico, however, a majority (40 percent) of respondents were in the category of "dreamers without a country," i.e., content with their own situations but despondent concerning the country's direction.[63] When compared with the nation, northerners were generally more optimistic,[64] but they also believed that they'd shared less in the country's wealth than people in other regions.[65] These findings confirm talk on the streets, which generally reflects a self-sufficient streak and mistrust of the central government in Mexico City.

An earlier survey in 2006 confirmed that border residents mistrusted Mexican institutions at levels higher than anywhere else in the country, as shown in Table 6.1.[66]

Many people have speculated why the border is different. Scholars and experts have drawn attention to the geographic proximity of the US as a factor. In oft-quoted words, Gloria Anzaldúa wrote in 1987 of a "third country" formed between the two nations:

> The U.S.–Mexican border *es una herida abierta* [is an open wound] where the Third World grates against the first and bleeds. And before a

**Table 6.1 Percentage of People with "No Confidence"
in Four Mexican Institutions**

NO CONFIDENCE IN	BORDER STATES	REST OF MEXICO
Police	36%	20%
Courts	26%	11%
Media	17%	3%
Army	14%	5%

scab forms it hemorrhages again, the lifeblood of the two worlds merging to form a third country—a border culture.[67]

Popular memory may also be at work in creating public perceptions of a distinct territory. Part of the third nation occupies the same land that once was "Aztlán," the spiritual homeland of Moctezuma, even though the precise location of the ancient homeland remains foggy. The term was later adopted by the Chicano movement in the US to symbolize cultural affirmation and promote civil liberties.[68] Today's social media are undoubtedly implicated in transforming regional awareness on both sides. In the spring of 2012, Robert San Jose tracked Twitter trends in the border twin cities. A cross-section from the most frequently trending topics in six twins included:

Tijuana: city-based political movements
San Diego: solidarity with Occupy movements across the US
Mexicali: celebration of medical students' scholastic achievements
Calexico: Dominican presidential candidate's appeal for support
Nogales, Sonora: grassroots movement for political reform
Nogales, Arizona: tickets to the taping of a popular Mexican television show
Ciudad Juárez: a march on both sides of the border against the ongoing femicide there
El Paso: discussion of Mexican President Calderón's billboard calling for "No more Weapons," posted on the Mexican side of cross-border Bridge of the Americas
Nuevo Laredo: travel show host's experience of border crossing into Laredo
Laredo: local news report
Matamoros: cheerleading team asking for support from both sides,
Brownsville: the Mr. Amigo Association, promoting and publicizing life in the twin cities

The topics represent the usual mélange of ephemera and quirky obsessions, but also reveal a diversity of cross-border exchange and topical concerns focusing on events from the other side.

THE THIRD NATION made a very public debut in 2004, at the opening of a multicultural exposition called *"Tijuana, La Tercera Nación"* (Tijuana, The Third Nation).[69] Publicity for the event referred to Tijuana as "a nation between two nations."[70] Explaining his motivation, exposition organizer Antonio Navalón recalled that when he first visited the border in 1978 (he is of Spanish birth), there was no fence separating the two sides. He spotted Border Patrol agents playing soccer with undocumented migrants who would attempt to cross the line later that evening.[71] On subsequent visits, when fences had sprouted, Navalón became aware of a developing cross-border consciousness on both sides of the line. People there never referred to the "United States of America" or to "Mexico," he wrote. Instead, they used only a single term for both: *"el otro lado,"* the other side.[72]

Navalón believed he was witnessing "...the birth of a community that had created an inevitable space for a joint civic life and a new social and artistic space." He dubbed it *"Tijuana, la tercera nación."* [73] Essayist José Manuel Valenzuela Arce expanded on the idea, calling the third nation:

> a metaphor, an allegory, a creative proposal or a manufactured provocation...that brings together and reconsiders the fears and desires that reside in cities and borders around the world in order to imagine and invent livable cities that shape new forms of multicultural life.[74]

The exposition attracted controversy partly because of the "third nation" label; some participants were suspicious that it represented another example of cultural takeover by the US. The term subsequently entered the vocabulary of local academics and artists, though the controversy lingered.

Almost a decade after the exposition, in 2012, Berkeley undergraduate Shannon Rieger talked with cross-border commuters about the Tijuana–San Diego connections, and explored ideas about a third nation mentality in the twin cities.[75] She uncovered a broad consciousness about connectivity across the border—perhaps unsurprising among frequent crossers. One woman lived in San Diego but went to the other side at least once a week in order to visit family, eat out, catch a movie, get a haircut, go to church, or see friends: "To me, [going to Tijuana is] like going anywhere else here in San Diego."

Another person said of people who crossed frequently: "Their lives are rooted in both sides of the border."

The reasons for the emerging transborder lives were frequently financial. Several commuters had moved to Tijuana from San Diego within the last few years because rents were cheaper, while *tijuanenses* worked in the US to take advantage of higher wages. A middle-aged Anglo man laid off from his job in San Diego had been unable to find work, and could no longer afford to live in the city. So he moved into a Tijuana apartment complex filled entirely with US citizens who were in similar financial straits. Many such apartment complexes existed along the border line in Tijuana, he claimed. The residents lived their lives in San Diego—working, shopping, seeing friends and family—and only rented sleeping space in Tijuana. The man was not altogether enamored with his binational arrangement, and expressed little affection for Tijuana. (The choice of Mexican residence by US citizens on fixed incomes is long-established. In the 1980s, I knew many veterans living in trailer parks on the beaches south of Ensenada, who had moved there to stretch their pensions.)

A stark contrast was provided by a considerably more affluent Anglo man who was travelling from an elite beach area in Tijuana to an upscale neighborhood in Coronado, near San Diego. He said that he took this trip to a second home every week, as did many wealthy *tijuanenses*. He felt comfortable in Tijuana, and considered it easy to move between the two cities.

Aside from money matters, cultural connections influenced people's cross-border calculus. Several mentioned that Tijuana and San Diego overlap culturally. San Diego's baseball and football teams are enormously popular in Tijuana, and fans from both sides cross to attend entertainment acts. (When a singer at a popular music concert in San Diego shouted out a conventional concert welcome: "Whaddaya say, San Diego?!" he was greeted with silence. Realizing his gaffe, he quickly amended his welcome to: "Whaddaya say, Tijuana?!" and was blitzed by tumultuous applause.)

One thoughtful woman began by saying that the two cities were obviously very connected through work, family, and shopping. But to explain deeper ties, she appealed to culture and shared history. The two cities were more similar than they were different, she concluded. The things that divided Tijuana and San Diego, in her mind, were the deterioration in public safety in Tijuana, and the racist manners of border crossing officials toward people of Mexican origin. She was emphatic that there was no racism between the peoples of the San Diego area and Tijuana.

Invited to describe the relationship between the twin cities, respondents offered words such as "positive" and "beneficial," referring to them as "*ciudades amistosas*" (friendly cities) and "*ciudades hermanas*" (sister cities). They were a "pair," and "friends," who "feel like they're together." Yet no one regarded the two cities as a single community. The gap between the two nations in terms of material wealth, living standards, and attitudes were simply too great. Added to this, the boundary line was itself a real divide. The two cities simply "felt different."[76]

One reason that people get close to one other is because they feel different from others. Rieger's respondents articulated these differences with precision, remarking that Tijuana and San Diego were different from their respective host nations because of their close relationship with each other, and because their relationship was positive, unlike that between the US and Mexico as a whole. Three young men who had moved from southern Mexico brought an outsiders' viewpoint to this issue. Tijuana, they asserted, was different from the rest of Mexico because of the influence from the north. Tijuana was not representative of Mexico because *tijuanenses* did not have the same pride in being Mexican, but instead wanted to be "American."

It was left to an elderly Anglo man crossing over to fill a prescription in Tijuana to reach the heart of the matter. He agreed with others that San Diego was different from the rest of the US because of its connections with Tijuana. To him, the towns that had grown up between Tijuana and the city of San Diego proper—San Ysidro, Chula Vista, and National City—"look like Tijuana" to such a degree that they "could be in Mexico." San Ysidro, the location of the principal border crossing, is neither American nor Mexican but somewhere in between, a product of both nations. He concluded that people on either side have their different ways of going about things, but with so many San Diegans having ties to Tijuana, San Diego looked and felt almost like Tijuana itself. Thus identities were not cleanly divided by the borderline: Tijuana is not fully "Mexican," nor is San Diego fully "American." Each city could only be understood in the context of its relationship with the other.

Rieger came away convinced that Tijuana and San Diego constituted a "separate space" between the two host nations, which could not be defined using conventional understandings of national affinity.[77] No matter what we call this shared space, certain features of the cross-border community stand out: border people are different from others in their respective nations, they are self-conscious about living in the spaces between two nations, and they understand that a shared identity is produced through interaction across the line.

I am confident in describing this place as a third nation. Its material connectivity is long-established and deep; and its cognitive foundations are articulated by residents with nuance and precision. A real estate agent who worked both sides of the line in the closely-connected housing markets of Tijuana and Chula Vista, California (the latter known as "Chulajuana"), caught something of the distinctive consciousness of the third nation dweller: "I am not successful because I am bilingual, but because I am bicultural."

Now, however, human events of cataclysmic proportions threaten the vitality of the third nation. The territory has been severed by a great wall built on the US side, and is being held hostage to unprecedented levels of violence in Mexico. The material and mental ties that bind the third nation are being severely tested.

7

Fortress USA

THE FOUNDATION OF contemporary immigration policy in the US was established by the Hart–Cellar Act of 1965. It abolished the country-of-origin quotas, installed family ties and needed skills as the principal criteria for entry into the US, and increased the overall number of migrants permitted to enter the country. As a result the total number of immigrants entering the country greatly increased. They were mostly people from Asia, Latin America, and the Caribbean, a mix that was much different from the predominantly European stock of earlier migration streams. An unexpected increase in Asian arrivals was due to immigration by those possessing skills that were in short supply (especially in health-related fields), and others escaping political persecution (especially from South Vietnam, Laos, and Cambodia). As time passed, many new immigrants took advantage of the law's provision allowing unification of families of permanent residents.[1]

Congress passed a second comprehensive law in 1986, the Immigration Reform and Control Act (IRCA), to stem the flow of undocumented migrants from Mexico. This act provided general amnesty for undocumented migrants who had been resident in the US since 1982, special entry provisions for migrant agricultural workers, and sanctions against employers of workers without papers. Over three million persons changed from illegal to legal status by the early 1990s. The number of undocumented residents continued to rise based on demand for their labor, however, and employer sanctions were rarely enforced by subsequent governments.

Together, the 1965 and 1986 acts dramatically diversified immigrant demographics in the US. The newcomers' race/ethnicity and skill sets altered (early waves of migrants tended to be highly skilled, the later less so). In addition, the geography of national immigration shifted. In 1910, more than half the arrivals were concentrated in five "gateway" cities: in order of importance these were New York City, Chicago, Philadelphia, St. Louis, and Boston. By 1990, the top five gateways had a distinctive west coast presence: New York

City, Los Angeles, Chicago, San Francisco, and Philadelphia. Ethnic mix varied widely according to region; for instance, in Los Angeles, since 1992 more than half the immigration came from Mexico, El Salvador, and Guatemala.[2]

By the early 1990s, the situation along the border had begun to deteriorate.[3] The scale of undocumented migration from Mexico to the US substantially increased as a result of reduced quotas, the seemingly endless demand for low-wage Mexican labor, and a severe economic downturn in Mexico (discussed in more detail in the following chapter). Television news coverage of the era showed crowds of would-be migrants massing in the vicinity of the crossings and then rushing the line under the assumption that a significant proportion of the crowd would evade capture. Such images provoked a sense that the border crossings were beyond control, ultimately causing a new era in border policing, when the US began to build fences designed to prevent illegal border crossings in major urban areas. In El Paso, "Operation Hold the Line"—formerly known as "Operation Blockade" but retitled because the name caused such offense—introduced unprecedented levels of border patrol officers and high-tech surveillance in 1994. Hold the Line was soon followed by "Operation Gatekeeper" in San Diego County, significant because it included the construction of fences between Tijuana and San Diego. A year later "Operation Safeguard" continued fence building, this time between the two Nogaleses, in Sonora and Arizona.[4]

Because of the new fortifications, migrants moved to more remote desert and mountain regions to cross. Deaths from drowning, heat stroke, and hypothermia increased in these parched lands.[5] As crossing became more hazardous, migrants also turned to human smugglers, known as *coyotes*, for assistance and so became unwittingly caught in a confusing fog of criminality.

For a brief moment, a more optimistic note regarding US–Mexico migration was heralded by the election in 2000 of George W. Bush and Vicente Fox, who met early in their presidencies and seemed to promise joint action on immigration reform. However, any optimism was short-lived, as the attacks of 9/11 caused the US to retreat to a more belligerent stance on matters of national security, creating (in 2002) a Department of Homeland Security (DHS), which included under its rubric immigration, customs, and border control, and other agencies dealing with terrorism and drug trafficking.

During Bush's second term as president, the US again contemplated comprehensive immigration reform. This attempt ultimately failed in 2007, largely because of the altered security climate and because opponents of reform rejected any actions that could be construed as "amnesty" for undocumented workers in the US. Subsequently, the Bush administration, without fanfare, undertook a version of immigration control based solely on enforcement principles, which aimed to stop unauthorized migrants from coming and to deport those already in the US, while sidelining other aspects of immigration, including human rights, earned citizenship, and US labor market needs.

The Secure Border Initiative

During his second term, President George W. Bush introduced the Secure Border Initiative (SBI) as a broadly-based effort to secure the nation's borders and reduce illegal immigration. Its goal was to gain "operational control" of both northern and southern borders within five years by increasing the number of agents in the US Border Patrol (USBP) and Immigration and Customs Enforcement (ICE) agencies; expanding detention and removal capacities to eliminate the former "catch and release" practices; upgrading technology and infrastructure to create a single "comprehensive detection suite" to deter border crossings; extending interior enforcement to places far from the border line, including workplace raids to apprehend criminal aliens; and cooperating with Canada and Mexico to accelerate repatriation.

Walls and Boots on the Border

Specific programs identified as part of the SBI included fortifying the border: increased physical layers of security, new access roads, and stadium-style lighting. In order to enable rapid deployment of the proposed changes, certain legal requirements (such as those related to environmental protection) were expected to be waived.[6]

Over the next few years, the nation's border protection budget expanded from $6 billion to $12 billion. In 2008, outgoing President Bush requested $775 million for *fencing* (making a grand total of $2 billion on fortifications to that point); $442 million to hire *additional border agents*, and $3 billion for ICE *enforcement* including work-site raids. The most prominent physical evidence of the SBI was undoubtedly the array of fortifications that was intended to separate Mexico from the US (see Figures 7.1–7.3). For the primary fence the estimated cost for 700 miles was $2.2–3 million per mile, although actual costs rose to $3.9 million/mile on average. Vehicle barriers—chest-high steel structures designed to stop cars and trucks—cost an average of $1 million per mile. One of the most expensive sections of new fencing required extensive landfill at Smuggler's Gulch near Tijuana and cost $16.5 million per mile. The price tag for maintaining the fence over the next 20 years was put at $6.5

FIGURE 7.1 The "Primary Fence" at San Luis Colorado, AZ, 2008.

This latest fortification is made from steel manufactured in Vietnam, and includes two noteworthy features: a 'lock box' in which a boundary monument is contained; and (at left) a gap that allows passage under the fence. Copyright © 2008 by Michael Dear.

billion. The number of USBP officers grew to almost 20,000 by decade's end, making it the fastest-growing category in federal employment.

DHS Dragnet

Before the SBI, Border Patrol agents usually returned undocumented migrants apprehended in the US to the nearest Mexican border town and released them. This practice was known as "catch and release." A keystone of the SBI initiative was to transform the practice of "catch and release" into "catch and return." For this to happen, undocumented migration was transformed into a criminal offense, enabling the DHS to identify, detain, prosecute, and deport offenders.

Identification was the priority of the "Secure Communities" program. It began modestly as a way of identifying migrants already in US jails who were

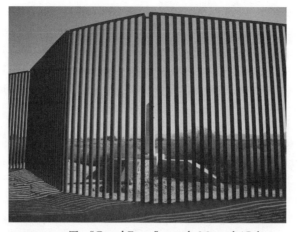

FIGURE 7.2 The "Caged Fence" outside Mexicali/Calexico, 2008.

The new fortifications are manufactured from diverse materials, but recent forms appear to favor some possibility of seeing through to the other side. The fences are invariably built on US soil to ensure ease of access and maintenance, but as a consequence they also conceal and isolate the boundary monuments. In this image, the fence swerves to accommodate a boundary monument. Copyright © 2008 by Michael Dear.

FIGURE 7.3 The "Floating Fence" at Algodones Dunes, California, 2008.

Conventional fence foundations are unworkable on the shifting sand dunes of south-eastern California, not far from Yuma. Buttresses have been attached to stabilize the fence structure, but this also allows sand to accumulate in the dead space below the fence. Copyright © 2009 by Michael Dear.

deportable under immigration law. However, it quickly (and controversially) grew to become the cornerstone of US anti-immigration enforcement practices. In the program, participating jails agreed to submit detainees' fingerprints to criminal and immigration databases. If the person was matched to an immigration violation, ICE would typically issue a "detainer" order against the jailed individual, requesting that the arresting agency notify ICE before it released the violator. ICE thus had the opportunity to decide whether the individual should be transferred to federal custody rather than released.[7] The arrangement gave ICE a technological (but not a physical) presence in prisons and jails across the country, although no local agents were deputized to enforce immigration law, nor were protocol agreements with local law-enforcement required.

Secure Communities did not quite work out as advertised. The program was supposed to focus on the removal of serious criminal offenders, the dangerous so-called "Level 1" criminals. However, only 15 percent of all matches identified in 2010 were immigrants charged or convicted of Level 1 offenses (out of a total of more than 248,000 database checks). The remaining 85 percent had been charged or convicted of Level 2 or 3 offenses such as traffic violations or juvenile mischief.[8] So while the numbers might have persuaded some observers of success, closer scrutiny revealed more of a "bait and switch" tactic, in which the program's ostensible target (dangerous criminal offenders) had been replaced by perpetrators of lesser offences.

Secure Communities also led to racial profiling and discouraged immigrant communities from cooperating with local police, who had their own doubts about the program, not the least of which was that it shifted the costs of detention onto local jurisdictions while ICE determined the status and disposition of a referral.[9] Some communities were so upset by the perversion of local policing that they opted out of the program.[10] Sanctuary cities across the country objected to any attempt to make participation mandatory.[11] And civil rights advocates worried that the program too often involved an abuse of police powers. For instance, one 15-year-old girl in San Francisco got into a school fight with her sister, and was referred to juvenile probation authorities, who reported her to ICE. She was transferred immediately to an internment center in Miami, from whence she would have been deported had it not been for rapid intervention.[12]

Borderland Prisons for Profit

Once identified, migrants have to be detained somewhere. As numbers grew, the ICE detention system quickly expanded into a far-flung network of more than 500 county jails, for-profit prisons, and federal jails, where detainees were held while the government took steps to deport them (see Figure 7.4).

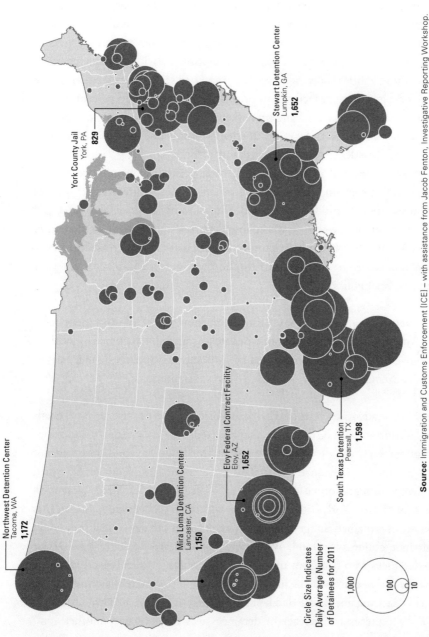

Northwest Detention Center
Tacoma, WA
1,172

York County Jail
York, PA
829

Stewart Detention Center
Lumpkin, GA
1,652

Mira Loma Detention Center
Lancaster, CA
1,150

Eloy Federal Contract Facility
Eloy, AZ
1,652

South Texas Detention
Pearsall, TX
1,598

Circle Size Indicates
Daily Average Number
of Detainees for 2011

1,000

100

10

FIGURE 7.4 Location of Private Detention Centers in the US, 2011.

Artwork by Dreamline Cartography, with assistance from Jacob Fenton.

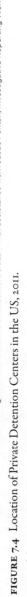

Source: Immigration and Customs Enforcement (ICE) – with assistance from Jacob Fenton, Investigative Reporting Workshop.

The facilities were geographically clustered along the southern border, but also extended into coastal zones where there was a large migrant presence.

In 2008, approximately 442,000 detainees passed through ICE's 32,000 detention beds at a cost of $2.4 billion per year, more than double the number in 2003, the program's first year.[13] ICE operated its own processing centers, holding about 13 percent of detainees; it contracted with privately operated detention facilities (holding 17 percent); and had service contracts with state and local government facilities to provide bedspaces (for 67 percent).[14] ICE also operated 186 unlisted and unmarked subfield offices, many in suburban office parks, referred to by political scientist Jacqueline Stevens as America's "secret ICE castles" in the "office park gulag."[15]

Many municipal governments regarded prisons as economic-development tools promising new jobs and revenues. ICE contracts with private agencies (such as the Corrections Corporation of America, and the GEO group, formerly known as Wackenhut), were so attractive that detention centers were soon being built on spec in anticipation of increased bedspace demand. According to Tom Barry, of the Washington DC-based Center for International Policy:

> These immigration prisons constitute the new face of imprisonment in America: the speculative public-private prison, publicly owned by local governments, privately operated by corporations, publicly financed by tax-exempt bonds, and located in depressed communities.[16]

Immigrant advocates reserved their most bitter complaints for privatized jails under contract with ICE.[17] These, they asserted, were underregulated and non-accountable, where detainees were sequestered in unsafe conditions without representation or adequate medical care. (Since 2004, 83 detainees have died while in immigration custody.)[18] For example, the Varick Street Detention Facility in New York City was charged with such inadequate nutrition that detainees remained hungry enough to work for $1 per day so that they could purchase commissary food. When asked to forward letters of legal advice to detainees who had been transferred, the Varick warden balked, claiming that he had to consider "the financial interests of his private shareholders"—a small Alaskan tribe whose dividends are linked to Varick's profits.[19]

The unnecessary transfer of detainees was the target of another complaint about detention practices. In 2009, the advocacy group Human Rights Watch (HRW) concluded that noncitizens, including illegal immigrants, were held unnecessarily and transferred needlessly within the detention system.[20] Through this process—known as "churning"—tens of thousands of residents from cities such as Los Angeles were removed to distant jails in Texas, Mississippi, and Louisiana, thus making it more difficult to maintain contact with legal counsel and families. According to officials, such transfers were caused by a lack of detention capacity in certain locations, but critics point out that transfer rates grew much more rapidly than the numbers of people in detention. In 2008, more than half the detainees were transferred at least once, and one quarter were moved multiple times. An HRW investigator put it this way: "ICE is increasingly subjecting detainees to a chaotic game of musical chairs."[21] Churning also had the effect of distributing the income derived from detention services.

Clogging the Courts

In the old days of catch-and-release, first-time border crossers were returned to their home countries through civil immigration proceedings. Criminal prosecutions were reserved for migrants with prior criminal records or those who made repeated attempts to cross the border. In 2005, "Operation Streamline" abandoned this distinction, requiring the criminal prosecution of *all* undocumented border crossers regardless of their history.[22] Not only were there hugely more numbers of identified and detained people, but each one of them now had to be brought to trial.

Unsurprisingly, during the Bush administration the annual rate of federal criminal prosecutions for immigration offenses more than quadrupled.[23] In 2008, the immigration courts received over 350,000 cases, with 186,000 cases pending, both record numbers. A shortage of judges contributed to an increase in the backlog of cases, as well as the time it took to resolve them.[24] In order to cope with the volume, many trials involved as many as 80 migrant cases at a single time, in violation of federal law.[25]

The justice system was actually in much worse shape than the numbers conveyed. By switching the justice system's focus to first-time offenders, Streamline diverted attention away from other crimes.[26] States began to take on cases that used to be prerogative of federal courts, including environmental, antitrust, and consumer fraud violations.[27] Morale reportedly declined precipitously in the overstretched US attorney offices; where once the focus had been on crime networks, international crime, and drug cartels, staff now dealt with improper and illegal border-crossings. Wiretap requests by US attorneys—usually regarded as a hallmark of complex federal drug investigations—dropped to a 14-year low, and requests for assistance from state and local prosecutors tripled.[28] In another effort to contain workloads, staff routinely declined to prosecute drug cases involving less than 500 pounds of marijuana, and drug traffickers responded by splitting their loads into smaller quantities to avoid federal attention.[29]

Deportation Nation

The culmination of the catch-and-return sequence is deportation of the convicted offender.[30] By the end of Bush's second term, the US had become a "deportation nation," removing a record number of 136,126 illegal immigrants with criminal records in 2008.[31] However, Human Rights Watch pointed out— once again—that not only criminal aliens had been caught up in the dragnet. Nearly three-quarters of the 897,000 migrants deported in this category for the decade up to 2007 were convicted of nonviolent offenses, typically driving while under the influence of alcohol, or immigration-related crimes such as selling false papers. One-fifth of those deported were legal permanent residents.[32]

So: deportation was another bait-and-switch situation, where a program directed toward criminals altered its focus to legal residents guilty of only minor offenses. Agencies were able to report inflated performance statistics, even though their performance was only tangentially related to the program's actual target. Flushed with success, ICE introduced a new deportation program entitled "Operation Scheduled Departure" in 2008. During the summer of that year, it offered anyone who surrendered for deportation a period of 90 days to get their affairs in order before departing. In effect, Scheduled Departure invited people to self-deport. Of the 457,000 people facing deportation orders, only eight took the bait, and the program was terminated after three weeks.[33]

More poignant were the ways in which unaccompanied children and so-called "medical repatriations" got caught in the deportation net.[34] Customs and Border Protection agents apprehended about 10,000 juveniles every year. They were mostly from Mexico and were returned voluntarily without detention.[35] In the first six months of 2008, 90,000 children were deported by US authorities.[36] Another growing category of children-at-risk consisted of those who were brought as children to the US by undocumented migrants and later in life found themselves subject to deportation despite having exemplary records of educational or other achievements.[37] There are also *private* deportations of patients discharged after hospital care but unable to find nursing homes willing to accept them without health insurance. Exact numbers of these medical repatriations are difficult to assess, and practices vary from state to state. One doctor critical of international patient dumping warned:

"Repatriation is pretty much a death sentence in some of these cases" where medical care is unavailable to meet patient needs.[38]

Spreading the Net

As well as enlarging the physical fortifications and numbers of border patrol agents and shifting to catch-and-return, the SBI extended enforcement operations across the nation and expanded its capacity for electronic surveillance.

The National Fugitive Operations Program (or NFOP), like many other SBI initiatives, began life as one kind of initiative and then morphed into another.[39] The program was initially portrayed as facilitating ICE raids of workplaces and homes in search of dangerous fugitive migrants. Beginning in 2003 with a budget of $9 million and 8 seven-member Fugitive Operations Teams (FOTs), by 2008 the program budget had grown to $218 million with 104 teams, dealing with approximately half a million "fugitive alien cases" across the country.[40]

The agency began to hit its stride in 2006 when quotas for arrests were raised to 1,000 per year, from a 2004 target figure of 124.[41] In a pattern familiar to SBI practices, the requirement that FOTs focus on criminal aliens was eliminated, allowing nonfugitives and fugitives without criminal records to be included in FOT counts. By 2007, fugitives with criminal records—the program's initial targets—accounted for only 9 percent of those arrested.[42]

An analysis by the Migration Policy Institute of five years of NFOP arrest data ending in 2009 concluded that three-quarters of the 96,000 people apprehended had no criminal conviction.[43] The major impact of the program had been to increase the number of noncriminal migrants held in detention.[44] Cardoso School of Law professor Peter L. Markowitz revealed that internal directives by immigration officials had altered the NFOP program *without* consulting Congress, causing Markowitz to conclude that: "It looks like what happened is that the law enforcement strategy was hijacked by the political agenda of the [Bush] administration."[45] He added that by targeting noncriminal undocumented workers, the NFOP favored the easy pickings of "low-hanging fruit."[46]

NFOP also took its fight against undocumented migrants deep into the nation's heartland in the form of workplace raids. The largest single workplace raid in US history occurred in August 2008 at a Mississippi electronics factory, where 592 migrant workers were arrested.[47] It was the biggest of many workplace raids that year, touching off fear and tensions in many small towns that relied on migrant labor.[48] The effects of such raids in small communities were often devastating. A 2008 raid in the town of Postville, Iowa, resulted in the arrest of 398 illegal workers at a kosher meatpacking plant. Nearly all the arrested men were deported, many claiming that they were deprived of adequate legal protection. Dozens of imprisoned Guatemalan women were later released to care for their children, but they remained in Postville unable to work and obliged to wear cumbersome ankle monitors. (They were known as *Las mujeres con grilletes elctrónicos,* or the women with electronic shackles.)[49]

One year later, the meatpacking plant was bankrupt and its managers faced prison time. Postville's resident population shrank by nearly half to 1,800. Local businesses associated with the plant were obliged to close, and in the face of stress and anxiety that townsfolk described as "relentless," families moved away and social networks unraveled. The town's mayor resigned from office, overwhelmed by constituents' difficulties. A former city councilman succinctly summed up the aftermath of the ICE raid: "We still haven't done anything about illegal immigration. All we've done is devastate north-eastern Iowa."[50]

The most pervasive insertion of ICE authority at the local level was through Section 287(g) of the 1996 Immigration and Nationality Act (INA), which authorized the federal government to enter into agreements with state and local law enforcement agencies in pursuit of immigration enforcement goals. Under the agreements, designated local officers could perform immigration enforcement functions so long as they had received appropriate training and operated under the supervision of federal officials. This was the only program that authorized state and local agents to partake in immigration laws,[51] allowing them to identify, process, and detain migrant offenders encountered during their regular law-enforcement activities.[52]

The 287(g) program was slow to get off the ground until former Attorney General John Ashcroft began touting funding availability.[53] In 2005, there were only 5 collaborating law enforcement agencies; by 2009, there were 67 in 27 states, with over 950 deputized officers.[54] There was also a wait list of 42 agencies that had applied to participate.[55] The program costs were $54 million in 2009.[56] The self-styled "nonpartisan" Center for Immigration Studies (CIS) championed 287(g), describing it as cost-effective bargain that provided "far more bang for the buck" than many other programs.[57] Dismissing opposition, the CIS regarded 287(g) as a "welcome addition" to US immigration law, and advocated that the program be expanded.[58]

Needless to say, not everyone admired 287(g). Hundreds of civil rights and advocacy groups urged cancellation of the program on the grounds of its racist orientation.[59] The Government Accountability Office (GAO) and the Police Foundation both criticized the program. Retiring chief William Bratton urged his City of Los Angeles Police Department to stay focused on fighting crime, not combating illegal immigration—a direct slap at the 287(g) mandate.[60] (The LA County Sheriff's Department maintained its contract with ICE.) Six local law enforcement agencies withdrew from the program, mistrustful of using police officers as immigration agents.[61]

Virtual Border

Not content to extend its geographical reach across the nation, the SBI unveiled plans to secure the nation's skies. The Secure Border Initiative Network (or SBInet) promised to "integrate multiple state-of-the-art systems and traditional security infrastructure into a single comprehensive border security suite."[62] Many exotic "toys" were made available to officers on the line (including new communications and surveillance equipment), but the program's centerpiece was a promised high-tech "fix."

In early 2008, the DHS announced that a pilot project to build a "virtual fence" along part of the Arizona border had been a success, although it did not intend to extend the capacity along the entire line. The project, known as P-28, constructed nine observation towers near Sasabe, Arizona, close to known smuggling routes but some distance inland from the boundary line. Local people were vociferous in their objections, complaining that the cameras were pointed in the wrong direction—at them and not toward Mexico! A $20.6 million contract was awarded to the Boeing corporation in order to develop and install the new technology, but it was much-delayed and failure-prone from the start—the instrumentation was activated by rain and small animals, for instance.[63] The GAO frequently called for better oversight and accountability in the project.[64] Only much later did DHS administrators concede that the government should have been "more specific" in its contracts with Boeing, while also blaming the contractor for "a series of mistakes."[65]

Despite the failure of P-28, the lure of technological fix persisted. In 2009 Boeing was awarded further contracts worth $1.1 billion (this time under the Obama administration) to continue development of the camera, sensor, and radar towers.[66]

THERE WAS MUCH less coherence about the execution of the SBI than I may have conveyed. In actuality, the initiative resembled a scatter-gun approach— an enormous fusillade of programmatic discharges, some of which hit targets (with varying degrees of precision and success), while others were blanks that missed targets completely. Among the many proliferating tryouts were programs named Operation Jump-Start, Operation Return-to-Sender, and Operation Reservation Guaranteed.

One of the more enduring of these minor programs was Operation Stonegarden, funded by DHS's Federal Emergency Management Agency (FEMA). Officially, Stonegarden offered federal assistance to state, local, and tribal law enforcement agencies in borderland counties. Introduced under a cloudburst of counterterrorism rhetoric, Stonegarden's rationale morphed quickly from being a "first-responder" against terrorists into a border security program focused on drugs and illegal immigrants.[67] In practice, it provided grants for additional law enforcement personnel, overtime pay, and travel and lodging expenses.[68]

Stonegarden attracted the same criticisms that beset the 287(g) program, namely that it led to racial profiling and community distrust of law enforcement.[69] For example, in Otero County, New Mexico, Stonegarden supported hunts for illegal immigrants in a largely Latino settlement near El Paso. In September 2008 a federal injunction barred the county sheriff's department from using Stonegarden dollars to enforce immigration laws through raids that targeted low-income Latino residents in a county that incidentally housed two government-owned but privately operated prisons that detained immigrants.[70] Other complaints against Stonegarden identified the lack of a clear mission or federal oversight and the misuse of funds. One apparently tireless Arizona police chief received $100,000 overtime pay on top of his regular salary by logging workdays of 14 hours over several months; elsewhere, Stonegarden funds were allocated to routine police duties such as issuing traffic citations, crowd control at parades, antiprostitution cleanups, and chasing motorcycle gangs.[71]

SBI in the Obama Era

The Obama presidency opened with expectations of a more humane approach to immigration and border policing.[72] Early in his administration, President Obama voiced support of immigration reform, saying "we can create a system in which you have strong border security and an orderly process for people to come in.... [and] for those already in the United States to be able to achieve a pathway to citizenship."[73] He held highly publicized meetings in support of Mexican President Calderón's fight against the drug cartels, promising financial aid, technological support, expanded law enforcement, shared intelligence, and criminal prosecutions.[74] Further deployments of the US National Guard along troublesome sections of the border were also undertaken.[75]

Initial expectations were boosted when Obama appointed Janet Napolitano as Secretary of the Department of Homeland Security Secretary.

Prior to her appointment, Napolitano was Governor of Arizona and in those days she frequently belittled Bush's plan to build walls along the US–Mexico border, saying: "You show me a 12-foot-high fence, and I'll show you a 13-foot ladder." (Sometimes in these quips, the height of the fence increased but the length of the ladder always stayed one foot ahead of it.) Once in office, DHS Secretary Napolitano conceded that the fence had helped gain "operational control" in some border zones, and she authorized completion of the final 60 miles of fencing at a cost of $4 million per mile (which had already been approved by Congress).[76]

Napolitano promised that her approach to immigration would be "very, very different" from her predecessor's. It was distinctive, she averred, because "it is more strategic, more cooperative, more multilateral, and in the long run, more effective."[77] In early 2009, she unveiled a revamped plan for border security, emphasizing support for Mexico's campaign against the cartels, limiting the flows from the north of firearms and cash into Mexico, and guarding against the spillover of violent crime from the south. The plan also promised periodic review and evaluation of the border initiatives, something that many local communities and law enforcement officials had long called for. However, there were also lingering traces of the programs of her Republican predecessor, including increases in personnel attached to cross-border collaboration, enhanced technologies, and improved interdiction efforts along the border.[78]

With hindsight, perhaps the most accurate guide to Napolitano's intentions during Obama's early years was when she injected a note of political realism into the national conversation. She warned that a "no-nonsense" approach to immigration was a priority in order to "persuade American voters to accept [later] legislation that would give legal status to millions of illegal immigrants."[79]

Certainly, by the middle of Obama's term (2010), few clear breaks with the practices of the previous administration were evident.[80] In many instances, SBI enforcement capacities had in fact expanded. The nationwide dragnet for undocumented migrants continued as the Secure Communities program grew to become something of a "poster child" for the incoming administration's hard line.[81] John Morton, ICE head, did not budge from the claim that Secure Communities "focuses our resources on identifying and removing the most serious criminal offenders first and foremost," even though his predecessor had transparently exceeded this mandate.[82] By October 2010, Secure Communities operated in 686 jurisdictions in 33 states, and ICE planned to implement the program in every one of the nation's 3,100 state and local jails by the year 2013.[83] The program's implementation continued to be plagued by mixed reviews and strong opposition.[84]

The upstream supply of migrant apprehensions showed few signs of slowing, but in August 2009 the Obama administration announced plans to overhaul the detentions system and review the performance of 350 local jails and private prisons with ICE funding.[85] The newly ensconced Napolitano established centralized authority over the detention system and opened a new Office of Detention Policy and Planning. One aspect of detentions that received immediate attention was the lumping together of criminal and noncriminal detainees. Among those in custody in September 2009, half had no criminal convictions; the other half were considered felons, but only 11 percent of them had committed violent crimes.[86] Napolitano insisted that nonviolent inmates should be housed in separate facilities and supervised in more appropriate ways. (She was considering converting hotels and nursing homes into detention centers.) ICE's John Morton grasped the nettle of civil versus criminal status and proceedings by promising to transform the penal network into a "truly civil detention system" separate from the criminal mainstream.[87] Meanwhile, criticisms of detention practices continued unabated, including accusations of unnecessary deaths in detention, coverups, and contracting with unaccountable private operators.[88]

As apprehension and detention policies remained essentially undisturbed during Obama's early years, levels of prosecutions inevitably rose. Despite the hiring of more immigration judges, by December 2010 the backlog of pending cases had reached an all-time high of over a quarter of a million, 44 percent higher than 2008 levels. The average length of time cases had been waiting was 467 days.[89] Many cases were now adjudicated by new "immigration judges" employed through the Executive Office of Immigration Review (EOIR) where, as one judge put it: "I'm afraid there's a premium on quotas and productivity, and not the truth."[90] The country's 238 adjudicators shared a massive caseload: 390,000 cases were initiated nationally in 2009 (over 1,600 cases per adjudicator). Intended to relieve the burden, the enlarged system actually aggravated judicial process by making procedures less transparent (e.g., hearings held in detention centers required that outsiders obtain security clearance in order to attend).[91]

Finally, greater numbers caught up in the criminal justice system inevitably meant increased pressure for more deportations. Who knew how to stop the conveyor belt? In the three years, 2009–2011, there were close to 1.2 million deportations from the US. And yet, in an early sign of tempering the fevered pace of deportation, ICE officials in 2010 canceled the expulsion orders of 17,000 immigrants who were likely to win legal status on review of their cases, primarily in order to reduce the huge backlog in the immigration courts.[92] Larger efforts to cut back on the deportation caseloads and to remove from the list those who posed no security risk were also promised.[93]

DURING ITS FIRST two years, the Obama/Napolitano DHS followed a hard line on identifying, detaining, prosecuting, and deporting undocumented migrants. However, around the midterm mark, efforts emerged to curtail the more flagrant abuses in some of the programs in the SBI armory.

In 2009, SBI executive director Mark Borkowski had restated his enthusiasm for SBInet, the virtual border, announcing plans to cover the entire line between Mexico and the US by 2014, at a cost of $6.7 billion.[94] Two years later, in January 2011, after a long string of delays and failures, Secretary Napolitano unceremoniously cancelled the ill-fated project, on the grounds that: "SBInet cannot meet its original objective of providing a single, integrated border security technology solution." The project had cost $1.9 billion, over five times the initial estimate.[95] But the DHS was not ready to abandon the promise of a technological fix. A vast array of communications, surveillance, and other equipment continued being issued to line officers. Promises were made to utilize mobile surveillance systems, unmanned aircraft, thermal imaging devices, and tower-based remote video surveillance. Just six months after SBInet was cancelled, as National Guard troops were once again arriving on the southern Arizona border, Napolitano announced the launch of her department's fourth Predator drone aircraft. The boots on the ground, she promised, would now be reinforced by surveillance from the skies.[96]

In another break with SBI precedent, the deeply unpopular workplace raids associated with the National Fugitive Operations Program (NFOP) were scaled back, and replaced by audits of employers to check their hiring practices regarding undocumented workers.[97] Through this altered emphasis, ICE hoped to introduce a "culture of compliance" among employers so that verifying the status of potential employees would become standard workplace practice. In these so-called "silent raids,"[98] human resource auditors had taken the place of sheriffs' posses.

In her most public departure from Bush era precedents, Napolitano confronted the 287(g) program, one of the most unpopular across the country. As in the cases of SBInet and NFOP, her about-face on a centerpiece of DHS policy required no small adjustment. Soon after taking office, Napolitano had voiced support of 287(g)'s "force extension" opportunity (by which federal immigration responsibilities were delegated to local law enforcement agencies). Bush's 2006 budget for 287(g) was $5 million; four years later in 2010,

Napolitano had helped grow its budget to $68 million, representing contracts with 72 police jurisdictions nationwide.[99] Yet a performance review confirmed what most people already knew—that 287(g)'s original goal of identifying criminal aliens had shifted to a focus primarily on noncriminals, and that racial profiling was standard 287(g) operating procedure in many localities.[100]

By mid-2009, Napolitano had altered 287(g) procedures, requiring ICE and its partnering agencies to sign revised agreements that heightened federal oversight of the program.[101] Contracting agencies would henceforward be obliged to abide by federal antidiscrimination law, and most importantly, the revised program would be redirected toward its original goal, that of detaining undocumented immigrants who had committed serious crimes.[102] One of the first consequences of the new rules was the termination of *street-based* enforcement of immigration law in Maricopa County, Arizona, which had by far the largest 287(g) program in the country, with 160 trained deputies.[103] Screening of the immigration status of *jail-based* inmates was allowed to continue.[104]

Perhaps unsurprisingly, some local partners in the modified 287(g) agreements remained reluctant to change their habits.[105] Many 287(g) partners (especially in the Southeast) continued to target noncriminal as well as criminal unauthorized immigrants; and agencies remained subject to local political pressures that enabled racial profiling to persist. Nationwide, at least 30,000 undocumented people stopped for common traffic violations had ended up in deportation, and this number was rapidly increasing.[106] The Migration Policy Institute extended its criticism to the Secure Communities program, concluding that the US continued to lack "a clear and comprehensive interior immigration enforcement strategy, even as interior enforcement has become an increasingly important component of US immigration policy in the post-9/11 period."[107]

REFERRING TO THE first half of her tenure as DHS Secretary, Janet Napolitano conceded that an enforcement agenda had expanded since she took office. Nevertheless, the second half of Obama's term saw some bold course corrections, particularly regarding the cancellation of SBInet, the shift from workplace raids to employer audits, and the containment of abuses by ICE-deputized local immigration police. Napolitano's actions were consistent with her earlier expression of political realism: that a no-nonsense approach was the first priority in order to ensure later acceptance of legislation giving legal status to eligible immigrants.[108] But as time went by, it became evident that no such legislation was imminent.[109]

SBI and the Third Nation

After 9/11, the US government moved to create a behemoth Department of Homeland Security, brandishing a Secure Border Initiative and charged with ensuring operational control over the nation's borders. The DHS agenda effectively recast immigration as a national security issue.[110]

The focus of the SBI under both Bush and Obama was enforcement. The fundamental break with past immigration policing was captured by the move from catch-and-release to catch-and-return—achieved primarily by transferring migrant offenses from the civil to criminal courts. Enormous efforts were henceforward directed toward building fortifications along the international boundary; doubling the number of US Border Patrol agents; identifying, detaining, prosecuting, and deporting undocumented migrants; upgrading technology and infrastructure to hold the line; conducting workplace raids and employer audits to capture undocumented workers; and extending enforcement capacities throughout the nation. Many programs that began by promising to identify and deport dangerous criminals or terrorists were amended to target ordinary people linked only with minor offenses. The latter pool was much larger and easier to catch, and quotas for line workers and judges ensured that the net would be widely and energetically cast, thereby boosting the agencies' performance statistics. There was strikingly little oversight and scarcely a nod toward program evaluation until much later.

The growth of the SBI was astonishing. At national, state, and local levels, a web of patronage and collaboration involving both public and private institutions rapidly evolved to absorb the dollars made available through the initiative. Under both administrations, the tentacles of the DHS stretched deeply into the fabric of national life. For instance, the DHS-inspired realignment of federal agencies incorporated parts of the Department of Justice, FEMA, and the National Guard, as well as conscripting agencies with no direct responsibility for immigration into the enforcement task, including the Department of Fish and Wildlife and the Bureau of Land Management. The legitimate mandates of some federal agencies not involved with national security were overridden by DHS prerogatives (including the suspension of environmental protection laws). Many federal agencies incorporated immigration-related costs into their own budgets, such as the millions of dollars spent by the Department of Justice on prosecuting immigration offenders and increasing the number of federal prosecutors. State and local governments were also obliged to bear a proportion of the growing costs of border control.[111]

The DHS apparatus was bolstered by contracts with private corporations such as the Corrections Corporation of America, Boeing, the GEO group, and Blackwater. Private subcontractors were enlisted for the construction of the physical and virtual fences, and to supply security training and services, equipment, the operation of detention facilities, and transportation and deportation functions. In addition, DHS contracted with local public agencies by outsourcing its immigration mandate and obligations to states and municipalities, thereby co-opting many borderland communities and their institutions within the protocols of national security. The delegation of many federal immigration responsibilities to subfederal agencies presaged the later barrage of state-sponsored initiatives aimed at usurping federal immigration prerogatives (discussed in chapter 9).

This congeries of public and private interests may be referred to as a "Border Industrial Complex" (BIC).[112] I use this term to invoke a famous speech by President Dwight D. Eisenhower in 1961, when he warned of the growing influence of the "military-industrial complex:"

> This conjunction of an immense military establishment and a large arms industry is new in the American experience. The total influence—economic, political, even spiritual—is felt in every city, every State house, every office of the Federal government. We recognize the imperative need for this development. Yet we must not fail to comprehend its grave implications. Our toil, resources and livelihood are all involved; so is the very structure of our society.
>
> In the councils of government, we must guard against the acquisition of unwarranted influence, whether sought or unsought, by the military industrial complex. The potential for the disastrous rise of misplaced power exists and will persist.[113]

Since Eisenhower's time, the term "military-industrial complex" has become common parlance, and its meaning has expanded beyond the nexus between defense contractors and the Pentagon. An analogous concept may be applied to the multidimensional, interrelated set of public and private interests now managing border security—encompassing flows of money, contracts, influence, and resources among a vast network of individuals, lobbyists, corporations, banks, public institutions, and elected officials at all levels of government. We must guard against the unwarranted influence of this Border Industrial Complex.[114]

THE THIRD NATION is where the burden of enforcement in "Fortress USA" is localized and experienced. The issue of national security has *distributed benefits and concentrated costs*, in that an entire nation stands to gain by the burdens borne and sacrifices made by a subset of its inhabitants. From the viewpoint of the third nation, the task of solving a nation's problems may have limited appeal if the task threatens the well-being of the impacted communities. This divergence of local and national interests is at the heart of the tensions observable in the borderlands today, as the third nation's integrity and viability are threatened by a host nation's obsessions with homeland security and immigration. The lives of people in the third nation are unlikely to improve so long as a the US pays little or no attention to the troubles it has foisted upon them. But this is only half the story: a different threat to the third nation emanates from the Mexican side of the border.

8

Mexico

NARCO-STATE OR FAILED STATE?

THE INFLUENCE OF organized crime and drug trafficking has provoked unprecedented levels of violence and brutality in Mexico.[1] To be sure, the manufacture and sale of illicit narcotics are long-established practices in Mexico, metastasizing into a binational issue only after the US passed a Marijuana Tax Act in 1937 that effectively outlawed marijuana by criminalizing its production and sale.[2] The Prohibition era in the US set in motion an undercover drug smuggling apparatus that would eventually become transformed into a multibillion-dollar industry in which organized criminal gangs (or "cartels") sought to monopolize territories (or "plazas") for the distribution and sale of illicit substances.

From 1929 to 2000, when Mexico was dominated by a single political party, the *Partido Revolucionario Institucional* (or PRI, the Institutional Revolutionary Party), the *narcos* reputedly enjoyed considerable leeway to conduct their business so long as they remained out of sight.[3] However, the PRI patronage networks faltered after the 2000 presidential election victory of Vicente Fox of the *Partido Acción Nacional* (or PAN, the National Action Party). Competition among cartels became more overt when there was no pliant partner to act as godfather. Fox later conceded that pressure from his government had contributed to a "terrible wave of violence among cartel leaders."[4]

Upon taking office in 2006, President Felipe Calderón made a highly public declaration of a "war on drugs," followed by manifest resolve and commitment of personnel and materiel to the struggle. As the narco-war body count spiraled into the tens of thousands, cartel influence paradoxically grew, and four years later, two-thirds of the Mexican public believed that the *narcos* were winning the war.[5] A character from Carlos Fuentes' novel *La Voluntad y la Fortuna/Destiny and Desire* gave voice to this dawning realization: "I grew up in a society in which society was protected by official corruption. Today...society is protected by criminals.... The great drama of Mexico is that crime has replaced the state."[6]

A Narco-State?

The wealth and power of organized crime has become Mexico's defining characteristic, according to US journalist William Finnegan.[7] He used the term "state capture" to describe the realities of power in parts in Mexico, such as the state of Michoacán. The notion of "capture" implies that state government has been taken over by cartels—not necessarily destroyed or closed down, but placed (we might say) under new management. After 2000, as police began arresting many in the top echelons of the drug lords,[8] cartels fought to divide the country into separate market areas where they would brook no competitor.[9] If in so doing they managed to elbow aside conventional political and police powers, so much the better. The result of this murderous enterprise was the partitioning of the nation into distinct territories (the *plazas*) where each cartel enjoyed a local monopoly. Scholar-activist Sergio Aguayo cogently expressed the consequences of this arrangement: "In some parts of Mexico, the state is no longer present." Others in Mexico feared that in its place, a "narco-state" was emerging.

A narco-state contains many interest groups besides the *narcotraficantes* themselves. Also engaged are local politicians and businesses anxious to preserve some semblance of civic order even if it means collusion with the cartels; terrified residents who mistrust local police and who are often intimidated into doing cartel work; millions of young people, known as *los ninis* (*ni estudian ni trabajan*), who don't go to school or have jobs, and are considered ripe for recruitment by cartels;[10] and the country's own drug addicts, only now becoming part of public debate.[11] The security forces responsible for prosecuting the war on drugs are, more often than not, suspected of working for the cartels.

Although images of the gory bodies of murder victims may dominate the headlines, a broadly based *narcocultura* (or drug culture) has also permeated the nation's psyche, normalizing and consolidating the place of cartels in Mexican society and reinforcing their influence even when their physical presence is absent. The culture flourishes, for example, in the proliferation of *narcocorridos* and movies that celebrate gangster wealth, power, and sexual potency.[12] It is confirmed by *narcotourismo* each time a taxi driver in Mazatlán offers a tour to a drug lord's neighborhood, or in a Brownsville trip to visit the site where a cartel leader was arrested after a shootout.[13] Fatalistic cults—most famously Jesús Malverde, patron saint of the drug world, and Santa Muerta, or Holy Death—have mushroomed beyond plazas and their prison-based franchises into Mexican neighborhoods and even abroad.[14]

However pervasive these influences may be, they do not add up to universal acceptance of the narco world. Many Mexicans tolerate the presence of cartels with a stoicism and passivity that derive from a sense of helplessness,[15] and personal security concerns remain uppermost in their minds.[16] A friend who once lived in a gated community in Playas de Tijuana moved out when a drug dealer built a fortified house next to hers because she did not want her children exposed to everyday narco culture in schools and on sidewalks. The key point is that while cartel presence in Mexico is indisputable, it is rarely universal or monolithic in its application; it has not penetrated Mexican society to the same degree in all places at all times.

This question of degree is important in deciding whether or not Mexico is a narco-state. Choice of definition has consequences for how national and international agencies approach relations with Mexico. Lorenzo Meyer, a respected commentator and scholar in the Colegio de Mexico, applied a forensic intelligence to the question of definition. A *narcoestado*, he began, is a nation where the power structure, economy, and culture are dominated by drug cartels. But what level of "domination" is sufficient to demonstrate cartel ascendancy over the other agencies of state or civil society? Meyer answered: when drug lords gain *some measure* of influence in the structures of government, become *relatively* powerful economically, and render *certain* of their cultural values acceptable to the population at large, then we can regard a political system as a narco-state. But he still left open the question of exactly *how much* political, economic and cultural domination was required to qualify Mexico as a narco-state.[17] Such indeterminacy may be unsatisfying, but it is also realistic because narco-control has to be determined on the ground, with a sensitivity to the specific characteristics of each place. This characterization of a *localized* narco-state better emphasizes the geographically bounded nature of cartel control, as applied to plaza, town, or neighborhood.

ONE PLACE THAT epitomizes the deep penetration of cartel influence is the border city of Ciudad Juárez, which until recently had a population of 1.3 million people.[18] In the five years after Calderón declared his war on drugs, 40,000 people were murdered in Mexico, a national murder rate of 14 per 100,000 inhabitants. In Ciudad Juárez, the rate was 189 per 100,000.[19] Journalist Ed Vulliamy regards Juárez as the most dangerous place in Mexico.[20]

Ciudad Juárez has long possessed a reputation for violence. In the ten years following 1993, over 430 women were murdered in the State of Chihuahua, and many hundreds more simply disappeared. One-third of the victims had been sexually assaulted, others had been mutilated or showed signs of torture, their bodies dumped in desolate deserts. No one is sure what caused the epidemic of femicide. Some criminologists suggested that it began as the work of a serial killer but mutated into a project involving a highly organized group of killers. From the outset, members of the Juárez police department were implicated in a growing list of malfeasance that included failure to investigate the killings, torture of suspects, and the assassination of witnesses and lawyers involved in related criminal proceedings.

In 2001, eight bodies were discovered *inside the city limits* of Ciudad Juárez, the consequence of what came to be called the "cotton-field murders." Eight tall pink crosses, bearing the names of the murdered women, were later erected on site (see Figure 8.1).[21] Three years after the murders, while photographing the commemorative crosses, I was held for a while by federal agents of the Agencía Federal de Investigaciones, because of my presence at what they described as the scene of an "active" criminal investigation.

FIGURE 8.1 Memorial to Eight Women Found Murdered in Ciudad Juárez.

Hundreds of women have been killed in Juárez over the past decade, but very few of the crimes have been solved. Copyright © 2004 by Michael Dear.

Police arrested two bus drivers in connection with the cotton-field murders. They were family men, poor and uneducated, seemingly not hardened criminals capable of dumping eight corpses at a busy city intersection. In 2002, one driver's attorney was shot to death by police after he became too critical of the city's inactions. Police confessed to the killing, but claimed it was a matter of "mistaken identity;" they were later exonerated for acting in self-defense. The second driver's attorney complained about the violations of his client's rights, and four years later he too was assassinated on a Juárez street.

There was a small decline in the murder rates of women during 2000–2003, after which the numbers began once again to rise. The lack of convictions invoked increasingly lurid and outlandish causes for the killings, involving trafficking in human organs or the interventions of religious and satanic cults. Perhaps unsurprisingly, the volume of media coverage devoted to the femicide declined when cartel-related carnage got top billing. Nevertheless, the murders of women continue.[22]

Today, after many years of living with many different kinds of death, Juárez is suffering from cartel-induced depopulation, business closures, and housing abandonment. One-fifth of its population (roughly 230,000 people) left the city over the past three years. A rise in domestic violence and crimes against children has been linked to the stresses of everyday life. A recent sequence of gruesome murders involved attacks on patients in drug rehabilitation clinics that were explained as cartel efforts to eliminate former members of rival gangs, or members of their own clan no longer regarded as loyal. They were also interpreted as a campaign of *limpia social*—an army-backed social cleansing designed to eliminate society's undesirables under the cover of a drug war.

In some Juárez neighborhoods, the entire process of urban living seems to involve criminal enterprises.[23] The culture of violence and impunity in Juárez became so intense that in 2010 a local newspaper, *Diario de Juárez,* published an unprecedented open letter, on its front page, addressed to the local *narcos* and entitled: "*¿Qué quieren de nosotros?*" (What do you want from us?):

> What are we supposed to publish or not publish,... You are at this time the de facto authorities in this city,... We do not want more dead. We do not want more wounded nor further intimidations.... Therefore, tell us what you expect from us as a medium...[24]

No guidance was forthcoming, but on many other occasions, cartels have not been shy about articulating their expectations.[25] When the La Familia cartel rose to power in the state of Michoacán, pickup trucks full of armed men were dispatched to several small towns. The local mayor in one such town, Zitácuaro, later reported that the invaders were respectful, telling him: "We want to work here. There will be no trouble, no crime, no drunkenness, nothing."[26] After that, they would proceed to take over the town and enforce their own laws. The mayor himself was offered *plato o plomo* (silver or lead)—take the cartel's money and cooperate, or be killed along with your family. Local police chiefs were sometimes assassinated, and many towns lost as much as half of their populations through out-migration. The residents who remained lived in fear among abandoned homes and businesses, staying indoors as much as possible in the absence of police protection or services of any kind.

A few towns hired women as police chiefs in the hope that criminals would be less likely to harm them, and because there were so few men willing to take the job. But this strategy did not work: Hermila García of Meoqui (in the state of Chihuahua) was shot in November 2010 after only one month on the job; and 28-year-old Erika Gándara, appointed chief in October 2010 at Guadalupe Distrito Bravos (population formerly 9,000, but now half that size), was abducted two months later and has not been seen since.[27]

I ASKED MANY people in Mexico what could or should be done about the drug cartels. Their most frequent response was that no one really had a solution or seemed able to provide the required leadership. Already, in 2009, a report from an international commission headed by former presidents of Brazil, Colombia, and Mexico declared flatly that the three-year war on drugs had failed, and called for an end to Mexico's purely repressive response in favor of an alternative based on reducing consumption.[28] More people began to favor direct negotiation with the cartels. In the influential magazine *Proceso*, for instance, Javier Sicilla advocated unambiguously for a *pacto*, or compact, with the cartels.[29] His son had not long ago been murdered by alleged cartel members, and his anguished appeals gained wide support.[30] Sergio Aguayo regarded Sicilla's intervention as a pivotal moment, an "epistemological watershed" that changed the way ordinary Mexicans understood the war and its aftermath. Now, he told me, Mexicans realized that: "There is no one there to protect me. I am on my own."[31]

Despite these pessimistic outlooks, there is no shortage of public debate about solutions to the drug problem.[32] Two examples demonstrate the range of such discussions. Pragmatic in his prognostications, Mexico City professor Jorge Chabat narrowed his country's drug policy options to three:[33] *simulación*, or pretending to enforce the law while tolerating the narcotics

industry up to some negotiated limit, which is what happened during the
PRI era; military confrontation, the policy instigated by President Calderón;
and legalization, openly discussed in Mexico as a way to reduce cartel income
and influence.[34] (Legalization rarely enters polite debate in the US.)[35] In his
sweeping manifesto, Enrique Krause pressed all the hot-button issues pertinent to the drug wars. He called upon the Mexican government to root out
corruption in local police forces, reform the prison and judicial systems, and
seek a more collaborative nonpartisan approach in national politics. The print
media, he continued, should abandon its flirtation with the "pornography of
violence" which sensationalized the worst aspects of the drug wars and contributed to perceptions that the Mexican state was "failing." Finally, Krauze
reminded the US to recognize its complicity in creating Mexico's problems,
both as the world's largest market for illegal narcotics and as the source of
most of the guns acquired by the cartels.[36]

The difficulties involved in implementing such recommendations go some
way to account for the deepening pessimism in Mexico. Take the legalization
issue, for example. Two questions matter in this debate: How much income
would cartels stand to lose through legalization? And would it be a crippling
blow to cartels if they were denied that income? Current estimates of the proportion of cartel income attributable to drugs vary between 50 and 60 percent.[37] To
restate the obvious: up to half of cartel income already comes from sources other
than narcotics. Cartels long ago diversified into other operations, including syn-
thetic drug manufacture, human smuggling, kidnapping for ransom, child pornography, extortion, and the sale of pirated goods.[38] Money laundering and oil
theft have also been identified as major sources of new income for cartels.[39]

Apart from cartels, the challenges of rooting out corruption in local
police forces, prison, and judicial systems are among the toughest confronting Mexican society.[40] How can compromised local security forces be cleaned
up or safely replaced, given the absence of trusted law enforcement? Some
appointees in positions of high authority in cleanup operations were found
to be on a cartel's payroll, and newcomers with unblemished records are often
expeditiously eliminated or intimidated into leaving office. Cartel members
boast that the entire corpus of Mexican politics is corrupt, and that even when
authorities make "real" arrests (as distinct from staging bogus show trials),
their reach extends only to the neck of an organization, not its head.[41] There
is a small *chiste*/joke in Mexico: "If you go to a police officer and say: 'I have a
problem,' then you've immediately got two problems."

Successful cleanup campaigns have usually employed an iron fist and dubi-
ous methods to eliminate local corruption. Following the 2008 appointment

of former Lieutenant Colonel Julián Leyzaola Pérez as Tijuana's Secretary of Public Security, life in the city changed dramatically. Leyzaola began by moving his family out of Mexico. In confrontations with cartels, he was fearless and brutal. He avoided a number of assassination attempts through intelligence provided by US law enforcement agencies. He banned the popular band Los Tucanes de Tijuana from their hometown because they performed *narcocorridos* that glorified local drug lords.[42]

Leyzaola purged downtown Tijuana of cartel operations and followed up with a large-scale *depuración* (purification) of rogue officers in the local police force. Many of them disappeared into local army bases or were transported to distant federal prisons; some were tortured; others were exposed as cartel employees, dismissed from the force, and left to fend for themselves (which was tantamount to a death sentence).[43] The corrupt cops were not missed by ordinary *tijuanenses*, who were fearful and exhausted after years of police arrogance and brutality. Local businesses regarded Leyzaola as a hero, and he enjoyed a great deal of personal immunity. Still, suspicions lingered. Community activists worried about the abrogation of civil rights under Leyzaola; conspiracy theorists suspected that Leyzaola was cleaning up the plaza for the benefit of the local drug lord, known as El Chapo; and cynics claimed that Leyzaola had been hired simply to produce *un espectáculo* (a show) for US agencies funneling money into Mexico's antidrug efforts.[44] Nevertheless, a respected local newspaper, *Zeta*, whose courageous coverage of the narcotics industry had marked its staff as cartel targets, named Leyzaola "Man of the Year" in 2009.[45] Leyzoala subsequently moved on to become police chief in Ciudad Juárez, after which Tijuana murder rates started to inch up once again.[46]

A final example of the problems confronting antinarcotics agencies is the binational nature of drug smuggling. El Paso-based Howard Campbell expressed a typical border-dweller's perspective on drug policy:

> a land so thoroughly bilingual, bicultural, miscegenated, and porous— despite the arbitrary demarcation of a border and the increasingly weird and futile attempts to seal it—can only be studied and understood as a united territory and a single problem.[47]

Yet US officials have only recently begun to talk openly about their nation's responsibilities in the drug nexus. Historically, the US has doggedly laid all blame at Mexico's door, insisting that solutions must originate with effective policing and prosecution south of the border. Change came only after Mexico bombarded the US with complaints about the impacts of its "bottomless" demand for illegal substances, and the "avalanche" of military-grade firearms that flowed illegally from the north into Mexico.[48] The trade was straightforward: drugs go north, and money and guns go south, following the so-called "iron river"—a chain of gun stores and dealers (mainly in Arizona and Texas) that served as the headwaters of a torrent of firearms flowing south to the drug lords, which was paid for by the proceeds of smuggling.[49] US Government attempts to stem this flow invariably encountered legal challenges from the National Rifle Association.[50]

The recent surge of US attention to Mexico's drug wars might be due to the spread of cartel influence north of the border.[51] Certainly any crime that bears the stamp of cartels gets prominent media coverage in the US,[52] such as that culminating in the labeling of Phoenix as the "kidnap capital" of the nation.[53] Through high-profile agreements such as the Mérida initiative, a variety of cross-border collaborations have been instituted, including plans to embed US intelligence agents in Mexican federal police units, and for US involvement in prosecuting and imprisoning cartel members. Such discussions usually occur beyond the media's glare due to political sensitivities regarding Mexico's sovereignty, but this has not prevented a growing US presence in the Mexican drug offensive.[54]

For the most part, Mexico has welcomed US assistance in combating the cartels, but there is a growing conviction that fortifying the border between the two nations did nothing to stop the transit of drugs.[55] Aguilar and Castañeda voiced a typical Mexican opinion on this issue: "*El costo de sellar la frontera norte de México es enorme; la eficacia, mínima.*"[56] ("The cost of closing the northern border of Mexico is enormous; its efficacy, minimal.")

A Failed State?

Complaints about a Mexican narco-state often seamlessly shift into accusations that Mexico is a "failed state," that is, a state incapable of carrying out its basic functions. Reporting to the US Council on Foreign Relations in 2008, Pamela Starr warned that Mexico was on its way to becoming a failed state, linking this condition to the rise of a lawless society ruled by drug cartels:

> The violence [in Mexico] threatens the government's ability to govern effectively. It threatens oil supply. It makes Mexico a potential transit point for terrorists. The worst thing in the world that could happen to the United States is to have an unstable country on its southern border.[57]

Notice how the stakes get raised in this assessment, moving from a concern with a single problem (drug-related violence), through potential failure of the state as a whole, to an invocation of national security. Starr was not alone in her prognostication. Former federal drug czar Barry McCaffrey warned: "Mexico is on the edge of an abyss."[58] A year later, Michael Hayden, former head of the US Central Intelligence Agency, put Mexico on top of his list of international worries with this heart-stopping sentence: "Mexico is one of the gravest dangers to American security, on a par with a nuclear-armed Iran."[59]

The notion of a "failed state" is poorly defined and controversial.[60] The cavalier manner with which the term is bandied about only adds confusion. It has been applied, for instance, to a small African nation governed by a brutal dictator engaged in bloody civil war while its citizens face starvation, but also to state governments in the US that are beset by partisan gridlock, bloated budget deficits, and disenchanted electorates (the roster includes New York and California).

A state may be said to have "failed" when it is unable to satisfactorily execute its most basic functions, including maintaining public order, resisting external threat, and ensuring the well-being of its population. If the breakdown is severe, in a democratic society the compromised government loses the consent of the governed and may be replaced by a successor in the normal course of electoral politics. In nondemocratic societies, the transition beyond a failed state may involve overt conflict to the point of revolution.

Even if it occurs, state failure is unlikely to apply equally across all sectors and levels of government operations, still less over an entire territory. After Hurricane Katrina, for instance, US federal emergency response proved to be inadequate; however, the remainder of Washington DC's government apparatus continued to function, and FEMA's failure was confined to the geographical region most severely affected by natural disaster. In other words, the nation-state's dysfunctionality was sector-specific and geographically localized; it did not warrant labeling the US a failed state. Another difficulty in understanding what state failure entails is revealed by contemplating what it means to talk about a "successful" state. For example, can a state be regarded as successful if its performance is based on the repression and suffering of its citizenry, or on the rapacious subordination of other nation-states?

The term failed state is deeply flawed, perhaps to the point of incoherence. The desire to label a country as a failed state has less to do with existing conditions in the country under examination and more to do with the motivations of the nation doing the name-calling. Identifying Mexico as a failed state allowed the US to fold that country into its national security rhetoric and protocols, thereby calling forth financial aid and justifying other kinds of intervention (such as cooperative law enforcement).[61] Even if inappropriately applied, the label may yet cause harm if other nations regard it as an acceptable pretext for intervention. Before awarding or condoning the failed state appellation, it is prudent to check who is doing the name-calling and why.

WHAT EVIDENCE IS there to support the claim that Mexico is a failed state? Since 2005, the US-based Fund for Peace and the magazine *Foreign Policy* have published an annual *Failed States Index* (FSI) based on twelve indicators measuring weaknesses in a country's social, economic, and political institutions.[62] The FSI does not purport to predict when a state will fail, but to provide a measure of its vulnerability to collapse; even a failing score need not imply that every one of the state's institutions is vulnerable. According to the 2010 FSI ranking of 177 countries worldwide, the most unstable nation in the world was Somalia, with a score of 114 out of a possible 120; the least unstable was Norway, with a score of 19. Mexico ranked 96th, placing it in a *warning* category (above the *alert* category—the worst—which included half the nations under review). The US ranked 158th, which put it in the *moderate* category, one step below the best category, *sustainable*. Mexico's FSI rating was hurt by its uneven economic development and levels of socioeconomic inequality and by the existence of internal militias, guerrilla forces or private armies in armed struggle against state security forces, e.g., drug cartels or the Chiapas rebels. (Mexico is not a poor country, but it is not as rich as the US, and neither country spreads its wealth around very evenly.)[63]

Other global indicators add nuance and perspective to Mexico's failings, but most of them point to the nation's consistently average performance. Thus, Transparency International's 2011 world *Corruption Perceptions Index* (CPI) ranked Mexico number 100 (out of 183 countries), and the US number 24. (In the CPI, the lower number is better.)[64] However, there are two exceptions to these generally average indicators, one unfavorable, the other more positive.

When the international Reporters Without Borders brought out its first *Press Freedom Index* (PFI) in 2002, Mexico was roughly at midpoint in the rankings; a few years later, it had tumbled almost to bottom place where it has been stuck ever since.[65] The PFI judged Mexico (along with Afghanistan, Somalia, and Pakistan) to be in a situation of "permanent chaos," where a culture of impunity had taken hold and where journalists who voiced critical opinions became targets. In a related 2010 *Impunity Index* compiled by the Committee to Protect Journalists, Mexico ranked ninth-worst nation the world. Noting that "more than 30 journalists and media workers were murdered or have vanished since 2006 when Calderón took office," the Committee claimed that a chilling veil of self-censorship had descended over reporters and editors who, in the face of threats, had chosen to put personal survival above reporting the news.[66]

Other international observers evince greater optimism about the state of Mexico's democracy. *The Economist*'s Intelligence Unit regularly examines 167 nations worldwide in a *Democracy Index* (DI). In 2010, the US ranked number 18 and was categorized as a "full democracy;" Mexico ranked 55th and was characterized as a "flawed democracy."[67] Aspects of Mexico's political culture and electoral practices negatively influenced its ranking, but the functionality of the Mexican government was not brought into question.[68]

Seasoned observers in Mexico bring much-needed perspective to overheated invocations of state failure. Alma Guillermoprieto, for instance, rejected the notion of Mexico as a failed state. Failed states, she protested, do not constantly build new roads and schools, collect taxes, and generate legitimate industrial and commercial activity sufficient to rank Mexico in the Top 20 largest economies in the world.[69] Mexican citizens may be less than surprised when government neglects to execute certain of its functions, but they worry more when cartels take over the functions of government and local policing and move into the business of building schools.[70]

Enrique Krauze countered the charge of failure by cataloguing the recent achievements of the Mexican state. It was a tolerant and secular state, he wrote, an inclusive society with no serious threat of regional secession or territorial dispute. It had overcome one-party political rule. Power had been decentralized, allowing much greater autonomy in the executive, legislative, and judicial branches. A transparency law had been passed to combat electoral corruption. The nation's institutions demonstrated resilience to crises such as currency devaluation, economic downturn, the murder of a presidential candidate, and postelection civil unrest. Still, Krauze conceded, Mexico's young multiparty democracy confronted many challenges, some old and some new. Poverty and inequality were stickily persistent. Alluding to the country's newest problem— the most serious crisis since the 1910 Revolution, in his opinion—Krause warned of the increasing power and viciousness of organized crime in drug trafficking, kidnapping, and extortion.[71]

On the evidence of the rankings, expert opinion, and the informal responses of virtually every Mexican I asked, Mexico is not a failed state.[72] However, there is a widespread consensus that the Mexican government is losing its capacity to govern. A 2011 Latinobarómetro poll placed Mexico last out of 18 Latin American nations in terms of satisfaction with the way democracy works in the country and close to last in terms of whether or not the country is "making progress."[73]

Too many of the nation's institutions have lost public trust, and too many ordinary people are alienated from their politics and politicians. When electorate dissatisfaction gains widespread traction, a government faces what is called a "legitimacy crisis," and risks losing the consent of the governed. Until recently, there was no tradition of public opinion polling in Mexico, but a poll in May 2010 discovered that *every* important national institution in Mexico failed to inspire confidence among a majority of respondents (see Table 8.1).[74]

Mexicans have always been distrustful of national institutions, with the possible exceptions of the church, military, and universities. Politics and politicians have traditionally drawn special scorn. Writing around the time of Mexico's 2009 influenza crisis, Mexico City-based commentator Denise Dresser gazed out on a disillusioned electorate where two-thirds of Mexicans thought that the country was headed in the wrong direction. She offered this diagnosis: that effective democracy was slow to materialize in Mexico because the old authoritarianism was not blending smoothly with the new ways, that the emerging political pluralism had not yet satisfied peoples' demands nor solved their problems, and that PAN politicians were perceived as being just as corrupt as their PRI predecessors. Dresser roundly blamed all major political

Table 8.1 Percentage of People Having "a Lot" of Trust
in Mexican Institutions, 2010

INSTITUTION	PERCENTAGE OF RESPONDENTS HAVING "A LOT" OF TRUST IN MEXICAN INSTITUTIONS
Church	40.0%
Army	37.7%
Universities	34.4%
Media	25.9%
Supreme Court	20.9%
Elections	18.8%
President	16.9%
Business leaders	15.5%
Labor unions	7.2%
Police	7.2%
Senators	6.9%
Political parties	6.5%

parties for being more concerned about maintaining power than addressing problems of inequality and lawlessness in the country.[75]

On another occasion, Dresser was equally fierce in her condemnation of private corporations in Mexico. In an open letter to Carlos Slim, the Mexican telecommunications billionaire and the world's richest man, she offered this stunning rebuke:[76]

> while you think that you are the solution to this country's problems, I must tell you that you are part of them....you stand between the current problems and the solutions....JFK once said that great crises produce great men. It's a shame that you are not interested in becoming one.

Slim later unapologetically defended his lack of philanthropic largesse: "What we need to do as businessmen is to help to solve the problems, the social problems.... To fight poverty, but not by charity."[77] Slim placed greater emphasis on investment, especially among small businesses, ignoring the criticism that his kind of market dominance squashed small entrepreneurs.[78]

Perhaps Dresser is too close to the travails of her home country? *New York Times* reporter Larry Rohter returned to Mexico in 2009 after a 20-year absence and found many positive changes. Comparing Mexico's prompt and effective handling of the swine flu outbreak with the secretive and inept bungling by China of the 2002 SARS epidemic, Rohter dismissed any thought of Mexico as a failed state. He recalled leaving a one-party state 20 years earlier, where suspicious intellectuals obsessed minutely about grievances against the US. Yet upon returning, he discovered a more democratic society where people were increasingly comfortable and confident. Although on track, Mexico was not yet a "model state," Rohter conceded, because corruption and impunity persist, and elites block necessary changes.[79]

Mexico's Second Revolution

Mexico is neither a narco-state nor a failed state. Viewed from the perspective of history, the condition of Mexico's democracy in the early twenty-first century is indicative of a vibrant political culture responsive to internal political pressures in ways that would have been unimaginable for most of the previous century. To outsiders, the nation's politics might appear tempestuous and crisis-prone, but it is hardly unexpected for a country at this stage of evolution (see Figure 8.2).[80]

After a period of adjustment following the Porfiriato and the Revolution, the PRI settled into a long reign that lasted for the remainder of the twentieth century. The PRI philosophy was nationalistic (involving a deep suspicion of the US), socialistic (espousing redistributive goals, especially in the case of land), and committed to *presidencialismo* (vesting supreme authority in a single chief executive). While claiming to be democratic, the PRI never bothered much with the typical trappings of democracy, such as free elections, competing political parties, or an independent press. Its overarching ethos was that PRI was destined to rule indefinitely. The decades of PRI hegemony that followed gave Mexico a period of stability based in control from the center, but disenfranchisement and hardship at the peripheries, reinforced by periodic recourse to violence and repression.[81] Seventy-one years later, Vicente Fox of the PAN was elected president. It was the first time in history that Mexico had achieved a peaceful transfer of power through free elections and full suffrage. Savoring victory, Fox reminded Mexicans: "Today is the culmination of many years of struggle."[82]

FIGURE 8.2 Mexican Democratic Traditions, Ensenada, Baja California.

Statues of three prominent figures in Mexican history greet visitors disembarking from cruise ships at the popular coastal resort of Ensenada: Benito Juárez, who restored the Republic and became president after the overthrow of Emperor Maximilian in 1867; Miguel Hidalgo, who on September 16, 1810, issued the *Grito de Dolores* ("Cry of Dolores") which marked the beginning of Mexico's struggle for independence; and Venustiano Carranza, a leader in the Mexican Revolution who became president in 1914. Copyright © 2006 by Michael Dear.

Cracks in the PRI's twentieth-century dynasty appeared on the evening of October 2, 1968. A students' National Strike Council had called for a protest rally in a downtown Mexico City housing project called Tlatelolco, at the Plaza de las Tres Culturas, famous as the site where the Spanish invader Cortés had conquered Cuauhtémoc, the last of the Aztec emperors.[83] The students that evening were confronted by soldiers who had planned in advance to crush the rebellion. Snipers fired on local police and demonstrators, causing confusion and provoking a lethal response. Perhaps 325 people were killed and over 2,000 were detained. As a consequence, the PRI lost credibility in the eyes of ordinary citizens as well as many prominent leaders, including Octavio Paz, who resigned his position as Mexican ambassador to India.[84] Thirty years later, Cuauhtémoc Cárdenas (then Mayor of Mexico City) was to commemorate the 1968 student movement as "a decisive factor in Mexico's democratic opening."[85]

Two catastrophes further altered the political landscape in the mid-1980s. In 1981, a drop in world oil prices caused economic collapse in Mexico. President López Portillo responded by nationalizing the banks and ordering deposits held in dollars to be converted to pesos at rates far below market. Many ordinary Mexicans lost their livelihoods and savings. In the northern states, prominent business leaders fled from the PRI to PAN, fearing the advent of socialism. Then, four years later, on September 19, 1985, an earthquake hit Mexico City with a devastating force of 8.1 on the Richter scale. Government agencies failed (or were slow) to respond, so earthquake victims organized self-help brigades, and student militants gained fresh energies.[86] The do-it-yourself politics that emerged during the earthquake's aftermath were independent of the PRI or other political parties, spawning a new generation of community leaders and nongovernmental organizations.[87]

The loosening of the PRI's grip presented opportunities for PAN.[88] The conservative National Action Party had been a minor presence in Mexican politics since the 1930s, a low-budget operation run by business interests and Catholic lawyers but never winning many seats in the federal government's Chamber of Deputies.[89] In the wake of the peso's devaluation, PAN candidates in 1983 won the mayoralties of six of the seven largest cities in the border state of Chihuahua.[90] PRI leaders vowed never to surrender a border state government to the *panistas* who had, they claimed, a history of "traitorous ties to the United States."[91] In 1986, the PRI managed to hold onto the governorship of Chihuahua state but only by fixing the election results. PAN politicians united with leftists to seek annulment of the election. PRI ballot-rigging was proved and the fraud gained international attention, its ripple-effect spreading across the country.[92]

The first phases of the 1988 presidential campaign were nothing out of the ordinary. President de la Madrid named Carlos Salinas de Gortari as his successor, and his election seemed the usual foregone conclusion. Except that early election returns showed that Cuauhtémoc Cárdenas, the candidate of a leftist coalition known as the *Frente Democrático Nacional*, was leading in the balloting. PRI leaders promptly announced that the election results would be delayed because of a computer malfunction. One week later Salinas was declared the victor. Cárdenas and the PAN united in an effort to annul the election, but the coalition split after Cárdenas declared himself the winner (that is, he sought to alter the election's result, not to annul it). Eventually Salinas prevailed, but Cárdenas had demonstrated that the PRI could be toppled by peaceful, democratic means. He went on to found the *Partido de la Revolución Democrática* (PRD) in 1989, which became a third force in Mexican politics. Henceforward, the PRI was obliged to deal with plurality in Mexico's politics.[93]

Salinas began his *sexenio* (a six-year term of office, nonrenewable) by advancing Mexico's modernization.[94] He sought neoliberal economic reforms to position Mexico as a global partner through economic integration with the US. For this, Salinas needed at least the semblance of an active political opposition, so he worked with PAN to promote greater participation. But then, in 1989, *panista* Ernesto Ruffo Appel was elected governor of another border state, Baja California, the first state to be governed by an opposition party since the Revolution. Salinas was applauded for loosening PRI's authoritarianism, but behind the scenes he later engineered brutal confrontations with PRD supporters and refused to quit the PRI habit of election fraud.[95] Other actions isolated Salinas from his electoral base. For instance, the allegiance of union workers was jeopardized by his privatizing of the national telephone company, Telmex, and by advancing land reforms that undercut farmworkers' unions.[96]

Salinas's final year in office began in January 1994, just as the North American Free Trade Agreement came into effect (it is known in Mexico as the *Tratado de Libre Comercio*, or TLC).[97] During the New Year's celebrations, the *Ejército Zapatista de Liberación Nacional* (the Zapatista National Liberation Army, or EZLN) seized several towns in the southern state of Chiapas, denounced NAFTA, and called for the overthrow of the federal government. Then in March, Salinas's chosen successor as president, Luis Donaldo Colosio, was assassinated in the border city of Tijuana; many suspected that his killers would be found within the ranks of his own party.[98] In April, Mexico was admitted to the Organization for Economic Cooperation and Development (OECD), but by then social unrest and the assassination had shaken the confidence of overseas investors. At home, the money markets were panicked, and in one day in December 1994 Mexico lost $4 billion off its reserves, leaving only $6 billion on hand. That same day, the peso was allowed to float, and by next morning its value had dropped by 20 percent, causing US intervention to stave off further collapse.[99]

For his successor, Salinas turned to Ernesto Zedillo, who went on to win a three-way election with just over 50 percent of the vote. Zedillo was born in Mexico City but grew up in a working-class family in the border town of Mexicali, Baja California. In those days, Baja was a peripheral outpost in the PRI domain. The young Zedillo was never very active in PRI affairs, so he ascended to the presidency with few political debts. With a doctorate from Yale, Zedillo was a dedicated neoliberal committed to free markets, global trade, and privatization. But unlike his predecessor, Zedillo was convinced that democracy was a prerequisite for healthy markets, so the old-style PRI had to go.[100]

Zedillo's presidency began ominously.[101] In 1995 José Francisco Ruiz Massieu, secretary-general of PRI and its second-highest official, had been assassinated on the streets of Mexico City. Salinas's brother Raúl was arrested for masterminding the murder. Raúl's arrest caused an irreparable rift between Salinas and Zedillo, whose relationship was already at a breaking point as a result of the peso crisis Salinas bequeathed to his successor. Zedillo's decision not to protect Salinas opened up major fault lines in the PRI foundations.[102] The prosecution and sentencing of Raúl demonstrated that corruption and criminal behavior had reached the highest level in Mexican government, but also that the politically well-connected in Mexico were no longer immune from law.[103]

Aside from this distraction, Zedillo's first task was to address the collapse of the peso, with assistance from the Clinton administration in the form of a $52 billion bailout in the spring of 1995.[104] Zedillo did not shy from further reforms. No less than seventeen constitutional amendments were passed in 1996, including the right of Mexico City residents to elect their own mayor. Zedillo also moved to require Congressional ratification of candidates for the posts of Attorney General and Supreme Court justices, and he named a *panista* as Attorney General—the first opposition member ever to serve in a PRI cabinet.[105] In 1997, the PRD's Cuauhtémoc Cárdenas became the first elected mayor of Mexico City, thereby planting another tree in Mexico's "Democratic Spring."

Momentum against the PRI was building. In the 1997 midterm elections the PRI lost its federal congressional majority for first time. Out of the 500 seats in Chamber of Deputies, 230 went to the PRI, and 261 went to opposition parties, principally the PAN and PRD. Unusually for Mexico, there were very few challenges to the election results.[106] Zedillo announced: "The nation has taken a definitive, irreversible, and historic step toward a normal democratic life."[107] Since there were no guidelines for the transition of federal political power in Mexico, a volatile period of adjustment followed. Members of the Mexican Congress began to contest the president's actions, decades of deferential self-censorship by local and national press ended, and Mexican intellectuals rediscovered their critical voices. Everywhere, talk was about how the PRI could be unseated.[108]

One important factor in the PRI's downward slide was the ongoing weakening of the party's traditional support, especially the labor unions. Historically, the PRI had favored unions when it was convenient but otherwise did not anguish about using the police, army, and imprisonment to discipline workers. Over time, aging union leaders had given up on seeking better wages and working conditions for the rank and file, focusing instead on maintaining their own privileges.[109] An important new chapter in the decline of centralized union power opened with the Border Industrialization Program, which ushered in the *maquiladora* industry in Mexico's northern states, and brought with it many jobs, better incomes, and new worker organizations.[110] Many unions cut their formal ties with PRI; employers began making independent deals with labor federations; and some unions allowed members, to decide their own political affiliations instead of requiring fealty to the union's choice. By the late 1990s, the old-style PRI unions had been rejected and they confronted mounting challenges from rival organizations.[111]

In the lead-up to the game-changing 2000 presidential election, Zedillo again surprised his party by abandoning the president's prerogative of naming his successor, establishing instead a system of primaries to elect a successor. Francisco Labastida became the PRI nominee. Cuauhtémoc Cárdenas resigned as mayor of Mexico City in order to run for the presidency on behalf of the PRD. But the front-runner was Vicente Fox, an exuberant PAN campaigner who pugnaciously donned the mantle of outsider, and transformed the election into a referendum on *el cambio* (change). The PRI tried to match Fox's spirit by inventing *El Nuevo* PRI (the New PRI), an echo of Tony Blair's "New Labour" campaign in Britain. However, this flagrant rejection of the past so offended the old guard that candidate Labastida was obliged to run as the proud heir of PRI traditions.[112] He then proceeded to lose the election.

The PRI's long reign in Mexico was formally terminated in 2000 with the election of PAN presidential candidate Vicente Fox. Fox gained 43 percent of the popular vote, PRI's Labastida took 36 percent, and PRD's Cárdenas 17 percent. Fox was strongly supported by younger, educated, urban voters swayed by his promise to dismantle the PRI monolith. He grabbed Mexico City by recapturing the working-class vote that in 1997 had gone to Cárdenas; he won every border state and 16 of the 19 electoral districts adjacent to the US border. A newly sophisticated Mexican electorate voted tactically, splitting their ballots to elect a minority Congress composed of the three principal parties and electing the popular leftist Andrés Manuel López Obrador (known as AMLO) as mayor of Mexico City.[113] The PRI dynasty was over, at least for now.[114]

During his presidency, Fox was criticized for not living up to his promises, but in truth the levels of expectation among his supporters were recklessly high, and he confronted a Chamber of Deputies that was dominated by a belligerent, aggrieved PRI. On the binational stage, Fox's goal of revitalizing relationships with the US was stalled by the events of 9/11.[115] After three-quarters of a century of one-party rule, the transition to multiparty democracy in Mexico was inevitably bumpy.[116] Nevertheless, Mexico achieved a peaceful "second revolution" in its move from a perfect one-party state to an imperfect plural democracy.[117] This remains a work in progress, even more so since the return of the PRI presidency in 2012.[118]

Not Narco, Not Failed, but Also Not out of Danger

Mexico's adventure in democracy was rudely interrupted by the infiltration of drug cartels into the apparatus of state and civil society. Luis Astorga, a Mexican authority on the drug trade, offered this prediction: "The narcos are threatening governors, the military, mayors. Eventually the state will find a way to prevail. In the end, war is not good for business."[119] In her conspiracy-minded account, Anabel Hernández concluded that the entire drug war in Mexico is a sham because drug lords operate only with the connivance of business, politicians, and police. Behind the smoke-screen of war, she claimed, government is in fact working to advance the interests of one cartel over all others.[120] Once a hierarchy is restored, a new equilibrium will emerge that may resemble the collusion between cartel and state that characterized the twentieth-century PRI era.[121] If Hernández's assessment is correct, the current violence is but the latest spike in an ongoing cycle of cartel struggles for supremacy. The war will last only as long as it takes to (re)establish a hierarchy of authority among competitors.[122]

Conspiratorial visions exist on the US side of the border, too. Journalist Ben Ehrenreich documented the common-interest alignments that could be emerging between Mexican cartels and what I call the US Border Industrial Complex. The war on drugs, he warned, was becoming more profitable than the drug trade itself, not only for the cartels but also for their hit men; for funeral directors, bankers, businessmen, weapons manufacturers, security consultants, and military contractors, as well as for the builders and operators of private detention centers; and for politicians of all stripes who can leverage campaign contributions from contractors, and win votes with alarmist rhetoric about immigrant hordes and the need for "comprehensive border security." The feeding frenzy, Ehrenreich surmised, will be hard to stop since so many people are vested in its continuation.[123]

Conspiracy or not, the Zeta cartel is now active in 17 out of Mexico's 32 states, and the Sinaloa cartel in 16 states.[124] Mexican governments appear to have ceded a certain degree of *de facto* control in some territories to the cartels, at least for now. Manifestations of cartel "governance" evince a remarkable adaptability to local conditions: in some rural places, cartel takeover has been complete and barely contested; but in larger cities with diverse centers of competing political and economic power, cartels gain only a share of influence while everyday democracy continues around them; and in places without strategic importance or profit, cartels have not bothered exerting influence. Residents in some of the occupied zones have been reticent about becoming subjects of the cartels; in Ciudad Juárez, for instance, those who were able fled to El Paso or elsewhere.

The challenge posed by drug cartels is immense, and the damage they have wrought in terms of human suffering is indisputable. Yet so many factors besides narcotics will determine Mexico's future, among them oil, the military, maquiladoras, the church, altered political fortunes, the billion-dollar businessmen, even natural disasters. Global interests, especially those of the US, also have the ability to radically alter Mexico's fortunes. No alternative future should be exempt from scrutiny, but let me be clear: I am not advocating international collusion with drug lords, nor the ceding of Mexican territory to cartel control. I am heartened by government-led efforts to reconstruct war-damaged lives, and by the actions of courageous individuals and communities to defend themselves against occupation and oppression.[125]

But the central question persists: How have the war against Mexican drug cartels and the fortification mania of Fortress USA impacted the lives of ordinary people in the third nation?

9

Third Nation Interrupted

THE FORTIFICATIONS ALONG the land boundary of the US–Mexico border are essentially completed. The landscape of the third nation is awash with the detritus of partition—steel walls, wire-mesh fences, closely spaced concrete pillars and bollards, vehicle barriers, and razor wire. In some places no fewer than three layers of fencing divide the two nations, their intervening spaces continually being groomed to permit high-speed chases by USBP vehicles. I will refer to this whole ensemble of fortifications as the "Wall," but it is important to remember that the Wall neither completely nor uniformly seals the land and water boundary between Mexico and the US. Yet already in 2010, Luis Ituarte, an artist who lives on both sides of the boundary line, was lamenting: "The relationship that once existed between the two sides is broken."¹ Could this be true, after so short a time?

After the Wall

Up against the Wall

It was inevitable that border residents would object to the Department of Homeland Security's plan to build fortifications across and through their communities, but what really drove them crazy was the way the DHS went about doing it. The 1996 Illegal Immigration Reform and Immigrant Responsibility Act provided broad authorization to construct barriers along the international boundary, and the Secure Fence Act of 2006 specified the construction of 850 miles of additional fencing. The Mexican government resolutely and repeatedly opposed the fortifications, saying on one occasion: "a wall is never the solution to problems" and that "all walls eventually get torn down".²

Border residents everywhere took great exception to the Wall. Mexicans described it to me as offensive, stupid, and inefficient. They regarded it as a flagrant anti-Mexican advertisement, adding that if the fence actually worked it might be possible to begin defending it. On the US side, those who crossed regularly had nothing positive to say about the Wall and its incursions. The uproar over the hideous screening was so intense in the Nogales twin cities that altered designs were introduced so that residents could see through to the other side. (This simple modification also resulted in a reduction of rock-throwing over the fence.)

The preponderance of private land-ownership in Texas led to a flurry of well-documented lawsuits objecting to DHS demands for land to build the riverside fortifications. Many complaints focused on the Wall's threat to cross-border communication. When the University of Texas at Brownsville and Texas Southmost College filed suit to prevent the fence from splitting their joint campus, court documents asserted that the proposed barrier would "disrupt the border institutions and undermine their efforts to unite communities on both sides of the border."[3] Longtime civic activist Elizabeth García conveyed similar sentiments about coexistence across the Brownsville-Matamoros line, saying: "*La frontera* [the border] is both sides of the river, not one side or the other."[4] Brownsville writer Oscar Casares articulated the lifestyle that was now under assault: "We learn both cultures as effortlessly as we do two languages. We learn as quickly that we can exist simultaneously in both worlds, and that our home exists neither here nor there but in the migration between these two forces."[5]

The construction of the Wall became a huge issue in Texas, where sentiments of cross-border connectivity and affection surface frequently and with passion. Singer-songwriter Shawn Kiehne grew up working on his family's ranch outside El Paso and learned to see the world through the eyes of Mexican farmhands. Known in the entertainment world as "El Gringo," Kiehne's autobiographical *El Corrido del Gringo* included these lines:

> I respect immigrants and of this I'm sure
> We need to be good neighbors and not build a wall.
> To my illegal friends who live in the U.S.
> As a gringo I want to tell you to keep dreaming and fighting
> This country needs your effort and your work.[6]

When he sang this song on a popular Spanish-language TV show, El Gringo went from being a novelty act to a star.[7]

The Rio Grande/Rio Bravo forms a natural boundary between Texas and four Mexican states. Its wide meanders made it impossible to build a continuous fence in the style of the land boundary; fence construction, where it was attempted, was an intermittent affair that left many sections of the river unprotected. The river's contorted curves often meant that fences were erected north of the river, deep inside US territory. As a result, the fence sliced off part of a nature reserve here, a few holes of a golf course there, and it cut a university campus into two.[8] People stranded on the "Mexican side" of the new barriers were left wondering if the fence was the new border, and whether they now lived in Mexico?[9]

An investigation into the Texas experience concluded that there had been "massive violations of human rights" in constructing the Wall.[10] The DHS work had involved:

> the unfair and discriminatory taking of private property without a clear and fair process and … [negatively impacting] the means of subsistence and way of life of persons living in border communities, including the members of several indigenous groups.[11]

While conceding that governments had the right to take private property for reasons of the public interest, the investigators concluded that the DHS had executed its takings in an "arbitrary, discriminating, and disproportional" manner, and that other less restrictive measures were available.[12] They provided examples where DHS plans placed an 18-foot-high fence through the property of a small farm-owner but not the adjacent property of a Dallas billionaire; where adjustments made to the fence in response to complaints from universities made it clear that the original plans had little rationale; and where the fence was scheduled to pass through a public city park but not a private industrial park.[13] Perhaps most egregiously, an examination of the fencing in Cameron County, Texas, showed that fences were disproportionately located in communities with lower incomes and lower levels of educational attainment, or those of predominantly Hispanic identity and noncitizen status.[14] The treatment of long-term indigenous peoples stirred up bitter memories of centuries of disrespect and maltreatment.[15]

Third Nation Lifelines

The Wall gave rise to a free-floating resentment among impacted communities, but in these compromised, damaged lands a burgeoning resistance flourished, spilling over into the nation as a whole. It took many forms, including community activism, street demonstrations, civil disobedience, and lawsuits.[16] For example, in 2006, National City, California, located just a few miles north of the Mexico–US border, proudly proclaimed itself a sanctuary city for immigrants and stated that it would leave the task of immigration enforcement to federal authorities. Another form of protest and support was the "New Sanctuary Movement," an extensive network of institutions in 18 cities (including Los Angeles) that pledged to harbor undocumented people and contribute resources to those who sheltered them. New Sanctuary planned to move migrants from church to church in order to share risk and responsibility, while bearing witness. Further from the border, in the Napa County wine district of northern California, some wine growers dependent on migrant workers—regardless of status—made sure they received decent wages, subsidized housing, and health care.[17]

Borderland communities had long offered material and moral support to undocumented migrants as part of a broad-based sanctuary movement.[18] Many humanitarian aid organizations along the California borderlands were spawned in the mid-1990s after Operation Gatekeeper sealed the Tijuana border. As migrants responded by moving eastward into more hazardous mountain and desert areas, aid organizations followed them. One of the earliest, founded in 1997, was "Angeles del Desierto," which undertook search and rescue work in mountainous areas of California and also provided food, medicine, and other aid to deported individuals through a cross-border alliance with Mexico's *Grupo Beta*. Another well-known California a group was "Water Station," established in 1999 to prevent deaths from heat exposure and dehydration in the Imperial Valley and Anza Borrego Desert State Park. The group also campaigned to prevent drowning deaths in the All American Canal, which runs parallel to the Mexicali border, but the Imperial Irrigation District for many years stonewalled their efforts to construct lifelines across the swiftly moving waters of the Canal.

Analogous aid groups sprang up elsewhere along the border. For instance, "Humane Borders" was founded in 2000 to save migrant lives in the Arizona deserts, and has since earned a national and international reputation for advocating better immigration policies. "No More Deaths/*No más muertes*" (NMD) was established in Arizona in 2003 to provide direct medical attention for migrants in distress, as well as food and water. NMD also set up partnerships with Mexican organizations to provide aid for repatriated migrants.

The USBP tended to regard humanitarian aid groups with suspicion, suspecting them of aiding and abetting undocumented migrants. Dr. Jose Garcia of New Mexico State University offered an explanation for the hostility: "There is an ideological bias...shared by many law-enforcement agents who find themselves on the border.... many agents may come with attitudes that are negative toward human-rights groups."[19] Uneasy accommodations were sometimes worked out between aid volunteers and border patrol agents, but in recent years the USBP adopted a tougher line. In one notorious case, it charged two NMD workers with felonies for transporting three severely dehydrated and injured migrants to medical attention. (The complaint was dismissed.) In another, volunteer Dan Millis was prosecuted for "littering" in the Buenos Aires National Wildlife Refuge while he was distributing plastic jugs filled with water for passing migrants.[20] Because the Refuge falls under the jurisdiction of the federal Fish and Wildlife Service (FWS), USBP agents called FWS officials to issue the citation.[21] Millis was found guilty but a judge suspended the fine and sentence. Not to be outdone, FWS charged a second litterer with "knowingly" littering, a distinction that carried a more onerous penalty of one year in jail.[22] The federal Bureau of Land Management (BLM) also established formal cooperative arrangements with the USBP.

In Washington DC, the Border Patrol's Mike Reilly insisted that "there's no policy to take a hard stance against any type of humanitarian group."[23] Yet faith-based groups were especially aggrieved by the ongoing hostility they encountered from government agencies. At the NMD Arivaca camp, a seminary professor put it this way:

> What I found frustrating…is that here we were providing medical attention, providing food and water for people in the desert, and that somehow, this is a crime. As Christians, we're practicing our faith, and we're detained for it in this country.[24]

In 2009, at Friendship Park between Tijuana and San Ysidro/San Diego, USBP agents interrupted a Methodist minister attempting to give communion through the border fence, and in a separate incident, priests were arrested simply for praying in the vicinity of the border fence.[25] The minister who led an ecumenical service that day complained that USBP officers "all of a sudden…aren't facing south; they're facing north," and using tactics that are "beyond the pale for dealing with non-violent activists."[26]

Tensions grew as the Wall sprawled over the landscape. The widening presence of Latinos across the US emboldened many citizens to adopt an increasingly activist stance on immigration issues. Enormous rallies in favor of immigration reform were a feature in many US cities in the mid-decade, frequently in response to state-level anti-immigrant legislation.[27] Other confrontations were ignited by students brought to the US as children by undocumented parents. Now approaching graduation from college, these students became increasingly vociferous about their status and expectations. "It's all about losing that shame of who you are," said one student, expressing her motivation to come out as an undocumented person.[28] In December 2010, the US Congress failed to pass the "Dream Act," which would have opened the way to legalizing undocumented young people who went to college or served in the US military.[29] (The State of California passed its own Dream Act in 2011, allowing undocumented students to apply for student aid.)[30] Meanwhile, a few courageous individuals continued to come forward to announce their undocumented status.[31] A very small number, identified as undocumented after a lifetime of secrecy and personal achievement, were permitted to stay in the US.[32] Informally, the federal government began allowing these numbers to grow. President Obama subsequently moved to suspend thousands of low-priority deportation proceedings against people with no criminal charges or convictions.[33]

Meanwhile, on the other side, Mexican perceptions of migrants and the migration experience began to adjust. For instance, increased awareness of the often-desperate plight of Central American migrants traveling across Mexico en route to the US led to the establishment of sanctuaries in Mexican towns along the train routes.[34] Such awareness might also have come from movies, including *La Bestia*, and even from a theme park outside Mexico City that gave patrons a simulated experience of crossing the border line.[35] In addition, Mexican immigration activists deported from the US were treated as heroes upon their return to Mexico.[36]

Economy and Crossings

Economic ties in the third nation remained strong despite the Wall. US trade with Mexico hit an all-time high of almost $395 billion in 2010.[37] Approval was granted for a three-year trial of a long-delayed NAFTA/TLC agreement allowing Mexican truckers to carry goods into the US instead of being obliged to transfer their cargoes to US carriers after crossing.[38] Tourism, one of Mexico's biggest sources of foreign income, was hard hit by concerns over security. The other big foreign exchange earner, remittances sent back to Mexico from migrants, remained important, although the growth in money transfers leveled off as recession took hold in the US.[39]

Despite the economic downturn in the US, investors remained bullish about the borderlands. Many large Mexico-based companies reported having no plans to leave, even though they were paying more for security services. Half of the firms surveyed by the US–Mexico Chamber of Commerce in 2011 confirmed they would go ahead with expansion plans in Mexico. However, business promoters conceded that there was currently next to no interest in opening *new* plants in Mexico.[40]

In some localities, times were harder. California's agricultural heartland suffered, nowhere worse than El Centro in the Imperial Valley north of Calexico/Mexicali. Here, in 2010, unemployment peaked at 32 percent, a consequence of lost agricultural jobs, housing market collapse, and longer border-crossing times that curtailed shopping and restaurant trips into Calexico.[41] Communities south of the border suffered particularly from the decline in tourist visitors, and many shops and restaurants closed as a consequence of lost patronage,[42] their losses aggravated as Mexican shoppers were heavily courted by US retailers aiming to tap into Mexicans' growing purchasing power.[43]

Border crossing statistics reflected the divergent fortunes of a robust international trade alongside depressed local economies. Truck traffic stayed at levels similar to previous years, but large declines were registered in personal vehicle traffic into the US, which dropped one-third from its peak in 2000. The number of pedestrian crossings fell by 20 percent from its 2001 peak.[44]

The gloomy state of the US economy contributed to a decline in unauthorized immigration to the US. By 2011, Professor Douglas Massey reported that interest in crossing to the US among first-time Mexican migrants had fallen to its lowest level since the 1950s.[45] Needless to say, anti-immigration hardliners credited the Wall for this decline, even though migrant numbers had peaked in 2007, some time before the Wall began making its presence felt.[46] The decline was also accounted for by alterations in US immigration rules that allowed more legal temporary agricultural workers. In addition, Mexican wages were up and family income was higher than in 2000; there had been improvements in local public services in many towns (such as trash collection); declining fertility rates led to smaller families and less mouths to feed; and expanding educational opportunities made the trip to *el norte* no longer a vital rite of passage for young people.[47]

Whatever the precise causes, by 2012 a new balance had been achieved in the US immigration accounts: the numbers of undocumented migrants crossing out of Mexico approached zero, while the amount of legal permanent migration continued to climb. The federal Office of Immigration Statistics estimated that there were still about 11.5 million undocumented persons in the US, but that number was not growing.[48]

In the Gulag

News of a deteriorating US job market travels fast in Mexico, as do stories of the experiences of apprehension, detention, prosecution, and deportation in the ICE gulag. Such news surely contributed to the decline in undocumented migration. In 2008, border expert Andrew Burridge attended many Operation Streamline prosecutions in Tucson, Arizona, providing a poignant account of the courtroom experience of mass-produced justice for apprehended migrants:

> [There are] seventy or so people seated in rows, shackled at the feet and hands.... Many limp from sprained or strained ankles and tired muscles caused by walking through the desert, some for up to a week, and failing to receive proper treatment from the US government authorities or the private contractors who had detained them....
>
> Most are called to the front of the courtroom, and through the use of an interpreter plead guilty... For those that have been previously caught crossing undocumented, each is given a sentence of between 10 and 180 days of prison time. The majority being convicted for their first time are typically given a sentence of "time served"... For those with previous deportation records... punishment ranges from two to ten years. It is doubtful that most truly understand what they are agreeing to, often encountering the US court system for their first time, dealing with an interpreter, and being rushed through the system.[49]

Migrants who are deported often entered a bizarre world of estrangement—to a country many do not know, a language they do not understand, and where no networks of family and friends exist to assist them. Benny Amón spoke with three men, two of whom were brothers, who were permanent residents in the US but were deported after serving jail time.[50] Until then, the brothers had lived most of their lives in US, having been granted amnesty after the 1986 immigration law. Upon release, they were separately dropped off without papers or money, wearing clothing that identified them as deportees. Their most immediate task was to obtain copies of Mexican birth certificates in order to establish citizenship and legal residence in Mexico, essential prerequisites for work. This involved copious amounts of time, energy, and money, as well as dealing with the convolutions of an unfamiliar bureaucracy.

The first brother arrived in Tecate after nine years in prison, and started selling clothes and other things to make ends meet. He opened a small auto repair shop based on skills learned in prison, using the tools bought by his mother, who lived in Los Angeles. The shop was only marginally successful, and he continued to sell clothing at street markets. The second brother was luckier, finding work as a janitor in a local casino, rising eventually to become a full-time floor attendant (he cautioned that this was not a typical deportee's experience). A third man, who had met one of the brothers in prison, joined the pair in Tecate. For all three, the network of deportees in Tecate was their sole support in this strange new world. One year later, their lives remained precarious. The loss of contact with their children on the other side gnawed at their peace of mind.

Border Fusion

Tijuana has more buzz than any other border city. Even though its tourism and retailing were hurt by reports of violence and long waits at the border crossings, its maquiladora and health industries prosper. For over a decade, it has enjoyed a reputation as a "creative city" where a combination of demographic dynamism, economic growth, and an innovative do-it-yourself cultural scene combined to produce an unprecedented explosion of contemporary art, music, photography, film, video, architecture, food, and fashion.[51] Many *tijuanenses* are very self-aware about their commitment to the city, and to changing outsider perceptions of their city. Chef Javier Plascencia, for example, vowed to reinvent Tijuana'a upscale dining scene. He and others are often supported in this crusade by government, as in the 2010 *"Tijuana Innodora"* festival showcasing the city as a center of finance, arts, ideas, and innovation (at the cost of $5 million for a two-week bash).[52] Tijuana appeared to be reinventing itself as a vibrant, even global presence.[53] There is certainly nothing like it along the Mexican border, even though its grassroots, self-help energy is in keeping with the frontier ethos characteristic of many border towns.[54]

Part of Tijuana's "edginess" derives from the fusion of formal and informal cultural collaborations across the border.[55] Art historian Jo-Anne Berelowitz traced the origins of these fusions in the San Diego–Tijuana borderlands: from the 1960s Chicano movement, through the Border Art Workshop's deliberately inclusive multicultural engagement with the borderlands, to the flexible "combinatorial binationalism" that marks the current postborder condition.[56] Many established artists now live and work on both sides of the border, including Luis Ituarte, Marcos Ramirez, Einar and Jamex de la Torre, Jaime Ruiz Otis, and Norma Iglesias. One San Diego artist, Shannon Spanhouke, referred to Tijuana as her creative home because San Diego is too conservative: "If it wasn't for Tijuana, San Diego would be unlivable," she says.[57] Commenting on the widespread hybridization of the Mexican and US art scenes, writer Lawrence Downes was optimistic: "Some have declared the surge in immigrant Spanish-speakers as the end of America as we know it. But...it's just another new beginning."[58]

At the opposite end of the country Matamoros continued its economic expansion because of the buoyancy of its auto and electronic industries, and its success in persuading US and Asian companies to open new plants there.[59] The Brownsville economy is less healthy than its Mexican neighbor, and local officials complain that media coverage exaggerates the city's woes.[60] Yet the fortunes of the twin cities remain closely intertwined,[61] and in 2011 two organizations, "United Brownsville" and "*Imagina Matamoros,*" announced the creation of a "Bi.NED zone," a joint economic development initiative intended to encourage capital improvements and integrate urban infrastructures. The cities' Charro Days event, held annually since 1937, was sparsely attended in 2011 on account of border unrest, but one local resident emphasized that the cities continued to share traditions, history, culture, and geography.[62] Another remarked that the celebration "brings the two countries together."[63]

The "Arizona Rangers" Ride Again

Arizona has just over 6 million people. The state supplies about two-thirds of US copper, or about 5 percent of world supply. In 2006, undocumented workers made up 11 percent of Arizona's workforce of 2.9 million, double the national average.[64] Four counties front onto the Mexico border. From west to east, these are: Yuma, Pima (including the city of Tucson), Santa Cruz (with border-town Nogales), and Cochise (including Douglas, site of the nation's largest Border Patrol Station). To the north of Tucson lies Maricopa County, which is not border-adjacent but includes the city of Phoenix and is among the fastest-growing counties in the US, with just under 4 million people, almost one-third of whom are Latino. Arizona is one of the most conservative of US states, even though there are pockets of liberal sentiments in cities such as Tucson. The border zone is regarded as politically aberrant: I have heard people from northern Arizona talk about secession from southern part of the state, referring to it disparagingly as "Baja Arizona."

Arizona matters in any account of the Wall's impact since it has been "ground zero" in the US border wars for many years. The state received enormous media coverage, mostly on account of its draconian approaches to anti-immigrant law-making and policing. The *Washington Post* neatly summed up Arizona's legal strategy by asking: How much pain is a state willing to endure and inflict in order to rid itself of a population that contributed so much to its economic growth and prosperity?[65] And the *New York Times* captured the essence Arizona's experiment in local immigration policing: "Arizona intends to become the first state to try to muscle its way out of immigration problems on its own."[66]

The sources of discontent in present-day Arizona have been the economy and immigration. In 2006, the state's economy was growing at rate of 6.7 percent, double the national average, but this slowed to 1.8 percent in 2007, mainly reflecting vagaries in copper prices and the collapse of the housing market.[67] In the 1990s diminished crossing opportunities in other states made Arizona a choke-point for migrants who were funneled into the desert. The scale of this diversion was remarkable. A decade later, in Douglas, over 25,000 illegal immigrants were arrested in just one month.[68] The USBP's Tucson sector in 2009 had roughly half of all apprehensions, migrant deaths, and marijuana seizures along the entire US–Mexico border.[69] Locals blamed the federal government for not accepting responsibility, financial or otherwise, for a situation it had created (this same complaint had been voiced a century earlier by immigration opponents).[70] Crime rates along the border were another source of perpetual irritation.[71]

Before the Wall, it was hard to tell where one Arizona town stopped and its Mexican twin began, but afterward neighbors began to regard each other with suspicion. Many border dwellers worried that new tensions were eroding decades of cross-border bonds. Father Bob Carney put it this way:

> When I first got here [to Douglas], people moved back and forth across the line very fluidly…But suddenly, with the increased presence of the Border Patrol, I think there was just a pall of fear that came over the border.[72]

Cochise County, where Douglas is located, became the "eye of the storm" for immigration-related conflict, the fallout from which had:

> wreaked sheer havoc on Cochise County, draining its budgets, trampling its landscape, implanting a quasi-police state and fraying a rural social fabric that reaches back to frontier days.[73]

The Tohono O'odham Indian Nation reservation, just west of Tucson, is unique along the border because it is bisected by 74 miles of the international boundary line. A larger chunk of the reservation is in Arizona, the rest in the Mexican state of Sonora. About 1,400 tribal members reside on the Mexican side. In 2007, tribe Chairman Ned Norris Jr. declared that Homeland Security officials would build a fence across O'odham land only "over my dead body."[74] But the construction went ahead and Norris stayed alive. Thereafter, as increasing numbers of strangers traversed the reservation, neighborly practices on Nation land became strained.[75] Over 70 corpses of migrants were found each year on reservation land. The O'odham became less trusting of border crossers and fearful of self-incrimination, and the old ways started breaking down. Nation members regarded the federal presence on the reservation as a mixed blessing. Some were tired of the heavy outsider presence, and criticized tribal leaders for acquiescing in an "oppressive federal occupation."[76] But others supported DHS-related development as ways of bringing employment and investment to the reservation.[77]

The biggest source of unease was the increasing involvement of Nation residents with drug trafficking. In the early 1990s, virtually all those arrested for drug smuggling were nontribal individuals; but by now at least 60 percent of arrests are Nation members. When unemployment on the reservation exceeds 25 percent and average income is only $8,100 per annum, the promise of cartel payments ranging up to $5,000 (according to the type of load carried) is difficult to resist. Some smugglers deliberately became romantically involved with Nation women because, as fathers of O'odham children, they could not be ejected from the reservation.[78]

THE ARCHITECT OF Arizona's legislative clamp-down on migrants was Russell Pearce, a former law officer who rose to become president of the state senate. Pearce played a role in most of Arizona's toughest lawmaking,[79] characterized as a "radical experiment in state-level border control."[80] He and others in Arizona politics and law enforcement have strong ties with the for-profit Corrections Corporation of America, which participated in writing Arizona's draconian anti-immigrant legislation.[81]

The first of Pearce's big plays was passage of the state's 2007 Fair and Legal Employers Act, which suspended the business license of any company knowingly hiring persons not authorized to work. A repeat violation would result in permanent revocation of the license. Companies would henceforward be obliged to use the federal government's E-verify data base in order to confirm a worker's status. Pearce stoutly defended the measure, saying that anyone who placed "profits above patriotism" should not be allowed to do business in Arizona.[82] Opponents of the law sued, but subsequent court challenges upheld it.[83]

Pearce followed with a broad attack on migrants via SB1070 in 2010. Its stated purpose was to "make attrition through enforcement the public policy of all state and local government agencies in Arizona."[84] SB1070 aimed to detain, prosecute, and deport illegal immigrants by allowing authorities to demand proof of legal entry into the US from anyone suspected of being in the country illegally.[85] A federal judge promptly blocked that part of the law which enabled police to check a person's immigration status while in process of enforcing other laws. One year later the US Court of Appeals upheld this ruling, calling the law a preemption of federal authority in immigration matters. Pearce promised to take his appeal to the Supreme Court,[86] where in 2012 most of its key provisions were struck down. The only exception was the "show me your papers" provision, which requires police to check the immigration status of anyone they stop if there is suspicion that the person is an illegal immigrant.[87]

SB 1070 generated intensely partisan debates across the country. In Los Angeles, Roman Catholic archbishop Roger Mahoney referred to the law as "the country's most retrogressive, mean-spirited and useless anti-immigration law."[88] In 2010, the Phoenix Suns basketball team demonstrated their opposition to the new law by wearing bilingual uniforms emblazoned with "Los Suns" on the court. They were supported in this action by their managing partner and the National Basketball Association.[89] Days earlier, anti-SB1070 protestors had picketed a baseball game between the Arizona Diamondbacks and Chicago Cubs at Wrigley Field in Chicago.[90] The major league baseball players' union opposed the law because of concerns for foreign-born players who make up fully a quarter of the union's members.[91]

The strategic use of a nationwide boycott was advocated by a variety of Latino and civil rights groups, newspapers, and local governments.[92] Even Representative Raúl Grijalva, democrat of Arizona, urged conventions to skip his home state; and the state's attorney general called the law a "tragic mistake."[93] The boycott threat was taken very seriously in a state where the tourism and convention businesses were struggling to bounce back from the recession. Pearce still managed to draw large crowds to hear him extol the virtues of his hard-line approach.[94] Mexico weighted in by issuing an advisory warning cautioning its citizens living or traveling in Arizona that they were subject to harassment on account of the law.[95]

Arizonans are no strangers to violence, but a string of murders caused them to ask broader questions about the climate of violence in the state. In 2009, small-town Arivaca was stunned when a gunfight left two locals dead and one badly wounded; the perpetrators were linked to a vigilante "rogue group" engaged in border protection.[96] Around that time, Arizonans were riveted by news of the murder of a rancher in Cochise County; the killing was attributed to a drug smuggler, though this was never proven.[97] But it was the 2011 shooting of US Representative Gabrielle Giffords that inspired deeper soul-searching. Pima County sheriff Clarence Dupnik came right out and bluntly called Arizona a Mecca for prejudice and bigotry.[98] Residents wondered if and when the state's more moderate factions would begin to assert themselves.[99] Lost in the shuffle was the fate of migrants themselves. In the first six months of 2010, 150 people suspected of being undocumented were found dead in the desert (a 50 percent increase over the previous year). The Pima County morgue could not cope with the numbers and called in a refrigerated truck to store the corpses.[100]

At the other end of the political spectrum, Cochise County sheriff Larry Dever condemned the violence, but also revealed that he was "frustrated and disheartened when the White House, which had failed to secure the border for generations" sued Arizona for trying to fill the legislative vacuum.[101] Dever followed up by forming a "Border Sheriffs Association" to assist police departments being sued by immigrant advocacy groups.[102] Kris Kobach, who helped draft SB1070 and similar legislation in other states, was another who blamed the Obama administration for failing to "enforce the laws we already have," and for not regarding immigration as a priority.[103]

Despite accusations of federal inaction, a concerted effort at immigration legislation reform had occurred during the administration of George W. Bush. In 2007, it met with Congressional rebuff, so Bush went ahead with his "enforcement only" option (described in chapter 7). Next, it was Obama's turn. A plan to introduce immigration reform was floated early during his administration. In 2010 Senate Democrats introduced their "conceptual proposal"—not a draft of proposed legislation—attempting to reengage both political parties in reform.[104] The Senate proposal included measures to monitor the departure of all immigrants, open the door to more highly skilled immigrants and foreign students, ease the reunification of families, and offer a simple route to legal status for undocumented people already in the country.[105] In response, House Republican leader John Boehner predicted that "There is not a chance that immigration is going to move through Congress" that year.[106] It didn't. Instead, several states moved to copy Arizona's 1070 anti-immigrant lead, sometimes devising even more stringent conditions of their own invention.

AT THE CENTER of Arizona's law enforcement is Maricopa County sheriff Joe Arpaio, who boasts about being the toughest sheriff in the country. Maricopa County is not a border-adjacent county, and Arpaio came late to immigration issues. First elected in 1993, Arpaio is reputedly a publicity hound who courts the limelight. Soon after his reelection for a fifth term, he appeared on a Fox Reality Channel television show.[107] Well-versed in media manipulation, he became famous for employing male and female chain-gangs, and parading prisoners dressed in pink across town to a "tent prison" erected to relieve overcrowding in the county jail.

Arpaio's police department had 4,000 employees plus a media-relations unit of five. He had the largest number of officers (160) trained to enforce federal immigration laws under the 287(g) program, plus a 3,000-person "volunteer posse" deputized by the sheriff himself.[108] The department's practices had long been criticized. Maricopa County paid $43 million over a six-year period to settle legal claims from prisoners, including families of prisoners who had died while in custody. In 2008, the National Commission on Correctional Health Care revoked its accreditation of prisons operated by Arpaio.[109] The county faced more federal prison-condition lawsuits than New York City, Los Angeles, Chicago, and Houston combined.[110]

Arpaio's anti-immigrant activities drew the heaviest criticism. Maricopa County officers who detained someone for, say, a minor traffic infraction could inquire about that person's immigration status, based on assessments of appearance and language. Bruce Sands, of the County Sheriff's Department, asserted that deputies had the ability "to make a quick recognition on somebody's accent, how they're dressed."[111] Such overt racial profiling was one reason why, in late 2009, federal officials rescinded that part of Maricopa County's 287(g) contract that gave its deputies authority to question immigrants arrested on the street.[112] Phil Gordon, mayor of Phoenix, referred to Arpaio's "reign of terror" against undocumented migrants in the county.[113] The City of Phoenix police department had a policy of not asking citizenship on arrest, unlike Maricopa County where every person booked was checked for citizenship against an error-prone ICE database called E-verify.[114]

People who challenged Arpaio's authority often found themselves subjected to investigation by his office. His belligerence seemed to know no bounds. When state attorney general Terry Goddard publicly sparred with Arpaio, the sheriff retaliated by announcing a corruption inquiry of Mr. Goddard's office. No charges resulted.[115] When deputies raided the small town of Guadalupe in Maricopa County in search of illegal immigrants, mayor Rebecca Jimenez objected. In response, Arpaio canceled the contractual agreement by which the town obtained policing services from the county,[116] claiming that even if Guadalupe contracted with another police agency, his deputies retained authority to round up undocumented migrants there.[117] Jimenez was later replaced as mayor for reasons ostensibly unrelated to the confrontation, and the new mayor of Guadalupe vowed not to question the sheriff's actions.

Arpaio relished the national attention brought by his notoriety, even though it inevitably attracted increased levels of scrutiny. An unflattering 2009 *New Yorker* profile suggested that Arpaio, with an assist from the Bush-era Department of Homeland Security, had turned the Maricopa County Sheriff's Department into a "freelance immigration-enforcement agency."[118] The profile also noted that because Arpaio had diverted so many resources into pursuing migrants that other police functions had suffered: response time to emergency calls increased; arrest rates dropped; and dozens of violent crimes went uninvestigated.[119] Protesters began to accompany Arpaio wherever he went, loudly voicing their opposition.[120] Some official investigations were opened into his conduct as sheriff.

THEN THE UNEXPECTED happened in Arizona. The Pearce crusade began to unravel.[121]

Over the course of a single day in 2011, the Republican-controlled Arizona Senate rejected no less than five anti-immigrant bills.[122] The rebuffed measures would have denied citizenship to children born in Arizona of undocumented mothers, required hospitals to check the citizenship of every patient, refused schooling to undocumented children, criminalized driving by undocumented persons, and evicted them from public housing.[123] The bills failed because of overt pressure from the business lobby. Sixty chief executives from the state complained publicly about the unintended consequences of the harsh immigration legislation: the boycotts, lost jobs, cancelled contracts, and nationwide bad publicity.[124] They called on Pearce to mend his ways.

Opponents were not prepared to wait for Pearce to change his ways. By the summer of 2011, they had collected sufficient signatures on a recall petition, obliging Pearce to face a special election. He lost, and was subsequently removed from office.[125] Sheriff Arpaio also ran into stiff opposition, finding himself the target of a 2010 federal Justice Department lawsuit, charged with failing to cooperate with an investigation into allegations of discriminatory practices in his office. In addition, a grand jury examined accusations of abuse of authority by Arpaio,[126] and federal prosecutors received documents alleging that Arpaio improperly redirected almost

$100 million of jail funds.[127] By 2012, Arpaio faced two trials,[128] and the federal government suspended all 287(g) programs throughout the State of Arizona.[129]

Arizonans had finally tired of Pearce's and Arpaio's reincarnation of the Arizona Rangers.

Ciudad Juárez and El Paso

Ciudad Juárez is a city already encountered in this book, for its status as ground zero in the drug wars. Juárez and its US twin, El Paso, provide acute insights into the cross-border synergies of the interrupted third nation.[130]

Ciudad Juárez was, until recently, a prosperous city of about 1.5 million people, but since 2008 about a quarter-of-a-million inhabitants have fled the city as a result of drug war-related violence—maybe as many as 30,000 to El Paso alone, the rest to other destinations in Mexico.[131] About 25 percent of Juárez homes have been abandoned. The sparsely populated neighborhoods left behind attract crime, and present a financial burden for the city, adding to Juárez's litany of woes. The new construction market has almost dried up.[132] Yet the city's maquiladora sector continues to add jobs, and trade between Juárez and Texas rose almost 50 percent in 2010 to over $71 billion.[133]

Juárez attracts considerable financial assistance from the Mexican government, anxious for victories of any kind in the drug wars.[134] President Calderón came to Juárez in 2010 with a list of social programs to aid the stricken city. Conceding that a military solution to cartel violence would not work by itself, Calderón sought to combine policing with judicial reform and social programming—an approach favored by the US.[135] A year later, Calderón was back in Juárez for his fourth visit since the violence began, in order to celebrate the 100th anniversary of the Mexican Revolution. Announcing a change in the city's name to "Heroica Ciudad Juárez," Calderón touted the benefits of his program *Todos Somos Juárez* (We Are All Juárez), which in one year had pumped over $250 million into restoring the city's bruised fabric.[136] The number of violent deaths in the city fell to 142 for the month of April 2011, down from its peak of 359 in the previous October, and the lowest total since the virus of violence blossomed. However, the number of deaths in the State of Chihuahua reached a high of 374 for the same month.[137] Still, Calderón welcomed any good news in his war.[138]

One reason why crime statistics were improving in Juárez was the new police chief, Julián Leyzoala, who arrived there after a successful cleanup of the streets of Tijuana (described in chapter 8). The Leyzoala strategy in Juárez was taken from his Tijuana playbook: within one year, a hard line had reduced the number of murders by one-third; about 200 police officers had been purged; and complaints had surfaced about increases in human rights abuses. Yet as in Tijuana, residents gave their police chief a lot of leeway in conducting his business. Morale at the city's police department improved. Using another tactic learned in Tijuana, Leyzoala banned the musical group Los Tigres del Norte on the grounds that their music glorified drug traffickers.[139]

A few miles downriver from Juárez lie the twin towns of El Porvenir, in Chihuahua, and Fort Hancock, in Hudspeth County, Texas. They are connected by an informal bridge crossing over the river. Many people fled from violence in El Porvenir, seeking political asylum or using whatever kind of visa or crossing card they could obtain. Initially, the asylum-seekers had been mostly journalists, police officers, and other officials who had received threats, but now most were ordinary people fearful for their well-being. The departures turned El Porvenir into a ghost town.[140]

Directly across the river in Fort Hancock, Hudspeth County commissioner and local farmer Jim Ed Miller refers to his family farm in an out-of-the-way corner of the county as "Almost America," because a new DHS fence ended at his property and migrants could walk around it and pass by unimpeded. His wife Karen insisted that: "We do not live in fear," even though the local sheriff had warned people to arm themselves against the potential spillover of cartel violence. Another local woman was more appreciative of the fence: "When a dog barks, you don't know what's going on out there... I sleep a little better because of that fence."[141]

In El Paso, the movement of Mexicans seeking sanctuary across the border created a miniboom in the real estate and restaurant businesses.[142] It was not unusual to hear people remark that the city had no real problems. In his 2011 State of the City address, El Paso's mayor was optimistic about efforts to revitalize the downtown and confident in the city's strong economy based in the maquiladoras and the military (nearby Fort Bliss is the fastest-growing US Army post in the country).[143] Despite the crowded restaurants and revitalized air of well-being, many El Pasoans are keenly aware of the difficulties confronting their sister city. In 2011, five members of the US Congress met with the mayor of Juárez at the US consulate in that city and offered assistance in promoting public safety and economic development. Earlier that same year, mayors of 13 border cities met in Tucson to form the US–Mexico Border Mayors Association, focusing initially on economic growth and reducing negative stereotypes of the borderlands.

For their part, *juarenses* (the people of Juárez) are resentful when visitors fly in to lecture them about their problems and what to do about them (especially if they are from Mexico City). Many *juarenses* believe that Calderón had little option but to confront the cartels, but their most prominent desire now is to get the military out of the city because its presence was perceived as having contributed to escalated levels of violence, as well as bringing its own brand of intimidation.

In conversations, many El Pasoans reflected on the changing relations between the twin cities brought about by drug wars and fortifications. David H. conceded that everyone is a bit more cautious these days, and although he enjoyed being close to the border and to nature, he was "put off by violence over there." David H. had not been to Juárez for over three years, even though his wife is Mexican and has family there. She was in Juárez at the time of our conversation. He outlined the precautions she took to avoid drawing attention: dressing in ordinary clothes that indicated a person of less affluence; parking her car on the US side and walking over the bridge to Mexico; and being met on the other side by a family member intentionally driving a decrepit car. David H. had noticed the population exodus from Juárez, as families sought temporary refuge in the US. He'd even seen people sleeping in parked cars in the desert to avoid night-time violence.

César was another person who had suspended family visits to Mexico. He had not been back to Juárez to see his *abuelita* (grandmother) in four years. His parents live in the US, where his father once served in the military. Apart from family, César most missed the flavor of fresh vegetables (especially avocados and mangos) that were more readily available in Mexican markets. The new fence had resulted in longer waits at the border, and he considered the Wall a huge waste of money since migrants and drugs still got through. César thought that as life became harder in Juárez, there had been more vandalism and break-ins in El Paso.

Catherine used to be regular on cross-border buses in previous decades, but she no longer shopped in Juárez mainly because so many stores and restaurants that she favored had closed. She'd seen advertisements claiming that Juárez restaurants were safe to visit, but she was discouraged by long lines at the crossing and the need to carry a passport. The number of family visits across the border seemed to be down, she agreed, but schoolchildren who were born in US and now lived with parents in Mexico still crossed in large numbers every day, using their special passes.

Kate and David T. lived about half an hour north of El Paso. Both felt that reports in national and international media did not reflect the reality of the local situation. They agreed that racial and ethnic groups harmonized well in the region. The migration of relatively affluent *juarenses* to El Paso had created a boom; there were more people on the streets and in restaurants, adding a European-style bustle to the city. They expressed some of the mixed feelings among residents: migrants were fewer on the streets these days only because they had moved to other locations; and while many El Pasoans did not like the Wall, it had reduced crime in the city and many were glad that cars were not being stolen with such frequency. Pointedly observing that "New Mexico is not Arizona," Kate and David T. remarked that even conservative El Pasoans admired the migrants' courage.

CROSS-BORDER INSTITUTIONAL ties have been hard hit by border tensions. National Park Service personnel in El Paso no longer officially enter Mexico without authorization, nor soldiers from Fort Bliss, nor the staffs of the US International Boundary and Water Commission, the University of Texas at El Paso, and the New Mexico State University.

The International Boundary and Water Commission (IBWC) and its Mexican counterpart CILA (*Comisión de Limites y Aguas*, located in Ciudad Juárez) share the responsibilities of maintaining the line over the land and water boundaries (the latter including the levees and buoys at Falcon and Amistad dams). The IBWC/CILA collaboration is something of a success story, since it involves binational federal agencies that still work together effectively after more than a century of collaboration. Of course, it helps that there are well-defined shared aims on both sides, and that many problems are of a technical nature that can be addressed by staff who speak a common language (it's called "engineering"). Sheryl Franklin, director of operations and maintenance at the national headquarters of the IBWC in El Paso, believes that the IBWC has a huge potential for protecting resources and promoting diplomacy. "The river provides the water that lubricates the junction between two continental plates," she told me. Even in difficult times, the IBWC had increased community outreach, and there were plans to reopen some informal border crossings that were closed after the inception of the DHS.

Nowadays, it is definitely more dangerous working along the line. There's a lot of rock-throwing from the Mexican side, and IBWC workers are more careful about arranging visits to the other side. Maintenance crews (always consisting of more than one operative) are often accompanied by security details. Gabe Duran, the IBWC's unofficial historian, told me that when he was a kid, his father would take him to Juárez once a week to get a haircut, and Mexican neighbors would bring their sheep to graze in the US. (Everybody along the line has childhood memories about freely crossing over the unmarked border to explore and play with friends.) However, Gabe also mentioned that when the car he was driving ran out of gas on a recent job in Nuevo Laredo, he and a CILA colleague were accosted by a Zeta cartel squad who were monitoring movement in and out of the city's west side. Gabe put in a call and, after a nervous standoff, gas was delivered to them by a colleague and they hurriedly drove off without further ado. On another occasion, this time in Big Bend, Texas, Gabe ran into what he sadly referred to as a "new breed" of young USBP officers, the kind who issued orders and brandished weapons thoughtlessly.

Many IBWC personnel expressed concern about the proliferation of ports of entry (POEs) along the international boundary at the same time that the US was trying to seal the border. (USBP officers voiced similar worries.) Whenever crossings were coupled with transportation improvements on either side, movement over the line would inevitably increase, and so would the problems of policing and security. However, pressure to grow the number of POEs is intense, mainly because crossing tolls are a lucrative source of revenue. Permission from US and Mexican authorities, including the IBWC/CILA, is necessary in order to open a new POE. Rarely is it refused, although when the city and county of Laredo once submitted competing proposals they were instructed by the US State Department to go away and come up with a single proposal.

Other institutions in the region are experiencing collateral damage relating to Wall- and security-related matters. For instance, the famous Chamizal Park in El Paso is operated by the US National Park Service (NPS). Catherine Johnson is attached to law enforcement at the park, which operates through an arrangement known as "proprietary jurisdiction," meaning that the Park Service has authority to enforce only its own laws within the park. (Different agencies deal with other law enforcement issues.) Chamizal is popular with folks on both sides of the border for its extensive year-round program of cultural events. Catherine pointed out that the nearby Bridge of America is toll-free, so even today it is always crowded. *Juarenses* still come to Chamizal for entertainment and socializing; she estimated that maybe a third of license plates of cars parked at Chamizal festivals are registered in the adjacent Mexican state of Chihuahua. However, the NPS no longer flies in visiting artists for Chamizal events through Juárez airport (even though airfares are cheaper), nor will NPS personnel drive over to Juárez in order to transfer visitors to El Paso. Many Mexican visiting artists themselves insist on flying via safer US airports and carriers.

Disruption of activates at the University of Texas at El Paso (UTEP) is much greater, simply because a lot more people are impacted. Many Mexican students from Juárez commute daily to classes at UTEP, but some have moved to El Paso partly through fear and partly because commute times had grown so long. Kate Bonansinga, former director of UTEP's Rubin Center for the Visual Arts told me that the Center had regretfully suspended its close collaborations with Juárez artists as a consequence of changed university policies. Kate responded by curating exhibitions portraying how artists were confronting the issues of border violence.[144] Kerry Doyle, assistant director at the Center, expressed her own cognitive dissonance between what she called the "militarized zone" of Ciudad Juárez and the "dream land" of a safe and booming El Paso. To underscore the difference, Doyle mentioned plans by the internationally famous Tecnológico de Monterrey to open a branch campus at El Paso.

AND WHAT IS the future of beleaguered Ciudad Juárez?

Many families who remained in Juárez, exhausted by living in fear, are once again venturing out into public places. They take children to visit the zoo, organize fashion shows, and stage dance events at community centers.[145] Young people are especially active in marches against violence. Members of a church-based group calling themselves "Messenger Angels" act as a public conscience, and have traveled to other hard-hit cities to spur a peace movement.[146] One woman in Juárez even ventured to suggest that: "The city has hope now.... Businesses are opening. People have shed their fear."[147] There is talk of bringing league soccer back to the city.[148] Some *narcocorridos* speak of joining the protest movements.[149]

Third Nation Endures

The disruption of the Wall's construction is over. The anti-immigrant purges in Arizona have hit roadblocks in the form of federal lawsuits. The suffering in Ciudad Juárez still smolders, but in El Paso the air is clear. The upheavals in the third nation have been undeniably massive, and they are not yet over. But communities have made adjustments, and now people wait.

In 2011, I revisited El Paso–Ciudad Juárez after most of the fortifications along the land boundary had been completed. Monument number 3, the nineteenth-century obelisk at the western edge of the metropolitan region, was closeted behind a tall fence. Monument number 2 had been stolen, and no one knew why. Monument number 1 still stood at the point where the land boundary meets the Río Bravo/Rio Grande. Mexican hero Francisco Madero

FIGURE 9.1 Ancient Monument No. 1 at El Paso.

This border location is especially noteworthy for its complete absence of fortifications. From the left, panel 1 shows the Casa de Adobe, restored headquarters of Mexican Revolution leader Francisco Madero; panel 2, a bust of Madero; panel 3, the berm (with a sign) marking the boundary between the two nations; and panel 4, the ancient monument no. 1. Collage by Michelle Shofet. Copyright © 2011 by Michael Dear.

had based his Revolutionary headquarters here, and his restored "Casa de Adobe" had been opened as a museum a year earlier (see Figure 9.1).

Accustomed by now to the Wall's shadow, I was taken aback to discover there was no fortification in the vicinity of the Casa. Instead, only a shallow earthen berm with a sign atop it that marked the boundary, plus a few low posts stuck in the ground. The ambience that day was relaxed. Nothing impeded communication across the line, so I chatted amiably with the museum attendant across the berm; he was proud of the new building. My companion—holding appropriate papers!—walked into México from the US side and took photographs of the Casa. I waved at museum visitors, exchanging courtesies in Spanish and English. Things were as they should be.

Everywhere along the line, cross-border lives continue. Why expect anything different? The borderlands have been a cooperative enterprise for millennia. Today the urgent practicalities of everyday life propel Tijuana to its future. Basic human decency is being reasserted in Arizona. The enormous reserves of goodwill in Texas seem bottomless. The twin cities of Matamoros and Brownsville embrace a common destiny, as they have since the day they were founded.

The third nation endures.

10

Why Walls Won't Work

THERE ARE NO magic words to solve the problems of immigration in the US or drug-related violence in Mexico. Instead, I offer one incontrovertible conclusion regarding the borderlands: the Wall will not work. Here's why.

Because the Border Has Long Been a Place of Connection

The borderline is a permeable membrane connecting two countries. The inhabitants of this "in-between" territory thrive on cross-border exchange and collaboration, both of which have flourished for many centuries. There are strong senses of mutuality and attachment to territory among border residents.

Throughout time, many great dramas have been played out along what is today the border zone, including cataclysmic invasion, war, and revolution. The current afflictions in this troubled geographical vortex pertain to immigration and drug wars. The region has survived past upheavals, and will undoubtedly outlast the present woes (see Figures 10.1–10.2).

A principal reason why border tensions are today so intense is that neither the migration nor drug problem has its origin in the borderlands. Instead, they originated from outside, and borderland communities have limited capacity for self-determination in these matters. At the national level, the US and Mexico each stand to gain from the sacrifices of that small subset of their populations that resides in the border zones. These are the people who must endure the exogenously-induced threats, with little assistance from their national and local governments beyond military and police actions. In the meantime, they have made what adjustments they can: some people have left, tired of the stresses and dangers; others simply await the future.

FIGURE 10.1 Monument 122A, viewed from the Avenida Internacional in Nogales, Sonora.

A fortuitous vertical stacking of boundary infrastructure portrays the 'deep archeology' of the line. The top panel reveals present-day electronic surveillance apparatus; below this is the 1990-era Operation Hold-the-Line fencing; in the third horizon is a monument from the late 19th-century boundary re-survey; and at its base lies a concrete retaining wall that has been spray-painted with symbols of birth and death characteristic of ancient Mesoamerican cultures. Collage by Michelle Shofet. Copyright © 2003 by Michael Dear.

FIGURE 10.2 Monument No. 122A (detail).

The skull symbol painted on the concrete retaining wall of monument no. 122A (on right) is reminiscent of a carving on the ball court wall in the ancient Maya city of Chichen Itza, Yucatan (on left). Collage by Michelle Shofet. Copyright © 2003 by Michael Dear.

Because the Wall Is an Aberration in History

For most of human history, there was no United States of America or *Estados Unidos Mexicanos*. Both nation-states arrived relatively late on the global scene, and the international boundary between them is little over a century-and-a half old. Before 1848, the borderlands were an open frontier where our prehistoric ancestors roamed widely over the land in search of sustenance, eventually evolving complex civilizations on a subcontinental scale, with extended kinship, settlement, and trade networks.

After 1848, the frontier became a formal geopolitical divide between two nation-states. Thereafter, the border was only casually observed. Even though the boundary line had shifted, borderland peoples had not. For many decades after the war they continued shuffling their affiliations and allegiances, all the while absorbing newcomers and re-forging connections through intermarriage, trade, and self-defense.

During the twentieth century, economic ties between Mexico and the US intensified, and increasing migration from south to north led to the establishment of the US Border Patrol, dedicated solely to policing the boundary. Such regulation was only intermittently successful, and was usurped by the vagaries of US labor markets and other government programs that maintained the cross-border migratory flows. Later decades witnessed economic and demographic expansion in the twin cities along the line, provoking enormous cultural and political shifts that created a modern, integrated transborder economy that was instrumental in the emergence of the third nation.

From the perspective of a long history of borderland connectivity, the Wall is an unprecedented historical aberration.

Because Twin City Prosperity Requires
There Be No Barriers

The twin cities straddling the US–Mexico boundary are the most prominent current legacies of shared interests and collaborations extending back to the prehistoric networks of the Chichimecan and Southwest pueblo cultures; to the centuries-long Spanish colonial heritage of fort, mission, town, and mine; and to the post-1848 founding of border twin towns. For most of the twentieth century, twin-town urbanization was a roller-coaster of consecutive boom-and-bust: fast-paced economic and demographic growth, and cultural and ethnic mixing. Synergies across the borderline were consolidated and intensified, and the policing mechanisms regulating the line eventually collapsed.

Today, ambitious infrastructure plans to upgrade twin-city connections are regularly announced: boosting international tourism, promoting international investment and economic development, and constructing ports and freeways to facilitate trade and speed vehicle and pedestrian crossings. For instance, a *Ruta* 2000 freeway connects Tijuana with Ensenada, pulling Tijuana's sprawl southward; and the Valle de Guadalupe north of Ensenada is being transformed into a wine-growing region to match California's Napa Valley.

Without the presence of an international boundary, each pair of borderland twin cities would each be instantly recognizable as a single, integrated metropolis. As it is, the long-established downtown border crossing, which used to be the core of the city, is now only one element of an emerging, region-wide urban network. The multiplying numbers of exurban ports of entry have deflected growth away from the traditional core. In addition, cities that are distant from the boundary line have become enjoined with the borderland urban network (the principal examples being Monterrey–Reynosa–McAllen, and Tijuana–San Diego–Los Angeles). These transnational city-regions are the dynamic centers of demographic and economic growth, as well as of fundamental shifts in cultural, political, and social life. Neither nation can afford to suspend these connections without jeopardizing the future prosperity of Mexico and the US.

Because People Always Find Ways over, under,
through and around Walls

As long as migrants hold onto an American Dream, and as long as Mexican labor is required in the US, people will cross the border with or without papers. Walls don't work simply because people are too inventive in circumventing them.

As the land border tightens, more people go *around* it by sea. The waters off San Diego have seen a doubling in the number of sea-borne undocumented migrants in recent years, plus a seven-fold increase in drug seizures.

Going *under* the border line is an increasingly popular option. Since 2008, almost 70 tunnels have been discovered connecting Mexico to the US, mostly in California and Arizona. Some stretched for over half a mile, revealing elaborate lighting, drainage, and ventilation systems, and even rail tracks and elevators.

The old-fashioned method of going *over* the fence remains popular, because even the most sophisticated barrier has weaknesses. The vehicles of some border-jumpers have been rigged with custom-made roof ladders that can be extended as ramps over a fence to allow easy passage of vehicles. Climbers have perfected the use of hand-held screwdrivers to scale steel-mesh barriers that were designed to inhibit hand- and toe-holds. Migrants with a bit more time remove panels in the fencing and carefully replace them after passage; some employ gas-powered leaf blowers to erase their footprints once they cross. By 2009, there had already been over 3,000 breaches in the fence, costing $4.4 million to repair.

If all else fails, border-crossers still bluff their way *through* official ports of entry. Some inventive smugglers hollowed out the seats in their SUVs and re-covered them with a migrant hidden inside. Others have crossed with a small child wrapped inside a *piñata* (a kind of large doll). Those with a professional interest in shepherding an illicit cargo through a check point will employ spotters and corrupt inspection officers to schedule their delivery without interference.

Because Governments and Private Interests Continue Opening Portals in the Wall

As the US government moved to seal the border, it was simultaneously increasing the number of sanctioned portals in the Wall. The term "port of entry" (POE) usually refers to a collection of facilities that regulate movement into and out of this country at vehicular, rail, air, and sea ports. The chief attractions of opening more of these "gates" in the Wall are related to increasing trade and reducing congestion at the aging POEs in downtown locations. Local governments are also seduced by the tolls they can collect from POE users, and regard POEs as a stimulus to economic growth. In some out-of-the-way places lacking POEs, consideration is also being given to reopening the informal border crossings that were closed after 9/11.

Other organizations maintain open portals of communication across the line. The number of private and public agencies that promote trans-border ties is seemingly endless. They include the state-level Border Governors' Conference, the Border City Mayors' association, private business councils, joint economic development alliances, nonprofit humanitarian aid agencies, law enforcement, cultural organizations, and education establishments.

International relations between Mexico and the US simply could not exist without these communication portals—private and public, formal and informal, real and virtual. The most interesting (but little known) example is the "International Boundary and Water Commission, United States and Mexico," (IBWC), mentioned in previous chapters. The IBWC originated under Article V of the 1848 Treaty of Guadalupe Hidalgo and was established in 1889. In Mexico, the equivalent agency is the *Comisión Internacional de Limites y Aguas* (CILA). Both are charged with jointly implementing the international boundary and water treaties and settling disputes along the border. Their wide mandate embraces oversight of the distribution of waters from the Rio Grande and Colorado Rivers; the regulation and conservation of storage dams, reservoirs, and hydroelectric power generation; protection of lands along the river from floods; sanitation and other border water quality problems; and the preservation of the land and river boundaries.

Because "Third-Nationhood" Is Already on People's Minds

Connectivity and continuity along the international boundary line is molded by the mental maps (or cognitive psychogeographies) of border-dwellers. I have described four phases in the evolution of borderland mentalities: frontier, border, line, and third nation. Once the 1848 boundary line was in place, the *frontier spaces* that the Spanish wished to conquer were reimagined as *border places* that Mexico and US sought to define and control. After the US Border Patrol was created, the space between Mexico and the US was no longer an open frontier, still less a permeable border. Instead it became a *line* of demarcation controlled by a dedicated police force that henceforward was institutionalized in US–Mexico mental maps. *La línea* (the Spanish-language word commonly used to refer to the border) defined not only an arc of physical separation but also delineated a cognitive transition from one citizenship to another, and from legality to illegality. Most recently, the consolidated histories of millions of border dwellers on both sides are crystallizing into a fourth psychogeography, a *third nation*.

Because Diaspora and Diversity Trump
the Border Industrial Complex

Demographic diversity and the diaspora of people of Latino origin are ines-
capable facts of public life in the US. This is why the refrain, "The border is
over" has entered dialogues about race, discrimination, and immigration. In
the meantime, the rise of a strict enforcement-only mentality in US immigration matters has given birth to a swiftly-growing Border Industrial Complex
(BIC), charged with defending the boundary of Fortress USA and imprisoning upstart invaders in a new American Gulag. The vacuous nature of this
public-policy response is less surprising when viewed in the context of this
country's current obsession with mass incarceration. The US has the highest
rates of imprisonment in the world, and people of color are disproportionally
impacted by this punitive culture. Why should undocumented migrants be
exempt from this national obsession?

There are acute moral and practical issues at stake here. Whose justice is
being served when people of color are being imprisoned in grossly dispro-
portionate rates, at the same time as they are becoming the demographic
majority, at least in some parts of the nation? Immigration has been a constitutive foundation of the US since its birth, and population diversity is
recognized as a source of energy, innovation, and strength. Nevertheless, a
resurgence of racist and nativist attitudes has targeted minorities, including immigrants. It does not have to be this way, and the simple arithmetic
of demographic change suggests it cannot always be this way. Among the
many valuable lessons that the third nation teaches is how we might all get
along.

Because Mexico Is Going Global and Democratic

In Mexico, national conversations are dominated by cartel-related violence,
but behind them are deeper issues relating to the resurgence of democracy
and the passage to modernity. Over the past several decades, Mexico boldly
undertook political and economic reforms that radically altered the practices
of democracy in that nation. In addition, rising prosperity led to demands for
greater transparency and justice in Mexican society. The power of prosperity
and democracy together was forcefully demonstrated by the rise of PAN in
border states during the late twentieth century.

Established elites in the Mexican economy, politics, military, and church
will not readily surrender their power and wealth. The inertia of tradition is

an additional brake on the pace of change, most notably the legacies of indigenous roots (*México profundo*) and the European heritage of the Spanish conquerors (*México imaginario*). But today, as Mexico goes global (*México global*), a more open society will likely continue emerging, even though the return of the PRI in 2012 might presage otherwise.

Because Walls Always Come Down

The Wall separating Mexico and the US will come down. Walls always do. Partition is the crudest tool in the armory of geopolitics, an overt confession of failed diplomacy.

The Wall won't work because the third nation has strong connecting tissue that partition cannot compromise. The third nation is the place where binational lives and values are being created—organically, readily, and without artifice. The third nation will prevail, and is worth nurturing. It is the place of being and becoming in the spaces between two nations.

What should be done about the Wall that so rudely interrupts the third nation? The Berlin Wall was torn down virtually overnight, its fragments sold as souvenirs of a calamitous Cold War; the Great Wall of China was transformed into a global tourist attraction. Left untended, the US–Mexico Wall would collapse under the combined assault of avid recyclers, souvenir hunters, and local residents offended by its mere presence. Nevertheless, we should preserve sections of the Wall to commemorate that fraught moment in history when the US lost its moral compass.

Acknowledgments

I HAVE BEEN extremely fortunate in the range of friends and colleagues who have contributed to this book. Two long-time collaborators were principally responsible for my Mexican education: Héctor Lucero and Gustavo Leclerc. Héctor accompanied me for most of my travels along the border, and Gustavo and I conspired on joint projects for almost two decades. Along the way, Norma Iglesias introduced me to border cultures, and Larry Herzog, to border cities. On many weekends before daybreak, Bob Steward and I drove out of Los Angeles into the desert searching for boundary monuments.

This project began when I was working at the University of Southern California, where Barbara Robinson of USC's Boeckmann Center for Iberian and Latin American Studies was amazingly resourceful and helpful. Selma Holo, then Director of the Fisher Gallery, encouraged me to take risks. The work of several colleagues provided insight and inspiration, including Manuel Castells, Marc Cooper, Greg Hise, Pierette Hondagneu-Sotelo, Josh Kun, Abe Lowenthal, Dowell Myers, Manuel Pastor, Jr., Octavio Pescador, Jr., Roberto Suro, and Carol Wise. Tyson Gaskill deserves special mention for his digital restoration of the mid-nineteenth-century maps that were so central to my work.

The National Geographic Society's Committee on Research and Exploration provided funds that enabled my travel during the formative stages of the project.

The book was completed after I arrived at Berkeley, where I encountered a congenial faculty at the College of Environmental Design. Closest to my interests were Nezar AlSayyad, Teresa Caldeira, Ron Rael, and Ananya Roy. Marc Treib provided endless tea and encouragement. The historian's insights of Brian DeLay, David Montejano, and Richard Cándida Smith proved indispensible. At the Center for Latin American Studies, Harley Shaiken and Beatriz Manz hosted many visitors to campus who immeasurably expanded my horizons. A year as Senior Fellow at Berkeley's Townsend Center for the Humanities brought fresh viewpoints to my endeavors. I thank Provost George Breslauer and Vice-Provost Sheldon Zedek for permitting adjustments in my schedule so that I could complete this work.

Numerous undergraduates and graduate students have assisted and informed me over the years. They are too numerous to mention, but I must note Andrew Burridge and Jacqueline Holzer, whose USC doctoral dissertations focused on the borderlands, and Oscar Sosa, who continued my Mexican education at Berkeley.

My wider professional debts are just as extensive. Thanks to Tito Alegría, Teddy Cruz, and René Peralta for my Tijuana education; Dan Arreola and Michael Yoder for giving me the keys to South Texas; and Tony Payan for introducing me to Ciudad Juárez. Jo-Anne Berelowitz and Paula Rebert were extraordinarily generous with their expertise in (respectively) border art and cartographic history. Friends in Los Angeles have been an inspiration for many years, even though they might not recognize their direct influence on this book. They include John Agnew, Dana Cuff, Mike Davis, Steve Erie, Ali Modarres, Jaime Regalado, Allen Scott, Ed Soja, and Californian-in-exile, Margit Mayer. The voluminous works of many scholars provided a knowledge base without which this book would not have been possible.

Journalists and other media reporters who cover the border provided me with a deep reserve of raw materials for my work. Many who report the drug wars have been caught up in a dangerous world, and some have suffered injury and death. I salute their courage and dedication.

Much of my understanding of border cultures derives from artists, curators, and writers. Over the years, I have had reason to be grateful to Kate Bonansinga, Ulises Díaz, Marjolijn Dijkman, Matt Driggs, Janet Owen Driggs, Robbert Flick, Guillermo Gómez-Peña, Anthony Hernandez, Luis Ituarte, Jesse Lerner, Rubén Martínez, Amalia Mesa-Bains, Rubén Ortiz-Torres, Jaime Ruiz Otis, Marcos Ramirez ERRE, David Taylor, Einar and Jamex de la Torre, Camilo José Vergara, and Tomás Ybarra-Frausto. Two treasures at the Los Angeles County Museum of Art were Virginia Fields (now sadly gone from us) and Ilona Katzew.

The US National Archives and Records Administration in Maryland (Raymond Cotton and Mary C. Ryan), and Mexico City's Mapoteca "Manuel Orozco y Berra" (Carlos Vidali) arranged access to many essential historical maps, photographs, and documents. Other important institutional resources were the Bancroft Library at Berkeley, the Getty Research Institute in Los Angeles, and the International Boundary and Water Commission in El Paso (where Michael Tarabulski was tireless in assisting with inquiries). I visited scores of enchanting regional and community museums everywhere along the border that were invaluable sources of insight and pleasure.

I was invited to make presentations about this work in many universities in the US, Europe, and Latin America, where I gained valuable feedback on my evolving ideas. I am especially indebted to friends who arranged discussions at Mexico City's Universidad Nacional Autónoma de México (UNAM) and the Universidad Autónoma Metropolitana–Azcapotzalco (UAM–A), at the Colegio de la Frontera Norte in Tijuana, and at the Universidad Autónoma de Baja California in Mexicali. I gratefully acknowledge helpful conversations with Sergio Aguayo, Michelle Bachelet, Cuauhtémoc Cárdenas, Néstor García Canclini, Octavio Pescador, Jr., Doug Massey, Lorenzo Meyer, the late Carlos Monsiváis, Manuel Perló, and Rodrigo Salcedo.

At the regional offices of the United States Border Patrol I was met with courtesy and assistance. And I must say this: the same was true for equivalent agencies on the Mexican side of the border.

Finally, I am grateful to Dave McBride and his production crew at Oxford University Press for guiding this book to publication. Simply stated, Dave is an expert editor, and this book is so much better for his skills and generous support. Thanks to Michelle Shofet, who prepared the manuscript and illustrations, and also undertook archival research and to David Deis of Dreamline Cartography. Jennifer Wolch read and commented on the manuscript, and demonstrated remarkable forbearance in tolerating my mental and material absences while this book was being researched and written.

I dedicate this book to people who live on both sides of the Mexico–US boundary line. Not everyone will agree with my perspective on the border, so I must emphasize that the interpretations and opinions expressed in this book are mine alone. But to everyone, whatever your sentiments: thank you. *¡Que viva la tercera nación!*

Notes

CHAPTER 1

1. An earlier version of this chapter appeared as: Dear, "Monuments, Manifest Destiny and Mexico," 32–41. The U.S. National Archives holdings on the US–Mexico borderlands include field notebooks, topographical sketches, maps, trigonometric and astronomical readings, photographs, memorandums, and letters, as well as official reports. Most sources are to be found in Records of Boundary and Claims Commissions and Arbitrations, Record Group 76. The significant cartographic records are: US–Mexico Boundary Survey, 1849–1855, final maps (54, in 13 folders, plus 4 index maps and 5 maps of islands in the Rio Grande). The principal Mexican report on the post-1848 survey maps is Salazar's short diary which addresses only the California section of the survey, *Línea divisoria entre México y los Estados Unidos*. The Mexican maps of the post-1848 boundary survey are held in Mexico City at the Mapoteca "Manuel Orozco y Berra," Servicio de Información Estadística Agroalimentaria y Pesquera. In this book, I reproduce sections of the Mexican maps—which are in superior condition to the US documents—by kind arrangement with the Mapoteca.

2. Johnson, "Baja California and the Treaty of Guadalupe Hidalgo," 330.

3. Ohrt, *Defiant Peacemaker: Nicholas Trist in the Mexican War*, 97.

4. Griswold del Castillo, *The Treaty of Guadalupe Hidalgo*.

5. Grant, *Personal Memoirs of U.S. Grant*, 41.

6. A biography of Nicholas Trist that seeks to set the record straight is by Ohrt, *Defiant Peacemaker*. Others who recognize Trist's pivotal role in achieving the Treaty include Chamberlin, "Nicholas Trist and Baja California," 49–63; and Johnson, "Baja California and the Treaty of Guadalupe Hidalgo," 328–347, who finds "only one fault with Trist, his extreme verbosity; if something could be said in ten words, he would use one hundred" (347).

7. The standard account of cartographic history in the American west is by Wheat, *Mapping the Transmississippi West*, 3:207.

8. The definitive historical narrative of the 1849–1855 US–Mexico boundary survey is by Rebert, *La Gran Línea*, 2–3.

9. Wheat, *Mapping the Transmississippi West,* 3:220.

10. Ibid., 218.

11. A lively, well-researched history of the border region to the present day (including both boundary surveys) is Metz's *Border.* It includes piquant descriptions of the outsize personalities involved in the post-Treaty boundary survey.

12. A concise history of Polk's presidency is Seigenthaler's *James K. Polk.* In recent years, Polk has received extensive reappraisals in biographies by Borneman, *Polk;* and Merry, *A Country of Vast Designs.*

13. John Russell Bartlett was the second U.S. Boundary Commissioner, who reputedly spent over half a million dollars of boundary survey money on personal travel throughout the American and Mexican West. He later produced a classic tale of travel in the region entitled *Personal Narrative of Explorations and Incidents in Texas, New Mexico, California, Sonora, and Chihuahua.*

14. Metz, *Border,* ch. 3–4, provides details on some of Bartlett's adventures. Bartlett's reputation as a scientist and artist are recounted in Hine, *Bartlett's West.* A broader view of the art and cultural politics of the boundary survey may be found in: Hall, *Drawing the Borderline.*

15. Emory's biographers note how he was "thoroughly disgusted by the way the surveys had been conducted under Commissioners Weller and Bartlett [and] was determined to avoid the mistakes of his inept predecessors. Looking at the records...he discovered that Bartlett had squandered approximately $500,000 on wasted side trips, idle workers, useless secretaries, and personal business." Norris, Milligan, and Faulk, *William H. Emory: Soldier,* 145. Several chapters in this book report on Emory's boundary survey experiences, making copious use of his letters, diaries, and reports.

16. Wheat, *Mapping the Transmississippi West,* 3:208–209.

17. The life of Mexican Commissioner Salazar is not well-documented, but see Tamayo Perez, Luz María O., and Moncada Maya, "José Salazar Ilarregui, 1832–1892," 116–125.

18. Metz, *Border,* 90; Rebert, *La Gran Línea,* 112–113.

19. Emory, *Report on the United States and Mexican Boundary Survey.* A useful overview of Emory's role in mapping the southwest is Thrower, "William H. Emory and the Mapping of the American Southwest Borderlands," 41–91.

20. Emory, *Notes of a Military Reconnaissance,* 122.

21. Ibid., 124.

22. Emory, *Report on the United States and Mexican Boundary Survey.* The 1987 facsimile edition of this Report includes an "Introduction" by William H. Goetzmann addressing the achievements of Emory and his collaborators (vii, and ix–xxx).

23. Salazar Ylarregiu, *Datos de los trabajos astronómicos y topográficos.*

24. Quoted in Rebert, *La Gran Línea,* 198.

25. Salazar Ylarregiu, *Datos,* 38. (My translation.)

26. Martínez, *Troublesome Border* discusses the controversies that required modifications to the Treaty of Guadalupe Hidalgo. Also see Metz, *Border,* ch. 7; and Utley, *Changing Course.*

27. Rebert, *La Gran Línea,* 34.

28. Some of the differences between the two nations' cartographic output is discussed in Rebert, "Mapping the United States–Mexico Boundary," 58–71. She also discusses the extent to which copying of the maps was practiced.

29. Werne, *The Imaginary Line* is an invaluable resource because it draws on documents recently made available from Mexican archives. It should be read alongside Rebert's *La Gran Línea,* and St. John, *Line in the Sand.*

30. Hughes, "'La Mojonera' and the Making of California's U.S.–Mexico Boundary Line, 1849–1851," 126–147; and Lesley, "The International Boundary Survey from San Diego to the Gila River, 1849–50," 3–18.

31. Rebert, *La Gran Línea,* 60–64.

32. Ibid., 101.

33. Hardcastle to Emory, March 28, 1851; quoted in Brown, "Survey of the United States Mexico Boundary, 1849–1855," 163.

34. Dobyns, *Hepah, California!,* 11.

35. Metz, *Border,* ch. 4, 8; Rebert, *La Gran Línea,* ch. 4; Utley, *Changing Course,* ch. 4; and Werne, *The Imaginary Line,* chs. VI–VII.

36. This portion of the survey is related by Werne, "Major Emory and Captain Jiménez: Running the Gadsden Line," 203–221. Werne provides a graphic account of the hardships endured by the survey crews, including disease (yellow fever and smallpox), poor roads, absence of military escorts, theft of mules by Indians, shortage of potable water, impenetrable timber stands, sand and dust storms, floods, price gouging by local suppliers, death from thirst, insufficient funds, and insect bites of such voracity that Captain Francisco Jiménez described the experience as a virtual martyrdom. Werne also noted the spirit of harmony and cooperation between the two sides.

37. Metz, *Border,* 90; Norris et al., *William H. Emory,* 163; Rebert, *La Gran Línea,* 53.

38. Rebert, *La Gran Línea,* 113; Wheat, *Mapping the Transmississippi West,* 3:240.

39. Emory, *Report on the Unites States and Mexican Boundary Survey.*

40. Aspects of the parallel survey of the boundary flora and fauna are discussed in Rebert, "Views of the Borderlands: The *Report on the United States and Mexican Boundary Survey, 1857–1859,*" 75–90.

41. Quoted in Wheat, *Mapping the Transmississippi West,* 3:216.

42. Hewitt, "The Mexican Boundary Survey Team: Pedro Garcia Conde in California," 171–196; Rebert, "*Trabajos Desconocidos, Ingenieros Olvidados*: Unknown Works and Forgotten Engineers of the Mexican Boundary Commission," 156–184; also Werne, *The Imaginary Line.* Mexican frustrations regarding the post-1848 boundary survey are discussed by Martínez, "Surveying & Marking the U.S.–Mexico Boundary: The Mexican Perspective," 13–22.

43. In contrast to the post-1848 boundary survey, there has been little scholarly investigation into the conduct of the second survey. Valuable but brief accounts are to be found in Metz, *Border,* ch. 9, and Rebert, *La Gran Línea,* ch. 6. Detailed reports by both Mexican and US boundary commissioners (see endnote 49 below) compensate for this omission.

44. Metz, *Border,* 115–116.
45. Rebert, *La Gran Línea,* 119–121, 128–131, 190–191. Rebert underscores the importance of the monuments on the ground in taking precedence over lines of latitude and longitude on maps in disputes over the location of the boundary line, stating: "The true boundary was the boundary marked on the ground" (191).
46. Metz, *Border,* 110.
47. Ibid., 111.
48. Ibid., 115.
49. U.S. International Boundary and Water Commission, United Sates and Mexico, *Report of the Boundary Commission upon the survey and re-marking of the boundary between the United States and Mexico west of the Rio Grande, 1891–1896.* A second volume with the same title but also identified as an "Album" contains a photographic record of every monument along the land boundary. Many of the same photographs appear in the *Memoria de la Sección Mexicana de la Comisión Internacional de Limites entre México y los Estados Unidos que restableció los monumentos de El Paso al Pacífico.* The principal Spanish-language source for photographs of the 1891–1894 resurvey is *Vistas de los monumentos, a lo largo de la línea divisoria entre México y los Estados Unidos de El Paso al Pacífico,* under the direction of Mexican Commissioner Jacobo Blanco. The documents governing the Mexican resurvey are collected in Luis G. Zorrilla, *Monumentación de la frontera norte en el siglo XIX.*
50. Metz, *Border,* 106.
51. Ibid., 114.
52. U.S. Department of State, International Boundary Commission, United States and Mexico, "Placing of additional monuments to more perfectly mark the international boundary line through the town of Naco, Arizona–Sonora," 6.
53. Ibid., 8.
54. This history is well-recounted in deBuys and Myers, *Salt Dreams.*
55. U.S. Department of State, International Boundary Commission, United States and Mexico, "Monumentation of the Railroad Bridges between Brownsville and Matamoros, and Laredo and Nuevo Laredo."; "Placing of an additional monument to more perfectly mark the international boundary line through the towns of Calexico, California, and Mexicali, Baja California."; and "Placing of additional monuments to more perfectly mark the international boundary line through the town of Naco, Arizona–Sonora."
56. There are two indispensable accounts of this early era in border fortification: Dunn, *Blockading the Border and Human Rights* for the El Paso–Ciudad Juárez experience; and Nevins, *Operation Gatekeeper,* for the Tijuana–San Diego case. A second edition of the Nevins book under the title *Operation Gatekeeper and Beyond* was published in 2010.
57. In 2011, yet another effort was made to close the ocean-side crossing opportunity with a new quarter-mile long, 18-foot high fence coated with rust-proof material that came with a 30-year warranty. See Marosi, "U.S. to extend border fence 300 feet into Pacific."

CHAPTER 2

1. A concise, accessible overview of recent archeological perspectives on the first arrivals is in Pringle, "The First Americans."

2. A general account is provided in Fagan, *The First North Americans*.

3. Enormous controversy is characteristic of discussions on early human settlement in the Americas. A popular summary of current thinking is in Pringle, "The First Americans;" typically combative overviews are Adovasio and Page, *The First Americans,* and Lekson, *A History of the Ancient Southwest*; for an example of the state of current archeological inquiry, see Waters, et al., "The Buttermilk Creek Complex and the Origins of Clovis." The reports of John Noble Wilford in *The New York Times* provide readily accessible and readable accounts of major shifts in prehistorical knowledge and interpretation; see for instance: Wilford, "Stone Said to Contain Earliest Writing in Western Hemisphere," and Wilford, "Arrowheads Found in Texas Dial Back Arrival of Humans in America."

4. Hodges, "Cahokia: America's Forgotten City," 127–145.

5. López Austin and López Luján, *Mexico's Indigenous Past*.

6. Ibid., 81–82.

7. A well-illustrated, accessible account is given in Ferguson, Rohn, and Royce, *Mesoamerica's Ancient Cities*; a comprehensive and authoritative overview of Mexican evidence is Uriarte, *Pre-Columbian Architecture in Mesoamerica*. Alan Knight's *Mexico: From the beginning to the Spanish Conquest* is a scholarly account of the period in one concise volume.

8. Coe and Koontz, *Mexico: From the Olmecs to the Aztecs*.

9. Berrin and Fields, *Olmec: Colossal Masterworks Works of Ancient Mexico*.

10. Diehl, *The Olmecs: America's First Civilization*.

11. Coe, *The Maya*.

12. Lyons and Pohl, *The Aztec Pantheon and the Art of Empire*. The rise of organized states has been related to the practice of war elsewhere in the Americas; see Stanish and Levine, "War and Early State Formation in the Northern Titica Basin, Peru."

13. A short, well-illustrated guide for the armchair traveler is Baldwin's *Legends of the Plumed Serpent: Biography of a Mexican God*.

14. Ferguson, Rohn and Royce, *Mesoamerica's Ancient Cities*; Uriarte, *Pre-Columbian Architecture in Mesoamerica*.

15. Bourbon's biography of Frederick Catherwood, *The Lost Cities of the Maya,* collects many of Catherwood's highly evocative nineteenth-century illustrations of the Mayan sites he visited with John Stephens.

16. León-Portilla, "Aztlán: From Myth to Reality," 20.

17. Notably, the term "Aztlán" has been adopted by the contemporary Chicano movement in the US to refer to the mythical homeland. See Anaya and Lomeli, *Aztlán*.

18. Sanders, Parson, and Santley, *The Basin of Mexico: Ecological Processes in the Evolution of a Civilization*.

19. Uriarte and Suzan, "The Central Altiplano," ch. 5, 83–119.

20. On the Triple Alliance, see López Austin and Luján, *Mexico's Indigenous Past*, ch. 5.
21. Lyons and Pohl, *The Aztec Pantheon and the Art of Empire*, 62.
22. Lister and Lister, *Those Who Came Before*.
23. Ibid., 48.
24. Fagan, *Chaco Canyon: Archaeologists Explore the Lives of an Ancient Society*, ch. 10; Whalen and Minnis, *Casas Grandes and its Hinterland: Prehistoric Regional Organization in Northwest Mexico*, 206–207.
25. Lister and Lister, *Those who Came Before*, 39.
26. Lekson, *A History of the Ancient Southwest*.
27. Much recent evidence from Mexican archeology is collected in Uriarte, *Pre-Columbian Architecture in Mesoamerica*.
28. Whalen and Minnis, *Casas Grandes and its Hinterland*, 35.
29. Much recent scholarship is collected in Foster and Gorenstein, *Greater Mesoamerica;* and Schaafsma and Riley, *The Casas Grandes World*. Also of interest are: Pohl, "Chichimecatlalli: Strategies for Cultural and Commercial Exchange between Mexico and the American Southwest, 1100–1521," 86; and Weigand and García de Weigand, "A Macroeconomic Study of the Relationships Between the Ancient Cultures of the American Southwest and Mesoamerica," 184.
30. A standard source of Casas Grandes in its regional context is by Whalen and Minnis, *Casas Grandes and its Hinterland*, 45.
31. Kelley, "The Aztalán Mercantile System: Mobile Traders and the Northwestward Expansion of Mesoamerican Civilization," 137.
32. McGuire, Villalpando, Vargas, and Gallaga, "Cerro de Trincheras and the Casas Grandes World," 134.
33. Spence, "From Tzintzuntzan to Paquimé: Peers or Peripheries in Greater Mesoamerica?," 255; Schaafsma and Riley, "The Casas Grandes World: Analysis and Conclusion."
34. Villalpando, "The Archaeological Traditions of Sonora," 241.
35. Kelley, "The Aztalán Mercantile System: Mobile Traders and the Northwestward Expansion of Mesoamerican Civilization," 137; and Foster, "The Aztatlán Tradition of West and Northwest Mexico and Casas Grandes," 149.
36. Sauer and Brand, *Aztatlán: Prehistoric Mexican Frontier on the Pacific Coast, Ibero-Americana: 1*; and Sauer, *The Road to Cíbola, Ibero-Americana: 3*.
37. An imaginative reconstruction of the connections between Paquimé and Chaco Canyon is by Childs, *House of Rain*, although his account is marred by a complete absence of sources for his speculations. Equally iconoclastic, Lekson, in *A History of the Ancient Southwest,* is much more firmly grounded in his historical reconstruction. Skeptics include Fagan, *Chaco Canyon*.
38. Lister and Lister, *Those Who Came Before*, 39; and Fagan, *Chaco Canyon*, 180, 213.
39. Lekson, *A History of the Ancient Southwest*, ch. 8.
40. Noble, *New Light on Chaco Canyon*.

41. Maugh II, "Earlier traces of cacao use found in Southwest," A12; Haederle, "Mysteries of Ancient Puebloan Jars Solved," A14.

42. Childs, *House of Rain*, 440. The fascinating present-day story of the Tarahumara is related by McDougall, *Born to Run*. Other indigenous peoples, including Coahuiltecan men, demonstrated similar stamina and athletic prowess; see, Sánchez, *A Shared Experience*.

43. León-Portilla, "Aztlan: From Myth to Reality," 33; Cortez, "The New Aztlan: *Nepantla* (and Other Sites of Transmogrification)," 358. For a general overview of Nahua views of the conquest, see Wood, *Transcending Conquest*.

44. An important regional synthesis of current archeological evidence on Baja is to be found in the collection edited by Laylander and Moore, *The Prehistory of Baja California*.

45. Laylander, "Toward a More Complex Understanding of Baja California's Past," 202.

46. Alvarez de Williams, *Primeros Pobladores de la Baja California*.

47. Laylander, "Issues in Baja California Prehistory," 7–8.

48. Ibid., 3.

49. The best, lavishly-illustrated, account of this region in English is by Harry Crosby, *The Cave Paintings of Baja California*.

50. Hyland, "The Central Sierras," 121. See also: Diguet, *Territorio de la Baja California*.

51. Gardner, *The Hidden Heart of Baja*. Gardner went on to write more books on Baja. He was occasionally accompanied by archeologist Clement Meighan: see Meighan, "Prehistoric Rock Paintings in Baja California," 372–392.

52. Hyland, "The Central Sierras," 122.

53. Ritter, "South-Central Baja California," 99.

54. Ibid., 107.

55. A good, accessible account of California's prehistory is by Fagan, *Before California*.

56. Erlandson et al., "Paleoindian Seafaring, Maritime Technologies, and Coastal Foraging on California's Channel Islands."

57. McCawley, *The First Angelinos: The Gabrielino Indians of Los Angeles*.

58. Fagan, *Before California*, 144–146.

59. Ibid., 357.

60. I have already alluded to many efforts being directed toward regional and subcontinental synthesis, including: Carrasco, *The Oxford Encyclopedia of Mesoamerican Cultures* (3 vols); Foster and Gorenstein, *Greater Mesoamerica*; Schaafsma and Riley, *The Casas Grandes World*; Uriarte, *Pre-Columbian Architecture in Mesoamerica*; Fagan, *Chaco Canyon*; and Lekson, *A History of the Ancient Southwest*.

61. Highly readable accounts of this epochal transition are to be found in two books by Charles Mann, *1491* and *1493*.

62. See Cabeza de Vaca, *The Account: Alvar Núñez Cabeza de Vaca's* Relación; and an interpretive history by Reséndez, *A Land So Strange*. A popular account of these epic travels is Lavender, *De Soto, Coronado, Cabrillo*.

63. Whalen and Minnis, *Casas Grandes and its Hinterland*, 36.
64. Quoted in Ibid., 27.
65. An excellent account published in *National Geographic* on the rise and fall of the classic Maya civilization is Gugliotta, "The Maya Glory and Ruin." Good examples of recent efforts in computer modeling and simulation to sort out the plethora of factors contributing to decline are: Kohler et al., "Simulating Ancient Societies;" and Ford et al., "Modeling Settlement Patterns of the Late Classical Maya Civilization."

CHAPTER 3

1. This chapter draws from previous publications on regional history and urbanism, principally: Dear, "In the City, Time Becomes Visible;" Dear, "Peopling California;" Dear and Leclerc, *Postborder City*; Dear, *From Chicago to LA*; Dear, *The Postmodern Urban Condition*; Dear, Schockman, and Hise, *Rethinking Los Angeles*; and Leclerc, Villa, and Dear, *Urban Latino Cultures*.
2. Knight, *Mexico: The Colonial Era*, 9–12. Knight's is a concise standard text for the era of the Spanish conquest of Mexico, and it is my basic source for the first section of this chapter.
3. Ibid., 14–28.
4. Ibid., 31–33.
5. Ibid., Part I, ch. II.
6. Ibid., 61.
7. Ibid., Part I, ch. VII.
8. Ibid., 175.
9. Introductions to urban growth in the colonial era are to be found in: Crouch, Garr and Mundingo, *Spanish City Planning in North America*; and Cruz, *Let There Be Towns*. For a brief overview of urbanism in context, see Weber, *The Spanish Frontier*, especially ch.11.
10. Knight, *Mexico: The Colonial Era*, 133–142.
11. Ibid., 110–116, 131, 181–185. Discussions of Spanish–Indian relations in this period are also available in Kessell, *Spain and the Southwest*, ch. 9; and Weber, *The Spanish Frontier*, ch. 8. Also see Weber, *Bárbaros* for more detail.
12. Lynch, *Bourbon Spain*, 21; on the arrival of the Bourbons in New Spain, see Knight, *Mexico: The Colonial Era* Part II, ch. II.
13. Knight, *Mexico: The Colonial Era*, 239.
14. Ibid., Part II, ch. III; and Weber, *Bárbaros: Spaniards and their Savages in the Age of Enlightenment*.
15. Knight, *Mexico: The Colonial Era*, 256–263.
16. Weber, *Bárbaros*, 3, 237.
17. Knight, *Mexico: The Colonial Era*, 266–267.
18. Ibid., 257.

19. Ibid., 279–285.

20. Ibid., 304–307.

21. Ibid., Part II, ch. V.

22. Crouch, Garr and Mundingo, *Spanish City Planning in North America*, 2.

23. Cruz, *Let There Be Towns: Spanish Municipal Origins in the American Southwest, 1610–1810*, 14.

24. Ibid., ch. 3.

25. Simmons, *The Last Conquistador: Juan de Oñate and the Settling of the Far Southwest*; also see Lamar, *The New Encyclopedia of the American West*, 824.

26. Kessell, *Spain in the Southwest*, 82–84; Weber, *The Spanish Frontier*, 86.

27. de Oñate, "Letter written by Don Juan de Oñate from New Mexico to the Viceroy, the Count of Monterrey, on March 2, 1599," 82.

28. Stavans, "Juan de Oñate, 1550–1626," 78.

29. These terms are used, respectively, by Kessel, *Spain in the Southwest*, 83; and Weber, *The Spanish Frontier*, 86.

30. One of the earliest and most devastating accounts is by Bartolomé de las Casas, *A Short Account of the Destruction of The Indies*.

31. McKeever, *A Short History of San Diego*.

32. Dear, "In the City, Time Becomes Visible," 86–87. For more on LA's establishment, see Crouch, Garr, and Mundingo, *Spanish City Planning*, ch. II.3; and Cruz, *Let There Be Towns*, ch. 6.

33. A good account of Baja history is by Lucero, "Peopling Baja California," 83–150.

34. The persistence of the mission-presidio tradition over two centuries of Spanish expansion is examined in Spicer, *Cycles of Conquest*.

35. Kessel, *Spain in the Southwest*, 332–334, 337.

36. Ibid., 106, 111, 114, 150, 201. For accounts of the cultural mixing in Alta California at this time, See Beebe and Senkewicz, *Lands of Promise and Despair: Chronicles of Early California, 1535–1846*; Gutiérrez and Orsi, *Contested Eden: California before the Gold Rush*; Haas, *Conquests and Historical Identities in California, 1769–1936*; Osio, *The History of Alta California*; and Pitt, *The Decline of the Californios*.

37. Kessell, *Spain in the Southwest*, 377.

38. A valuable collection of essays on this emerging *mestizaje* world is in Hackel, *Alta California*.

39. Morales and Tamayo-Sánchez, "Urbanization and Development of the United States–Mexico Border."

40. More details on the twin towns' founding may be found in Arreola and Curtis, *The Mexican Border Cities*, ch. 2.; and Gasca Zamora, *Espacios transnacionales*, 82–83.

41. Reséndez, *Changing National Identities at the Frontier, 1800–1850*, 2. The absolutely indispensable account of Anglos and Mexicans together in Texas is by David Montejano, *Anglos and Mexicans*. Mora's *Border Dilemmas* is a valuable account of post-1848 adjustments in borderland New Mexico, especially in the Las Cruces–La Mesilla region.

42. Cruz, *Let There Be Towns*, ch. 5.

43. Kearney and Knopp, *Border Cuates: A History of the U.S.–Mexican Twin Cities*, especially ch. 5. This may be the only book that examines the borderland twin-town history from inception to the present day.

44. Ibid., 97–99, ch. 6.

45. Ibid., ch. 6. For additional coverage of the pivotal El Paso region, see Ortiz-Gonzalez, *El Paso: Local Frontiers at a Global Crossroads* and Timmons, *El Paso: A Borderlands History*.

46. Kearney and Knopp, *Border Cuates*, ch. 7.

47. Ganster and Lorey, T*he U.S.–Mexico Border into the Twenty-first Century*, 35–45.

48. Lucero, "Peopling Baja California."; for further detail on Mexicali, see Lucero Velasco, *Mexicali Cien Años*.

49. Anderson and Gerber, *Fifty Years of Change on the U.S.–Mexico Border: Growth, Development, and Quality of Life*, ch 2. A broad data set associated with this book is generously provided by the authors at http://latinamericanstudies.sdsu.edu/BorderData.html.

50. One of the best "travel guides" to the Lower Rio Grande Valley is actually a 336-page technical document on the history, architecture and historical designations of the valley's "heritage corridor." See Sánchez, *A Shared Experience*.

51. The early battles of the US–Mexican war in the Lower Rio Grande Valley are described in Eisenhower, *So Far from God*, chs. 5–9.

52. Chatfield, "The Twin Cities of the Border."

53. Ibid., 2, column 4.

54. Ibid., 14, column 4.

55. Ibid., 15, column 2. On Cortina, see Saldaña, *Diccionario Biográfico de la Heróica Matamoros*, 122–132.

56. Chatfield, "The Twin Cities of the Border," 33, column 1.

57. Ibid., 29, column 1.

58. Ibid., 29, column 3. Earlier in the almanac, Chatfield reported the Mexican population at nearly two-thirds of the Brownsville total; see page 16, column 4.

59. Ibid., 25, column 1.

60. Ibid., 3, column 1.

61. Ibid.

62. Ibid., 33, column 2.

63. Ibid. 29, column 4.

64. Ibid., 19, column 2.

65. Ibid., 36, column 4. Even today, Matamoros residents still avail themselves of Brownsville's postal services.

66. Ibid., 32, column 2.

67. Ibid., 33, column 1. On Mejía, see Saldaña, *Diccionario Biográfico de la Heróica Matamoros*, 381–383.

68. Chatfield, "The Twin Cities of the Border," 37, column 1.

69. Ibid., 38, column 1.

70. Adams and Knopp, *Portrait of a Border City*, 17.

71. Kearney and Knopp, *Border Cuates,* 151–157.

72. Lucero, "Peopling Baja California," 96–98; Kearney and Knopp, *Border Cuates,* 184.

73. Kearney and Knopp, *Border Cuates,* ch. 8.

74. More information on the Brownsville–Matamoros twins is available in Kearney and Knopp, *Boom and Bust: The Historical Cycles of Matamoros and Brownsville*; Adams and Knopp, *Portrait of a Border City*; and Saldaña, *Diccionario biográfico de la heroica Matamoros.*

75. Kearney and Knopp, *Border Cuates,* ch. 9.

76. Balderrama and Rodriguez, *Decade of Betrayal: Mexican Repatriation in the 1930s.*

77. Kearney and Knopp, *Border Cuates,* ch. 10.

78. Ganster and Lorey, 126–127.

79. Kearney and Knopp, *Border Cuates,* 219–233.

80. Ibid., ch. 11.

81. Iglesias Prieto, *Beautiful Flowers of the Maquiladora: Life Histories of Women Workers in Tijuana.*

82. The most recent history of the International Boundary and Water Commission (IBWC) is Bustamante Redondo, *La Comisión Internacional de Límites y Aguas entre México y los Estados Unidos.* The IBWC is discussed further in chapters 9 and 10 of this book.

83. The terms of NAFTA are still the source of contention between Mexico and the US, and it remains difficult to provide a comprehensive accounting of the treaty's full impacts. Useful starting points are: Fernández-Kelly and Shefner, *Annals of the American Academy of Physical and Social Science,* "NAFTA and Beyond;" Bacon, *The Children of Nafta*; Ruiz, *Mexico: Why a few are rich and the people poor*; and Wise, *The Post-NAFTA Political Economy.*

84. Audley et al., "NAFTA's Promise and Reality: Lessons from Mexico for the Hemisphere."

85. Polaski, "The Employment Consequences of NAFTA."

86. Ganster and Lorey, 117. Also see Gasca Zamora, *Espacios transnacionales,* capítulo 2.

87. Kearney and Knopp, *Border Cuates,* 265.

CHAPTER 4

1. Martínez, *Troublesome Border.*

2. The nauseating violence of this era is masterfully captured in the works of Cormac McCarthy, whose *Blood Meridian* tells a story of the border region immediately following the 1848 treaty. His "Border Trilogy" (*All the Pretty Horses, The Crossing,* and *Cities of the Plain*) continues the narrative into the twentieth century.

3. Martínez, *Troublesome Border,* ch. 2.

4. Our understanding of conflict and *connection* during these difficult times has been immeasurably improved by recent scholarship in new history of the American West, most especially concerning the roles of Indian peoples, including Comanche and Apache. In this chapter, the following examples have been particularly useful: Anderson, *The Conquest of Texas*; Calloway, *One Vast Winter Count;* DeLay, *War of a Thousand Deserts;* Hämäläinen, *The Comanche Empire*; Hine and Faragher, *The American West* (a concise version of this book is published as Hine and Faragher, *Frontiers*); and Jacoby, *Shadows at Dawn.*

5. Anderson, *The Conquest of Texas*, 15.

6. DeLay, "Forgotten Foes," 14.

7. See Hämäläinen, *The Comanche Empire*, for an excellent account of the powerful Comanche empire and its vexed relationships with other Indian tribes, Mexicans, and Anglos.

8. Ibid., ch 1, especially 20–22.

9. Ibid., 27–37.

10. Ibid., 3–5. Hämäläinen emphasizes how these arrangements were exactly the reverse of conventional colonial practice in many parts of Central and North America.

11. Ibid., 9.

12. An overview of Spain's pragmatic approaches to pacification of Indians in the Americas is by Weber, *Bárbaros.*

13. Pace and Frazier, *Frontier Texas*, 37.

14. Jacoby, *Shadows at Dawn*, 57–59. DeLay discusses the rise of local response to the Indian Problem and the lack of a coordinated Mexican approach in DeLay, *War of a Thousand Deserts*, 145–147, and 154–158.

15. Ibid., 61.

16. Ibid., 39; see also De León, *They Called Them Greasers.*

17. Quoted in DeLay, *War of a Thousand Deserts*, 228.

18. Anderson, *The Conquest of Texas, 1820–1875*, 3.

19. Ibid., 49–93.

20. DeLay, "Forgotten Foes," 15.

21. Ibid., 18–19.

22. Informe General de la Comisión Pesquisidora, "Depredaciones de los bárbaros en Nuevo Léon," 229. There are so many typographical errors in this English-language extract from a Spanish-language source that I have taken the liberty of adjusting them in order to render the text more readable.

23. Griswold del Castillo, *The Treaty of Guadalupe Hidalgo*, ch. 4 and 190–191. Also: DeLay, *War of a Thousand Deserts*, Epilogue.

24. Jacoby, *Shadows at Dawn*, 78–80.

25. Ibid., 105.

26. Pace and Frazier, *Frontier Texas*, 40.

27. Anderson, *The Conquest of Texas*, 9.

28. Ibid., 226–227.

29. Ibid., 228–229.
30. Ibid., 7.
31. McMurtry, "Texas: The Death of the Natives," 63.
32. McMurtry, "Indian Terror on Our New Frontier," 57.
33. For a measured history of Texas through this period, see Montejano, *Anglos and Mexicans.*
34. Jacoby, *Shadows at Dawn*, 1–2.
35. Ibid., 226.
36. Ibid., 183–188.
37. Ibid., 208–209.
38. O'Neal, *The Arizona Rangers*, 2.
39. DeSoucy, *Arizona Rangers*, 10.
40. Ibid., 8–9.
41. O'Neal, *The Arizona Rangers*, 36.
42. Ibid., 21.
43. Ibid., 64. On Kosterlitsky, see Meed, *Bloody Border*, ch.1
44. O'Neal, *The Arizona Rangers*, 45.
45. DeSoucy, *Arizona Rangers*, 31–33.
46. Bell, *Reminiscences of a Ranger*, 99–100.
47. Ibid., 13.
48. Ibid., 80.
49. Ellis, "Introduction," n.p.
50. Ibid., 143.
51. Kitchens, "Some Considerations on the Rurales of Porfirian Mexico," 443; and Vanderwood, "Genesis of the Rurales: Mexico's Early Struggle for Public Security." The many works on the Rurales by Paul Vanderwood have been invaluable to this section.
52. Meyer, Sherman, and Deeds, *The Course of Mexican History*, ch. 24.
53. Vanderwood, "Mexico's Rurales: Image of a Society in Transition."
54. Vanderwood, *Disorder and Progress.*
55. Quoted in Kitchens, "Some Considerations on the Rurales of Porfirian Mexico," 441.
56. Quoted in ibid., 442.
57. Vanderwood, "Mexico's Rurales: Image of a Society in Transition," 62–64.
58. Vanderwood, "Mexico's Rurales: Reputation versus Reality,"104; also Vanderwood, "Los Rurales: Producto de una necesidad social," 37.
59. Kitchens, "Some Considerations on the Rurales of Porfirian Mexico," 454.
60. Vanderwood, "Mexico's Rurales: Image of a Society in Transition," 68.
61. Vanderwood, "Los Rurales: Producto de una necesidad social," 39.
62. Ibid., 43.
63. Kitchens, "Some Considerations on the Rurales of Porfirian Mexico," 449; Vanderwood, "Mexico's Rurales: Reputation versus Reality," 106.
64. Vanderwood, "Genesis," 336.

65. Meed, *Bloody Border*, 28.

66. Meyer, Sherman, and Deeds, *The Course of Mexican History*, 682.

67. Vanderwood, *Disorder and Progress*, 123.

68. Vanderwood, "Mexico's Rurales: Image of a Society in Transition," 82–83.

69. Vanderwood, "Los Rurales: Producto de una necesidad social," 49.

70. Meyer, Sherman, and Deeds, *The Course of Mexican History*, 520–522.

71. Torres, *Twenty Episodes in the Life of Pancho* Villa, Episodo XII.

72. Ibid., xi.

73. Ibid., 62.

74. "Villa Invades the U.S.: Bandits Burn and Kill in Columbus."

75. Ibid.

76. "Army Crosses into Mexico."

77. Lacey, "In Echo of Pancho Villa: Modern raid shakes town on the verge of extinction."

78. Romo, *Ringside Seat to a Revolution*, 223–244.

79. Hernández, *Migra!*, 32. This section draws heavily on Hernández's account because it one of the only scholarly accounts focused on the agency's history. A highly-regarded account of Mexico's national history published in 1984 by Anglo journalist Alan Riding (*Distant Neighbors*) contains only two short references to border-related issues and none to the border patrol. By 2004, in Preston and Dillon's *Opening Mexico*, the situation had altered but not by much. The absence of attention to the USBP (and other border institutions such as the IBWC) by historians is hard to explain.

80. Broyles and Haynes, *Desert Duty*, 8–9.

81. Hernández, *Migra!*, 88–93.

82. Ibid., 93–97.

83. Ibid., 6–7, 83–85. The theme of cross-border collaboration is common in border studies. Especially relevant to the topic of this chapter are: Dunn, *The Militarization of the U.S.–Mexico Border*, 94–98; and Nevins, *Operation Gatekeeper*, 130–134.

84. Hernández, *Migra!*, 32–37.

85. Ibid., 45–51.

86. Ibid., 49.

87. Ibid., 59.

88. Ibid., 65–69.

89. Ibid., 103–106. It should be recalled that the 1930s was a time of large-scale repatriation; see Balderrama and Rodriguez, *Decade of Betrayal*.

90. Ibid., 109–114. Also: McWilliams, *North from Mexico*, ch. XIV. Although the Bracero Program was introduced as a wartime effort, it lasted until 1964 and involved more than 2 million guest workers.

91. Hernández, *Migra!*, 137–140.

92. Ibid., 117–124.

93. Ibid., 130–132.

94. Metz, *Border*, 388.

95. Hernández, *Migra!*, 130–140.

96. Ibid., 155–157.

97. Ibid., 171–175.

98. Operation Wetback's legacy in the US includes racist attitudes and difficulties of assimilation for migrant workers. See, for instance, Chacón and Davis, *No One is Illegal*; Rodriguez, *Mongrels, Bastards, Orphans, and Vagabonds,* especially chapters 6–9. A classic account of adaptation and assimilation is Sánchez, *Becoming Mexican American.*

99. Hernández, *Migra!*, 184–188.

100. Ibid., 196–211.

101. Ibid., 211–213. The consequences of the USBP's engagement with narcotics control could hardly have been foreseen; for perspectives on this issue, see Campbell, *Drug War Zone*; and Vulliamy, *Amexica.*

102. Magaña, *Straddling the Border.*

103. Quoted in Hernández, *Migra!*, 217.

104. Detailed accounts covering this important historical moment may be found in: Andreas, *Border Games*; Dunn, *Blockading the Border*; Nevins, *Operation Gatekeeper*; and Payan, *The Three US–Mexico Border Wars.*

105. Examples of personal accounts by agents who served in the early years of the USBP include: Moore, *Border Patrol*; and Jordan, *Tales of the Rio Grande*. Oral histories by the current generations of line officer may be found in Broyles and Haynes, *Desert Duty.*

CHAPTER 5

1. This chapter and the next draw on previous published work, most especially Dear and Burridge, "Cultural Integration and Hybridization at the U.S.–Mexico Borderlands," 301–318, but also: Dear, Leclerc, *Postborder City*; Dear, *The Postmodern Urban Condition*; Leclerc, Villa and Dear, *Urban Latino Cultures*; Dear and Holzer, "Altered States: The U.S.–Mexico Borderlands as a Third Nation," 74–93; Dear, "La tercera nación," xiv–xx; and Leclerc and Dear, "Hitting Soft and Looking South/Golpes suaves cara al sur," 14–31.

2. See Anderson, *Imagined Communities.*

3. A brief introduction to these ideas may be found in Grosby, *Nationalism: A Very Short Introduction.*

4. A history of the Tohono O'odham is told by Erickson, *Sharing the Desert;* some of the dynamics of shifting borderland identities among Indians, Mexicans, and Anglos in Arizona are revealed in Meeks, *Border Citizens.*

5. Gómez-Peña, *The New World Border*, 70.

6. Gómez-Peña, quoted in Rouse, "Mexican Migration and the Space of Postmodernism," 248.

7. In an influential early work on cultural hybridity, García Canclini defines the term *hybridity* as encompassing "all the processes that combine discrete social structures or practices, which already exist in distinctly separate forms, to create new structures, objects and practices in which the antecedents merge." See García Canclini, "Rewriting Cultural Studies in the Borderlands," 279. For a fuller treatment of his approach, see García Canclini, *Hybrid Cultures*. Flusty underscores the role of place in the blurring of previously existing cultural norms, describing cultural hybridity as "the coalescence of new personal and collective identities from novel combinations of previously disparate cultural attributes, practices, and influences… [e]merging from conditions of being cut off from one's roots and left without a place of one's own," Flusty, "Miscege-Nation," 109. Leclerc and Dear observed how hybrid Latino cultures in Los Angeles emerge from a complicated conjunction of identity, memory, and cultural mix; Leclerc and Dear, *Urban Latino Cultures*, 1–6. The universality of the hybrid is emphasized in Burke, *Cultural Hybridity*, and Kapchan and Strong, "Theorizing the Hybrid," 239–253. Also relevant to this idea are general investigations in many fields on the nature of borderlands, borders, and nation states, and ideas of borderlands as "third spaces." See, for instance, Stoddard, "Frontiers, Borders and Border Segmentation;" Adelman and Aron, "From Borderlands to Borders," 814–841; and Grayson, "Mexico's Southern Flank," 53–69. For an excellent account of long-distance hybrid connection between indigenous Mexican communities and US destinations (in the case of California), see Velasco Ortiz, *Mixtec Transnational Identity*. A more general anthropological perspective is in Alvarez Jr., "The Mexican–U.S. Border," 447–470.

8. The analysis in this section is based on field surveys on both sides of the US–Mexico borderland, and more particularly, a content analysis of border-related coverage in *The Los Angeles Times* and *The New York Times* (national edition) over a five-year period, July 2000–July 2005. The analysis comprised 337 articles, the majority of which was from *The Los Angeles Times* (69 percent). A number of other publications on both sides of the border were also reviewed on a more opportunistic basis. See Dear and Burridge, "Cultural Integration and Hybridization."

9. Weiner, "Border Custom Agents Are Pushed to the Limit," A14.

10. Torres and Momsen, "Gringolandia: The Construction of a New Tourist Space in Mexico," 314–335.

11. Weiner, "Americans Stake Claims in a Baja Land Rush," A1.

12. Baum, "The Man Who Says Keep Out," 9–17.

13. Chu, "Journey into U.S. Turns Deadly for Brazilians," A5.

14. For accounts of this era, see Dunn, *Blockading the Border and Human Rights*; and Nevins, *Operation Gatekeeper*.

15. Zeller, "Migrants Take Their Chances on a Harsh Path of Hope," 14; Kraul, "Illegal Immigrants Receive a One-Way Ticket to Mexico," A1.

16. Nevins, "How High Must Operation Gatekeeper's Death Count Go?" M2.

17. Richardson and McDonnell, "Immigration Crackdown Ineffective, Study Finds," B8.

18. Alonzo-Zaldivar, "U.S., Mexico OK Deportation by Air," A11; Kraul, "Illegal Immigrants Receive a One-Way Ticket to Mexico," A1.

19. Wilson, Reza, and Murillo, "Immigration Arrests Not Policy Shift," B1. Also see ch. 4 in this volume.

20. Wilson and Murillo, "Inland Latinos Alarmed by New Border Patrol Sweeps," A1.

21. Pavlakovich-Kochi, "Cross-border Cooperation and Regional Responses to NAFTA and Globalization."

22. Shatz and López-Calva, "The Emerging Integration of the California–Mexico Economies." Also see Lowenthal, *Global California*.

23. Iritani, "U.S. Reaps Bittersweet Fruit of Merger," A1.

24. Dickerson, "Funds Sent to Mexico Hit Record," C1.

25. Thompson, "Money Sent Home by Mexicans is Booming," A12.

26. Suro, "Breadwinners Who Know No Borders," B11.

27. Ibid.

28. Gorman, "Mexico Cuts Gas to Regain Sales Lost to U.S," B5.

29. A convincing demonstration of the growth of Tijuana's national and international ties is provided by Herzog, "Global Tijuana."

30. Ellingwood, "U.S. Mail Delivers—for Tijuana Residents," B6.

31. Romero, "Mexican wealth gives Texas city," B1. This example serves as a reminder of the twin-city connections that always need to be borne in mind when examining borderland urbanism: cf. Kearney and Knopp, as well as chapter 3 in this book.

32. Janofsky, "Burden Grows for Southwest Hospitals," A14.

33. Yardley, "A River That United Lives Is Now A Barrier," A12.

34. Weiner, "Water crisis grows Into a Test of U.S.–Mexico Relations," A3.

35. Bustillo, "Border Pollution Fight Gets New U.S.–Mexico Commitment," A24.

36. Bustamente Redondo, *La commission internacional de límites y aguas entre México y los Estados Unidos*. The IBWC is discussed elsewhere in this book, most notably in chapters 9 and 10.

37. Jameson, *The Story of Big Bend National Park*.

38. Good overviews of borderland environmental issues are: Herzog, *Shared Space*; DeBuys and Myers, *Salt Dreams*; and Blake and Steinhart, *Two Eagles/Dos Aguilas*.

39. Dear and Burridge, "Cultural Integration and Hybridization at the U.S.–Mexico Borderlands," 309.

40. Briscoe, "Marchers Want Changes in U.S.–Mexico Extradition Pact," B3.

41. Mena, "A Great Familial Divide," A14.

42. Kraul and Quinones, "Mexican Voting May Extend into U.S.," A1.

43. Thompson, "'Tomato King' Seeks a New Title," A4.

44. Ibid.

45. Cooper, "On the Border of Hypocrisy," 27–33.

46. Moore, and Becerra, "House Crammed With Illegal Immigrants Raided in Watts," A1.

47. Kelly, "Fight for Human Freight," A1.

48. Thompson, "Littlest Immigrants, Left in Hands of Smugglers," A1.

49. Ballinas and Becerril, "Establece el Senado protección para niños indocumentados deportados," 49.

50. Kraul, Lopez, and Connell, "L.A. Violence Crosses the Line," A28.

51. Miranda, "Fifteen Candles," 70.

52. Hernandez, "A Hybrid Tongue or Slanguage?" A29–A31.

53. Stavans, "The Gravitas of Spanglish," B7; see also Stavans, *Spanglish: The Making of a New American Language.*

54. Kun, "The New Border Aesthetic," 18, 20–34. The continuing strength of this trend is recorded by Iglesias Prieto, *Emergencias.*

55. For more on InSite, see Garza and Garza, *Parajes Fugitivos/ Fugitive Sites*; Berlowitz, "Border Art since 1965;" and Dear and Leclerc, *Postborder City*, Introduction.

56. Wald, *Narcocorrido.*

57. Fuentes-Berain, "Where Roma Soap Meets Dove," A27.

58. Johnson, "A 'Saint' of last Resort," E21.

59. Weiner, "McTaco vs. Fried Crickets: A Duel in the Oaxaca Sun," A2.

60. Murphy, "New California Identity Predicted by Researchers," A13.

61. Friedman, "Narcos, No's, and Nafta," WK10.

62. Lovato, "Fear of A Brown Planet," 17–22.

63. Weiner, "Of Gringos and Old Grudges: This Land is Their Land," A4; see also Fields and Zamudio-Taylor, *The Road to Aztlan.*

64. Chavez, *The Latino Threat*, ch.6.

65. Freedman, "Latino Parents Decry Bilingual Programs," A21.

66. Myers, "Demographic Dynamism," 21–53; Brooks, "The Americano Dream," A27.

67. Appendini, "Promuven neonazis exterminio de cholos," 14A.

68. Two volumes allow for an interesting comparison of cross-border lives for different time periods: see Dusard and Weisman, *La Frontera* for the mid-1980s; and Hendricks, *The Wind Doesn't Need a Passport*, for the mid-2000s.

CHAPTER 6

1. On matters of cognitive mapping, memory, and film, this chapter utilizes previous work in: Dear, Leclerc, *Postborder City*; Dear, *The Postmodern Urban Condition*; Leclerc, Villa and Dear, *Urban Latino Cultures;* and Dear et al., *Geohumanities.* Specific sources include: Dear, *"Es una frontera, no una barrera;"* Dear and Dijkman, "Here Be Dragons: the Art of Place;" Dear, "Rediscovering Reyner Banham's Los Angeles;" Dear, "Photography's Geography;" Dear, "Los Angeles and the Democratization of History;" and Dear and Leclerc, "Tijuana Desenmascarada."

2. Recinos, Goetz and Morley, *Popul Vuh*, 81; this remains my favorite translation. A more contemporary translation is by Tedlock, *Popul Vuh*, 72–73.

3. Some of these are discussed in Fields and Zamudio-Taylor, *The Road to Aztlán.*

4. Chávez, "Aztlán, Cíbola, and Frontier New Spain."

5. Katzew, *Casta Painting*.
6. Martínez, *Genealogical Fictions*. An insightful concise history of racism is Fredrickson, *Racism*.
7. For a fuller discussion, see Katzew and Deans-Smith, *Race and Classification*.
8. The founding of the US is concisely recounted by Wood, *The American Revolution*.
9. Two excellent sources on this topic are: Evans, *Romancing the Maya*; and Carrera, *Traveling from New Spain to Mexico*.
10. Spain also sought to trace the origins of Mesoamerican architecture and art to seeming precedents from Classical Rome; see Pohl and Lyons, *The Aztec Pantheon and the Art of Empire*, x. The fascinating history of Spanish cartographers' efforts to trace the history of New Spain after their own fashion is recounted in Mundy, *The Mapping of New Spain*, and Carrera, *Traveling from New Spain to Mexico*. An excellent general account of writing the historical geography of Modern Mexico is *Cartographic Mexico*, by Craib, who illuminates nineteenth-century French geographer Elisée Reclus's contention that: "Geography is not an immutable thing. It is made, it is remade everyday; at each instant it is modified by men's actions;" quoted in Craib, *Cartographic Mexico*, 1.
11. Stephens, *Incidents of Travel in Yucatán*; and Stephens, *Incidents of Travel in Central America, Chiapas and Yucatán*.
12. Evans, *Romancing the Maya*, 3–5, from which book I draw these examples.
13. DeLeón, *They Called Them Greasers*.
14. Ibid., 12.
15. Ibid., 3.
16. Ibid., 5.
17. Quoted in Weber, *Foreigners in their Native Land*, 79.
18. Ibid., 80.
19. Ibid.,84.
20. Beebe and Senkewicz, *Lands of Promise and Despair*.
21. Among many sources, see Hurtado, *Indian Survival on the California Frontier*; Jackson, *Indian Population Decline*; and Jackson and Castillo, *Indians, Franciscans, and Spanish Colonizations*.
22. Haas, *Conquests and Historical Identities in California*.
23. Good accounts of this era are in Osio, *The History of Alta California*; Hackel, *Alta California*; Gutiérrez and Orsi, *Contested Eden*; and Pitt, *The Decline of the Californios*.
24. Dana, Jr., *Two Years Before the Mast*, 125.
25. Ibid.
26. Quoted in Weber, *Foreigners in their Native Land*, 72.
27. Quoted in Simmons, "Attitudes toward the United States Revealed in Mexican Corridos," 34. My translation.
28. DeLeón, *They Called Them Greasers*, 104–105.

29. Quoted in Weber, *Foreigners in their Native Land*, 189.

30. Ibid., 258–259.

31. Ibid., 260.

32. Simmons, "Attitudes toward the United States Revealed in Mexican Corridos," 38; Lomnitz, "Modes of Citizenship in Mexico," 269–293.

33. Quoted in Simmons, "Attitudes toward the United States Revealed in Mexican Corridos," 40. My translation.

34. A good survey of attitudes is reported by Morris, *Gringolandia*.

35. Ibid., especially chapter 5.

36. The metaphor is developed in Davidow, *The Bear and the Porcupine*.

37. Morris, "Exploring Mexican Images of the United Status," 105.

38. For an overview of Mexican perspectives, see Florescano, *National Narratives in Mexico*.

39. Bonfil Batalla, *México Profundo*, xv.

40. A concise history of Mexico in global context is Beezley, *Mexico in World History*.

41. The broader significance and context of these debates are discussed in two books by Chávez: *Covering Immigration* and *The Latino Threat*.

42. Brookings Institution, *A Report on the Media and the Immigration Debate*.

43. Witt, "Immigration debate a new symptom," A21.

44. A steady supply of broad coverage during the past five to ten years is to be found in the *Arizona Daily Star*, the *Los Angeles Times*, and the *New York Times*.

45. See, for instance, Martínez, *Crossing Over: a Mexican Family on the Migrant Trail*.

46. Anzaldúa, *Borderlands*.

47. From a growing literature, several accounts by Vila stand out. See Vila, *Crossing Borders, Reinforcing Borders*; Vila, *Ethnography at the Border*; and Vila, *Border Identification*. Also: Davidson, *Lives on the Line*.

48. Durand and Massey, *Crossing the Border*; Massey, Durand, and Malone, *Beyond Smoke and Mirrors*; Perlmann, *Italians Then, Mexicans Now*. Also see White, "Race Relations in the American West," 396–416. On the topic of immigration and adjustment, see Myers, "Demographic Dynamism and Metropolitan Change;" in addition, the work of Manuel Pastor and his associates should not be overlooked.

49. Gomez-Peña, *The New World Border*; and Stavans and Alcaraz, *Latino U.S.A.*

50. Morris, *Gringolandia*, 279.

51. Associated Press, "Mexico's net migration down 50%," A9.

52. These programs are coordinated through the *Instituto de las Mexicanos en el Exterior* (IME, Institute of Mexicans Abroad). The US Migration Policy Institute refers to the IME's work as one of the "most significant, if overlooked, factors in US immigration policy." Laglagaron, *Protection through Integration*.

53. Engardio and Smith, "Business is Standing its Ground," 24.

54. Chávez, *The Latino Threat*, ch. 7.

55. This legacy is discussed by Ybarra-Frausto, "El Movimiento," 23.

56. An insightful perspective on present-day popular culture in Mexico is found in a collection of essays (called *crónicas*), *Mexican Postcards*, by the incomparable Carlos Monsiváis. An extended critique of Monsiváis' work, which at the same time is a meditation on Mexican cultural life is by Egan, *Carlos Monsiváis*.

57. Lyall, "Vigilante State," 257.

58. See Doty, *The Law into Their Own Hands*, on contemporary nativist and anti-immigrant movements in the US.

59. Chávez, *The Latino Threat*, ch. 6.

60. Neiwert, "The Fence to Nowhere," 16; Steller, "Disputes splinter border watchers,"

61. Brooks was an entertaining host and quite a comedian. See the *Penthouse* article by Rico, "The Prisoner of Patriot Point."

62. Nexos en línea, "Sueños y aspiraciones."

63. Ibid., 77–81.

64. Ibid., 52 and 79.

65. Ibid., 35 and 78.

66. Data cited in Johnson, "Political Culture and Public Governance in the Third Nation," n.p., from Latinobarómetro.

67. Anzaldúa, *Borderlands*, 3.

68. Anaya, Lomeli, *Aztlán*, 1.

69. Editorial Santillana, Tijuana, La Tercera Nación. My translations.

70. Valenzuela, "Tijuana, ¿la tercera nación? . . . pastiches y palimpsestos," 169.

71. Navalón, "La Frontera," 11.

72. Ibid., 14.

73. Ibid., 12.

74. Valenzuela, "Tijuana, ¿la tercera nación?…pastiches y palimpsestos," 25.

75. Rieger, "Re-imagining Urban Structure." There is no information on public opinion regarding the concept of a third nation in the Mexico–US borderlands. Very few people on either side are familiar with the term, and I've never heard the term used by the general public in casual speech. Rieger's pilot study was designed to collect preliminary ideas as a prelude to more in-depth analysis. She conducted 30 formal interviews as well as many more informal conversations, which were supplemented by my own. The direct quotes are drawn from Rieger, 89–98.

76. Such perceptions (and emotions) are strongly influenced by contemporary visual representations of the city in architecture, art, film, and television. Some examples of relevant work that relates to the border are: Adler et al., *Border Film Project;* Cruz, "Border Tours"; Cull and Carrasco, *Alhambrista*; Fox, *The Fence and the River*; Iglesias, *Entre hierba, polvo y plomo*; Maciel, *El Norte*; Mraz, *Looking for Mexico*; Noriega, "Border Crossings"; Teagle and Feliu-Moggi, *Strange New World*; and Uribe, *MiMéxico imaginado*.

77. This observation applies equally, in my judgment, to the example of the Tohono O'odham nation. See, for instance, Erickson, *Sharing the Desert*, and elsewhere in this book.

CHAPTER 7

1. Magaña, *Straddling the Border*, has an extensive appendix summarizing the history of US immigration law. See Waldinger and Bozrgmehr, *Ethnic Los Angeles*, for a good general account of immigration history and how it played out in Los Angeles.
2. Batalova, Mittelstadt, Mather and Lee, *Immigration: Data Matters*.
3. Authoritative accounts of the recent Mexico–US migration history are contained in a series of volumes from the Mexican Migration Project. See for instance: Massey, Durand, and Malone, *Beyond Smoke and Mirrors*; Durand and Massey, *Crossing the Border*; and Zúñiga and Hernández-León, *New Destinations*. Also: Nevins, "The Remaking of the California–Mexico Boundary in the Age of NAFTA;" and Magaña, *Straddling the Border*.
4. Good accounts of this era are in Dunn, *Blockading the Border and Human Rights*, chs. 3–4; Vila, *Crossing Borders, Reinforcing Borders*, ch. 5; Hernández, *Migra!*, 228–232, and Nevins, *Operation Gatekeeper,,* ch. 6.
5. It is worth recalling the growth of migrant deaths at this time, which doubled to 472 per year between 1995 and 2005, and mostly occurred in the mountains and deserts of the USBP's Tucson sector in Arizona. Mexican sources reported 5,607 deaths between 1994 and 2008; the USBP counted 4,111 deaths since 1998, though US agencies typically undercount because of inconsistent classification practices. The ACLU concluded that the increase in migrant deaths was a predictable outcome of fencing off the border and moving migrants into harsher crossing situations. The major causes of migrant deaths by crossing (in 2008) were: exposure (30 percent); water-related, including drowning (14 percent); and motor-vehicle related (11 percent). Three quarters of the dead were males.
6. For a general introduction to the SBI, see US Department of Homeland Security, "Fact Sheet: Secure Border Initiative."
7. Ibid. ICE reported that as of September 30, 2010, 4.2 million fingerprint submissions had resulted in 343,829 database matches (8 percent). Subsequently, ICE deported just over 64,000 persons (i.e., 19 percent of matches, or 1.5 percent of the total fingerprint submissions).
8. "Secure Communities: A Fact Sheet," *Immigration Policy Center*.
9. "Secure Communities," *National Immigration Forum*.
10. "Confusion Over Secure Communities," A26.
11. McKinley, "San Francisco Changes When Police Must Report Immigrants," A19.
12. Phelan, "Crossing the line," 10.
13. Bernstein, "Immigrant Jail Tests U.S. View of Legal Access," A1.
14. Ibid.
15. Stevens, "America's Secret ICE Castles," 13.
16. Barry, *Border Wars*, 6–7.
17. Joaquin, Natarajan, Tumlin, *A Broken System*.
18. Gorman, "Immigrant detention facility is considered," B5.
19. Bernstein, "Two Groups Find Faults in Immigration Detentions."

20. Parker, "Locked Up Far Away: The Transfer of Immigrants to Remote Detention Centers in the United States." See also Bernstein, "Two Groups Find Faults in Immigration Detentions," A23; Gorman, "Feds sues over detention conditions," A4.

21. Bernstein, "Two Groups Find Faults in Immigration Detentions."

22. Lydgate, "Assembly Line Justice: A Review of Operation Streamline."

23. "Operation Streamline Fact Sheet," *National Immigration Forum.*

24. Preston, "Study Finds Immigration Courtrooms Backlogged," A20; also "Operation Streamline Fact Sheet," *National Immigration Forum.*

25. Lydgate, "Assembly-line Justice," 12–14.

26. Ibid. According to Syracuse University's TRAC (Transactional Records Access Clearinghouse), during the period 2003–2008 prosecutions of white-collar crimes are down 18 percent; weapons prosecutions, down 19 percent; organized crime prosecutions, down 20 percent; public corruption prosecutions, down 14 percent; and drug prosecutions, down 20 percent.

27. Moore, "Focus on Immigration Crimes Is Said to Overtax U.S. Prosecutors," A1 and A15.

28. Ibid.

29. McCombs, "Pot Smugglers with Smaller Loads being Prosecuted Now."

30. Gorman, "A life divided by borders," A1.

31. Archibold, "Immigration Officials Arrest 300 in California," A10. The federal government repatriation program deported by plane 50,000 illegal immigrants to Central and South America in 2006 at a cost of $96 million. The same program repatriated 72,000 people in 2007, the budget growing to $135 million by 2008.

32. Parker and Root, "Forced Apart (By the Numbers): Non-Citizens Deported Mostly for Non-Violent Offenses."

33. "That's 8 Out of 457,000," A20.

34. US Department of Justice, "Unaccompanied Alien Children in Immigration Proceedings."

35. Three other countries: Guatemala, Honduras, and El Salvador, were the origin states of 85 percent of the 7,200 children who remained in custody. See Haddal, *Unaccompanied Alien Children: Policies and Issues.*

36. US Department of Health and Human Services, "Unaccompanied Children's Services."

37. These are the young people whom the DREAM Act was intended to assist. See Downes, "Don't Deport Benita Veliz," A16.

38. Sontag, "Deported, by U.S. Hospitals," A1.

39. Ibid.

40. US Immigration and Customs Enforcement, "Fugitive Operations."

41. Mendelson, Strom, and Wishnie, *Collateral Damage.*

42. US Department of Homeland Security, *An Assessment of United States Immigration and Customs Enforcement's Fugitive Operations Teams.*

43. Mendelson, Strom, Wishnie, *Collateral Damage.*

44. Bernstein, "Effort on U.S. Immigrant Raids Cast Wider Net," A1.

45. Ibid.

46. Gorman, "No longer rounding up just fugitive immigrants," A12.

47. Lydersen, "Breaking the ICE Record," 8.

48. Zucchino, "Immigration arrests roil small town," A18; Bustillo and Fausset, "Immigrant raid splits Miss. Town," A15.

49. The Postville saga is recounted in Grey et al., *Postville, U.S.A.* A brief update is available in Jones, 2012.

50. Olivo, "Raid leaves town worn, torn," A9. In 2010, the plant manager was cleared of charges that he had knowingly employed under-age workers. Most of the 29 young people who had stayed in the country to testify at the manager's trial were sent back to Guatemala; see Preston, "Former Manager of Kosher Slaughterhouse Is Acquitted of Labor Charges," A13. A few weeks later, the plant manager was sentenced to 27 years in prison for financial fraud charges; see Preston, "27-Year Sentence for Slaughterhouse Manager in Financial Fraud Case," A18.

51. Capps, Chishti, Rodriguez and Rosenblum, "Delegation and Divergence."

52. US Immigration and Customs Enforcement, "Delegation of Immigration Authority Section 287(g) Immigration and Nationality Act."

53. Edwards, Jr. and Vaughan, "The 287(g) Program: Protecting Hometowns and Homeland."

54. Gorman, "Immigrant focus of police is questioned," B5.

55. Archibold, "Report Questions Immigration Program That Uses Local Police," A12.

56. Preston, "Opposing Immigration Program," A13.

57. Edwards, Jr., and Vaughan, "The 287(g) Program."

58. Ibid.

59. Ibid.

60. Phelan, "Crossing the line," 13.

61. Archibold, "U.S. Alters Disputed Program Letting Local Officers Enforce Immigration Law," A9.

62. US Customs and Border Protection, "SBInet: Securing U.S. Borders."

63. Preston, "Officials Split on Viability Of Border-Fence Project," A20.

64. US Government Accountability Office, "SBInet Expenditure Plan Needs to Better Support Oversight and Accountability."

65. Serrano, "Delays, failures trip up high-tech border fence," A1.

66. McCombs, "US to revisit glitch-prone 'virtual fence' set for border."

67. Barry, "Operation Stonegarden's 'Friendly Forces' on the Border."

68. "Operation Stonegarden Fact Sheet," *National Immigration Forum.*

69. Barry, "The Failed Border Security Initiative."

70. Barry, "Operation Stonegarden's 'Friendly Forces.'"

71. McCombs, Brady, "Operation 'Stonegarden' a Euphemism for Cemeteries, is Poorly Supervised Homeland Security Border Program." See also: Schulz, "Texas counties claiming exclusion from security grants cashed in."

72. Kerwin and Meissner, "DHS and Immigration."

73. Lacey and Thompson, "Obama Says Immigration Changes Remain on His Agenda, but for 2010 Enactment," A6.

74. Rotella, "Joint Effort Targets Border Crime;" also, Mazzetti and Thompson, "U.S. Drones Fly Deep in Mexico To Fight Drugs," A1.

75. Preston, "Obama Signs Border Bill to Increase Surveillance," A8.

76. Thompson, "A Shift to Make the Border Safe, From the Inside Out," A12.

77. McKinley, Jr., "Napolitano Focuses on Immigration Enforcement, Not Overhaul," A11.

78. US Department of Homeland Security, "Fact Sheet: Southwest Border: The Way Ahead;" Thompson, "A Shift to Make the Border Safe"; Marosi and Meyer, "Border czar to try to repeat success," A20.

79. Preston, "Staying Tough in Crackdown on Immigrants," A1.

80. "Who's Running Immigration?," A20; "More Immigration Non-Solutions," A16; TRAC, "Federal Criminal Enforcement and Staffing: How Do the Obama and Bush Administrations Compare?"

81. Preston, "Immigrants Are Matched To Crimes," A13. The program's expansion was also roundly criticized, see, for instance, Frosch, "In Colorado, Debate Over Program to Check Immigration History of the Arrested," A12.

82. "Immigration Bait and Switch," A20. The local variation in arrest rates was startling: the national average of Secure Communities deportees without criminal record was 26 percent, but it was 56 percent in Maricopa County, Arizona, and 82 percent in Travis, Texas.

83. Immigration Policy Center, "Secure Communities".

84. See Preston, "Mixed Reviews of Program for Immigrants;" and Preston, "Despite Opposition, Immigration Agency to Expand." Also: DHS Office of Inspector General, "Communication Regarding Participation in Secure Communities;" and DHS Office of Inspector General, "Operations of United States Immigration and Customs Enforcement's Secure Communities."

85. One of Napolitano's first acts was to stop sending families to the T. Don Hutto Residential Center—one of only two such facilities in the country—which had been severely criticized for abusive treatment of children. Hutto was operated by the private Corrections Corporation of America in a former state prison near Austin, TX, under a $2.8 million-per-month federal contract. The 512-bed facility was sued by the ACLU, which documented imprisonment of children for as long as a year, with only one hour of schooling per day and disciplinary threats that included separation from parents. Since legal action, the number of individuals detained at Hutto dropped from 450 to 127. (See Talbot, "The Lost Children," 57; and Bernstein, "U.S. to Overhaul Detention Policy for Immigrants," A1.)

86. Bernstein, "Ideas for Immigrant Detention Include Converting Hotels and Building Models," A16.

87. Ibid.

88. "Salvaging Immigration Detention," A26; Bernstein, "Officials Obscured Truth Of Migrant Deaths in Jail," A1; Bernstein, "Lawsuits Renew Questions on Immigrant Detention," A20.

89. "Immigration Case Backlog Still Growing in FY 2011," *Transactional Records Access Clearinghouse.*

90. Stevens, "Lawless Courts," 18.

91. One immigration attorney complained about being deflected to GEO, a private security firm under contract to the DHS, for answers to his questions concerning public access to hearings concerning a Texas detention center; ibid., 20.

92. Preston, "Immigration Agency Ends Some Deportations," A14.

93. Preston, "In Test of Deportation Policy, 1 in 6 Get a Fresh Look and Reprieve" A11.

94. Associated Press, "Feds ready to build virtual fence along Arizona–Mexico border."

95. Perera, "DHS cancels SBInet;" also, Kephart, "Secure Border Initiative Proves Itself Again;" Kephart, "USA Today Op-ed: Keep SBInet."

96. Lacey, "National Briefing," A14.

97. Gorman and Meyer, "U.S. agents will target bosses over immigrants," A1.

98. Preston, "Illegal Workers Swept From Jobs In 'Silent Raids,'" A1.

99. US Immigration and Customs Enforcement, "Fact Sheet: Updated Facts on ICE's 287(g) Program."

100. In 2009, about two-thirds of the people turned over to ICE through 287(g) were noncriminals. See Bernstein, "Report Critical of Scope and Cost of Immigration Detention," A17.

101. Gorman, "New edict on immigrant arrests," A14.

102. US Immigration and Customs Enforcement, "Fact Sheet: Updated Facts on ICE's 287(g) Program."

103. Archibold, "Report Questions Immigration Program."

104. Archibold, "U.S. Alters Disputed Program."

105. Capps, Chishti, Rodriguez, Rosenblum, "Delegation and Divergence."

106. Gebeloff and Preston, "Unlicensed Drivers Who Risk More Than a Fine," A1.

107. Capps, Chishti, Rodriguez, Rosenblum, "Delegation and Divergence," 4. Commenting on the MPI analysis, the Center for Immigration Studies referred to the MPI as "the Obama administration's pro-amnesty think tank," and claimed that its findings actually proved that 287(g) worked; see Vaughan, "New Report: 287(g) Works."

108. Preston, "Staying Tough in Crackdown on Immigrants," A1.

109. The other program I mentioned, Operation Stonegarden, was incorporated into Napolitano's revamped border security initiative. She allocated $90 million to Stonegarden programs in 2009, over 80 percent of which went to Texas, Arizona, and California. A similar allocation was planned for 2010, although a declining budget was anticipated for later years. The program remained focused

on paying operating expenses (including overtime wages). See US Department of Homeland Security, "Fact Sheet: Southwest Border: The Way Ahead;" and National Immigration Forum "Operation Stonegarden Fact Sheet."

110. Tony Payan drew early attention to the problems of conflating national security and immigration issues with the drug issue. See Payan, *The Three U.S.–Mexico Border Wars.*

111. For example, between 1999 and 2006, the 24 US border counties spent over a billion dollars to process illegal immigrants in the justice system. They claimed that the federal government paid only a fraction of these charges, and even then rarely reimbursed the full amount. See Archibold, "Border Counties Shortchanged In Immigrant Costs, Study Says," A14.

112. Nevins' reference to a "boundary- and immigration-enforcement complex" may be regarded as a proto-BIC. See Nevins, "Security First: The Obama Administration and Immigration 'Reform.'"

113. The text of Eisenhower's speech is available at: coursesa.matrix.msu.edu/~hst306/documents/indust.html

114. The place of the BIC in the current era of mass incarceration in the US is worth fuller attention than is possible in this book. The US has the highest incarceration rate in the world, and the State of Louisiana's rate is more than twice the national average. The State's is a largely private system that has an incentive to keep the numbers high. See Blow, "Plantations, Prisons and Profits," and Gopnik, "The Caging of America." Two devastating critiques of criminal justice and incarceration in the US are: Alexander, *The New Jim Crow*; and Stuntz, *The Collapse of American Criminal Justice.*

CHAPTER 8

1. A concise overview of the war on drugs is Aguilar V. and Castañeda, *El Narco: La Guerra Fallida*; this should be read in conjunction with Aguilar Camín and Castañeda, *Un futuro para México*. In the English-language literature, a somewhat chaotic accumulation of evidence regarding the cartels is Grayson, *Mexico: Narco-Violence and a Failed State?*; see also Campbell, *Drug War Zone.*

2. Schrag, "Blowback at the Border," 23.

3. Beaubien, "As the Drug War Rages On, Will Mexico Surrender?" The point is also made by Grayson, *Mexico.*

4. Fox, Allen, *Revolution of Hope*, 321.

5. Finnegan, "Silver or Lead," 45.

6. Fuentes, *Destiny and Desire*, 381–382.

7. Finnegan, "In the Name of the Law," 71. A similar viewpoint is presented by Campbell, *Drug War Zone*, 271.

8. Finnegan, "Silver or Lead," 44.

9. Ehrenreich, "A Lucrative War," 18.

10. Ibid, 16.
11. Elizondo Elizondo, "Monterrey's habit," WK9.
12. The most comprehensive study is by Wald, *Narcocorrido*. Also see Guillermoprieto, "The Narcovirus," 3–9.
13. Lacey, "For Some Taxi Drivers, A Different Kind of Traffic," A10.
14. Guillermoprieto, "Troubled Spirits," 54–73; and Guillermoprieto, "Days of the Dead," 44–51. For a perspective on cartel penetration in the Catholic church see Cave, "Mexican Church Looks Closer as Its Benefactors," A1.
15. "Suenos y aspiraciones de las Mexicanas."
16. Cave, "A Mexican City's Troubles Reshape Its Families," A1.
17. Meyer, "Petroestado, narcoestado y estado falido," 2.
18. The nightmare situation in Ciudad Juárez has received a great deal of attention—very often sensationalistic and lurid—from fiction and non-fiction writers, including Bolaño, *2066*; and Bowden, *Murder City*. A more measured account is by Campbell, *Drug War Zone*.
19. Guillermoprieto, "The Murders of Mexico," 47. For comparison, the murder rate in Mexico City is 8 per 100,000 inhabitants, comparable to Wichita, Kansas, or Stockton, California, but still twice the national average in the US.
20. Vulliamy, "As Juárez Falls," 42.
21. Rodriguez, The Daughters of Juárez, ch. 9.
22. Cave, "Wave of Violence Swallows more Women in Juárez." Even though so much remains unresolved in Juárez, the murders attracted national attention in Mexico as well as international protests. For a perspective that considers femicide and drug wars together, see González Rodríguez, *The Femicide Machine*.
23. Vulliamy, "As Juárez Falls," 42.
24. Quoted in Guillermoprieto, "The Murders of Mexico," 48.
25. Padgett and Grillo, "Mexico's Meth Warriors," 30–33.
26. Finnegan, "Silver or Lead," 48–50.
27. Archibold, "Bit by Bit, a Mexican Police Force Is Eradicated," A1.
28. Comisión Latinoamericana sobre Drogas y Democracia, "Drogas y democracia: hacia un cambio de paradigma." Also: Statement by the Latin American Commission on Drugs and Democracy, "Drugs and Democracy: Toward a Paradigm Shift."
29. Sicilla, "Carta abierta a políticos y criminales."
30. Krauze, "Can this poet save Mexico?" SR-6.
31. This kind of desperation might explain why people of Guatemala are willing to contemplate voting for the return of a detested military strongman from an earlier repressive regime. See Cave, "Former General to Face A Runoff in Guatemala," A6.
32. The search for solutions led, for instance, to a plea to establish a unified national police command, essentially doing away with about 2,200 local police departments, but many localities balked at the recentralization of police authority. See Archibold, "Mexico Seeking Unified Police," A1.
33. Lawson, "The Making of a Narco State," 88.

34. Elizondo Elizondo, "Monterrey's Habit," WK9.

35. This is in contrast to so many European nations, where greater degrees of permissiveness are reported; see "Drugs: Virtually Legal," 70–71. For a statement in favor of legalization, see Perkinson, "Drug of Choice," 21.

36. Krauze, "The Mexican Evolution."

37. Longmire, "Legalization Won't Kill The Cartels," WK10.

38. Longmire, "Legalization Won't Kill The Cartels," WK10; Guillermoprieto, "Mexico's Widening War," WK9; Meyer, "Cartels snatch coyote trade," A1.

39. "U.S. Says Refineries Bought Oil Smuggled From Mexico," B7; Baker and Joly, "Illicit Money: Can It Be Stopped?" 61–64; and Bajak, "Prepaid cards are magnets for drug-money laundering," 6A. These trends should be understood as part of a widespread network of transnational crime: Farer, *Transnational Crime in the Americas*; and Andreas, *Border Games: Policing the U.S.–Mexico Divide*. Peter Schrag makes clear that drugs still form a major source of cartel incomes: "If marijuana were treated like alcohol or tobacco, the largest revenue sources of Mexican gangs would dry up." See Schrag, "Blowback at the Border," 24.

40. Guillermoprieto, "The Murders of Mexico," 47.

41. Lawson, "The Making of a Narco State," 61.

42. Tijuana-based writer Heriberto Yepez supported a ban: "*Narcocorridos* are war propaganda," he wrote. "Drug dealers reinforce their role-model status thanks to the music that portrays them as heroes. With no positive role models around and plenty of misery, cartel music is exactly what we don't need on our streets." Jorge Castañeda, former minister in the administration of Vicente Fox, criticized *corrido* bans: "You cannot blame *narcocorridos* for drug violence. Drug violence is to blame for *narcocorridos*." See Kun, "Minstrels in the Court of the Kingpin," 22.

43. Finnegan, "In the Name of the Law."

44. Ibid. Similar arguments are made for other cities/plazas; see Ehrenreich, "A Lucrative War," 18 and Vulliamy, "As Juárez Falls," 44.

45. Finnegan, "In the Name of the Law," 65.

46. Archibold, "Tijuana Killings Erode Image of a City Recovering From Past Woes," A11.

47. Campbell, *Drug War Zone*. Also see Vulliamy, *Amexica*.

48. Finnegan, "Silver or Lead," 46.

49. McKinley, Jr., "U.S. Stymied as Guns Flow to Mexican Cartels." The "iron river" theme is becoming a feature in popular fiction, e.g. Parker, *Iron River*.

50. Such was the fate of, for instance, a regulation requiring arms dealers to report multiple sales of semiautomatic rifles; see Savage, "New Reporting Rules on Multiple Sales of Guns," A13; and Savage, "N.R.A. Sues Over Rule," A15.

51. Krauze, "In Mexico, a War Every Century," A25; also Aguilar and Castañeda, *El Narco*.

52. See, for example: Lacey and Malkin, "Mexican Arrested in Killing of U.S. Consular Employee," A6; McKinley Jr., "On the Border, a Fishing Paradise Gains a Deadly Reputation," A14; and McKinley, Jr., "Killing of Missionary Rattles Texas Border," A11.

53. "The Reach of Mexico's Drug Cartels;" Serrano and Quinones, "No Longer 'Next Door", A1, A30. The flagrant sensationalizing of such trends by the media concealed the fact that violent crime in Arizona actually declined in recent years (even though the state's rate of crimes against property increased, it later fell again); see Archibold, "In Border Violence, Perception Is Greater Than Crime Statistics," 16.

54. Thompson, "U.S. widens its role in battle;" Mazetti and Thompson, "U.S. widens role in Mexican fight."

55. Aguilar and Castañeda, *El Narco*, 79–81. See also Astorga, *Seguridad, Traficantes y Militares: El poder y la sombra.*

56. Aguilar and Castañeda, *El Narco*, 79.

57. Starr, quoted in Lawson, "The War Next Door: As Drug Cartels Battle the Government, Mexico Descends into Chaos," 111.

58. McCaffrey, quoted in Lawson, "The Making of a Narco State," 61.

59. Ibid.

60. Draper concludes that only its own people can decide if a state has failed or not: "If their eyes say 'we have been deserted,' the verdict has been rendered." See Draper, "Shattered Somalia," 98.

61. Ehrenreich, "A Lucrative War," 18.

62. See "The Failed States Index 2010."

63. For the closing gap between the US and Mexican inequality score: "Gini Coefficient: An Indicator of Income Inequality;" and for a quick guide to comparative international figures on inequality: "List of countries by income equality."

64. See "Corruption Perceptions Index 2010."

65. On the press freedom index, see "Europe falls from its pedestal, no respite in the dictatorships."

66. "Getting Away With Murder."

67. The two other categories used in the DI were "hybrid regimes," and "authoritarian regimes."

68. "Democracy Index 2010: A report from the Economist Intelligence Unit."

69. Guillermoprieto, "The Murders of Mexico," 48.

70. Finnegan, "Silver or Lead," 39.

71. Krauze, "The Mexican Evolution," A25.

72. During a 2010 visit to Berkeley and not in the mood to celebrate independence or the Revolution, Lorenzo Meyer said: "Mexico began independence as a failed state and continued that way until the 1880s;" quoted in Novaes and Frenk, "Limited Independence, Limited Democracy," 58. Online editor Raymundo Riva Palacio is also unequivocal that contemporary Mexicans "have a failed state;" see Palacio, "Mission to Mexico," A31.

73. The Economist, "The Discontents of Progress."

74. Novaes and Frenk. "Limited Independence, Limited Democracy," 60.

75. Dresser, "Why Mexico Is Sick." Also see "Testimony of Denise Dresser."

76. Dresser, "Carta abierta a Carlos Slim."

77. Sorkin, "Dealbook; The Mystery of Jobs's Giving." On Slim's wealth, see Hawley, "The richest man you've never heard of."

78. Wright, "Slim's Time," 52–67; Preston, "Carlos Slim Is Skeptical About Philanthropy." Slim has established two philanthropies, Fundación Telmex and Fundación Carlos Slim, both focused on children.

79. Rohter, "The Crisis Came. Mexico Didn't Fail. Surprised?" WK3.

80. In this section, I draw heavily on two fundamental English-language sources: Preston and Dillon, *Opening Mexico: The Making of a Democracy*, 5, 407; and Riding, *Distant Neighbors: A Portrait of the Mexicans*. The latter covers the period up to the mid-1980s; the former continues to the story up to the Fox presidency. For an alternative history of Mexico as a case of underdevelopment, see Ruiz, *Mexico: Why a few are rich and the people poor*.

81. On PRI monolith, see Riding, *Distant Neighbors*, ch. 4.

82. Preston and Dillon, *Opening Mexico*, 501.

83. Ibid., 69.

84. Ibid., 79.

85. Ibid., 379.

86. Ibid., 95–97.

87. Ibid., 113–114.

88. Ibid., 117.

89. Riding, *Distant Neighbors*, 108–112.

90. See Ibid., ch. 7, on the aftermath of the post-1982 economic crisis.

91. Preston and Dillon, *Opening Mexico*, 127.

92. Ibid., 122–139.

93. Ibid., 149–150, 170–174, 179–180.

94. Ruiz, *Mexico*, ch. 9.

95. Preston and Dillon, *Opening Mexico*, 199–203. Also Cárdenas, "The Promise and Legacy of the Mexican Revolution," 55.

96. Preston and Dillon, *Opening Mexico*, 219–222.

97. A scathing critique of NAFTA's impact in Mexico is to be found in Ruiz, *Mexico*, ch. 10. Also see Warnock, *The Other Mexico: The North American Triangle Completed*.

98. Preston and Dillon, *Opening Mexico*, 230–231.

99. Ibid., 248–249.

100. Ibid., 258, 260–261.

101. Edwards, *Left Behind: Latin America and the False Promise of Populism*, ch. 6, outlines the depth of the economic crisis bequeathed to Zedillo by Salinas.

102. Preston and Dillon, *Opening Mexico*, 233–238, 314.

103. Ibid., 304–320.

104. Ruiz, *Mexico*, 195–197.

105. Preston and Dillon, *Opening Mexico*, 275–279.

106. Ibid., 291–298.

107. Ibid., 299.

108. Ibid., 405–406, 414, 426.

109. Ibid., 465–466.

110. Some aspects of these maquila-related adjustments are examined in Cravey, *Women and Work in Mexico's Maquiladoras.*

111. Preston and Dillon, *Opening Mexico,* 473–476.

112. Ibid., 483–492.

113. Ibid., 500–501.

114. The best documentary history of the 1910–2010 period is Aguaya Quezada, *La Transición en México: una historia documental 1910–2010.* A standard Mexican narrative history is that by Aguilar Camín and Meyer, *In the Shadow of the Mexican Revolution: Contemporary Mexican History, 1910–1989.*

115. Preston and Dillon, *Opening Mexico,* 503–515.

116. In 1985 Alan Riding's influential account of modern-day Mexico reported that many foreigners talk about the "inevitability of a new revolution" in Mexico due to the wide gap between rich and poor, but also reminded us of the resilience of the country's political system. See Riding, *Distant Neighbors,* 364.

117. Ibid., 516–517.

118. As soon as he was elected, Mexico's new president, Enrique Peña Nieto, wrote in the *New York Times:* "I would welcome the implementation of comprehensive immigration reform in the United States." See Peña Nieto, "Mexico's Next Chapter." All candidates in the presidential election called for the withdrawal of the military from the cartel wars; see Beith, "Generals in their Labyrinths," 28. For a critical assessment of the continuing challenges in Mexico's democracy, see Aguaya Quezada, *Vuelta en U: Guía para entender y reactivar la democracia estancada.*

119. Astorga, quoted in Lawson, "The War Next Door," 110. A key source on Mexican drug trafficking is Astorga, *Seguridad, Traficantes y Militares: El poder y la sombra.*

120. Hernández, *Los señores del narco.* An English-language review of this book is by Wood, "Silver and Lead."

121. If a new collusive "peace" returns, it will mark neither the achievement of a failed state, nor an indication of the Mexican state's "failure." I propose to retire the concept of a failed state from discussions about Mexico.

122. Hernández, *Los señores del narco.*

123. Ehrenreich, "A Lucrative War," 18.

124. Finnegan, "The Kingpin," 48.

125. Steinberg, "The Monster and Monterrey," 27–33.

CHAPTER 9

1. Quoted in Lacey, "Lost at the Border," 3.

2. Nuñez-Neto and Kim, "CRS Report for Congress, Border Security: Barriers Along the U.S. International Border."

3. Mangan, "Texas Colleges Argue That a Border Fence Would Divide a Community," A24.
4. Campo-Flores and Murr, "Brownsville's Bad Lie," 40.
5. Casares, "Crossing the Border Without Losing Your Past," A29.
6. Kun, "Born in America, Heart in Mexico," Music 20.
7. Ibid.
8. Eriksson and Taylor, "The Environmental Impacts of the Border Wall."
9. Barry, "A Natural Treasure That May End Up Without a Country," A14.
10. Benavides et al., "Obstructing Human Rights: The Texas–Mexico Border Wall."
11. Gilman, "Background and Context," 2.
12. Nedderman, Dulitzky and Gilman, "Violations on the Part of the United States Government of the Right to Property and Non-Discrimination Held by Residents of the Texas Rio Grande Valley," 7.
13. Ibid., 12–13.
14. Wilson, et al., "An analysis of demographic disparities associated with the proposed U.S.–Mexico border fence in Cameron County, Texas."
15. Guzman and Hurwitz, "Violations on the Part of the United States Government of Indigenous Rights Held by Members of the Lipan Apache, Kickapoo, and Ysleta del Sur Tigua Tribes of the Texas–Mexico Border."
16. See Jimenez, "Humanitarian Crisis: Migrant Deaths at the U.S.–Mexico Border;" and Bustamante, *Report of the Special Rapporteur on the human rights of migrants.*
17. James, "Aware of Its Dependence, Napa Takes Care of Migrant Workers," A23.
18. Hondagneu-Sotelo, *God's Heart has no Borders.*
19. Vanderpool, "Border Brush."
20. Ibid.
21. Vanderpool, "The Activist Question"
22. Ibid.
23. Ibid.
24. Ibid.
25. McCombs, "$7.2M added for AZ cops' border efforts."
26. Vanderpool, "The Activist Question."
27. Preston, "Fueled by Anger Over Arizona Law, Immigration Advocated Rally for Change," 13.
28. Preston, "After a False Dawn, Anxiety for Illegal Immigrant Students," A15.
29. "Dreaming of Reform," *New York Times*, A16.
30. "A Sensible Path in California," *New York Times*, A22.
31. Vargas, "Outlaw: My life in America as an undocumented immigrant," 22. Also Jones, "Coming out Illegal."
32. Berger, "An Undocumented Princetonian," 28.
33. This program was warmly received in US Latino communities, but it has been slow to make an impact, and is applied unevenly across the country. See Preston, "In Test of Deportation Policy, A11–12.

34. Tobar, "Mexico's immigrant sanctuary: The mayor of Ecatepec says those on their way north illegally are safe and welcome in his city," A5.

35. Johnson, "Unreal Ordeal."

36. Marosi, "Deported immigration activist is toast of Tijuana," B9.

37. Archibold, "Despite Violence, Mexico Plants Hum at Border," A1.

38. Applebaum, "U.S. and Mexico Sign Trucking Deal," B1.

39. Malkin, "Mexicans Miss Money from Relatives Up North," A1.

40. Mendoza, "US businesses reluctant to open in Mexico."

41. Medina, "Economic Downturn Holds Fierce Grip on Border Town," A20.

42. Mendoza, "US businesses reluctant to open in Mexico."

43. Dougherty, "Crossings From Mexico, Legally, With Money," B1; Hsu, "Speaking the shopping language of immigrants," C1; Gorney, "How do you say 'Got Milk' en Español?," 58.

44. "Border Crossing/Entry Data: Query Detailed Statistics," *Research and Innovative Technology Administration, Bureau of Transportation Statistics*. Texas crossings showed increases in truck and rail traffic during the years 2009–2010 in both directions across the border. However, the number of non-truck crossings (including personal vehicles) fell by about 17 percent in both directions during the same period. The number of pedestrians crossing to the north increased by 6 percent, and to the south declined by 10 percent. "Border Trade Vehicle Crossings."

45. Cave, "Better Lives for Mexicans Cut Allure of Going North," A1.

46. Since the early 2000s, the influx of unauthorized immigrants fell significantly by about two-thirds. In the early part of the decade, about 850,000 migrants entered each year; but by the decade's end, the inflow averaged 300,000 per year. The Pew Research Center judged this to be the first significant reversal in the growth of this population over the past two decades. In addition, the numbers of undocumented migrants returning home from the US more than doubled since the decade began. As a consequence, the population of unauthorized migrants in the US fell from its 2007 peak of 12.5 million people to about 11 million. See "Border News."

47. Ibid.

48. These data are from the Mexican Migration Project; see Castañeda and Massey, "Do-It-Yourself Immigration Reform," A19.

49. Burridge, "Differential Criminalization under Operation Streamline," 81.

50. Amón, "'Life After Death' in Tecate, Baja California: Re-Humanizing Criminal Deportees."

51. Valenzuela, *Paso del Norte: This is Tijuana!*

52. Kun, "Master of a New Tijuana," D6.

53. Iglesias Prieto, *Emergencias: Las artes visuales en Tijuana.*; Sánchez and Garza, *InSite 2000–2001/Fugitive Sites*. Ochoa Palacio, *"Notas sobre el desarollo cultural de Tijuana."*

54. Johnson, "A new direction south of the border," E28.

55. Walker, "The Cultural Economy of a Border Renaissance: Politics and Practices in the City," 185–200.

56. Berelowitz, "The spaces of home in Chicano and Latino representations of the San Diego-Tijuana Borderlands," 323–350.

57. Johnson, "A new direction south of the border," E30.

58. Downes, "American Stories, From Mexican Roots," A36.

59. Archibold, "Despite Violence, Mexico Plants Hum at Border," A1.

60. Roebuck, "Mayors decry 'culture of fear' on border."

61. Armendariz, "Border influences Brownsville economies."

62. "The History of Charro Days," *Charro Days Fiesta*.; and "Hands across borders ceremony unites sister cities."

63. Armendariz, "Parade wraps up Charro Days in style."

64. Archibold, "Arizona Seeing Signs of Flight by Immigrants," A13.

65. "Immigration Ground Zero," A20.

66. "Blazing Arizona," A30.

67. Howley, "The One-Man Wall," 34–44.

68. Vanderpool, "Eye of the Storm."

69. McCombs, "No Sign of Letup in Border Deaths."

70. Vanderpool, "Eye of the Storm."

71. Scarpinato, "Problems of Border: The Focus is Shifting." For an alternative view on crime statistics, see Arana, "The Border Violence Myth."

72. Vanderpool, "Eye of the Storm."

73. Ibid.

74. Martínez, "Don't Fence Them in," A17.

75. McCombs, "'Deadliest migrant trail in U.S.' is right on Tucson's doorstep."

76. Eckholm, "In Drug War, Tribe Feels Invaded by Both Sides," A1.

77. In 2009 the San Xavier district (one of eleven in the Nation) proposed opening a 750-bed immigrant detention facility in its district, to be operated by an outside agency. See Pedersen, "O'odham hope to build prison near Sahuarita."

78. McCombs, "O'odham increasingly drawn to drug smuggling for money."

79. Finnegan, "Sheriff Joe," 50.

80. Howley, "The One-Man Wall," 34–44.

81. Umali, "The Devil to Pay: the relationship between Arizona and the CCA."

82. Ibid.

83. "The Constitution Trumps Arizona," A20.

84. Downes, "The Hunt for American Decency in the Arizona Quicksand," A18.

85. Archibold, "Arizona Enacts Stringent Law on Immigration," A1.

86. Lacey, "Injunction on Arizona is Upheld," A12. Status of this appeal is unclear since Pearce's recall.

87. Liptak, "Court Splits Immigration Law Verdicts," A1.

88. Cathcart, "Los Angeles Archbishop to Lead a Rally Against the Arizona Measure," A9.

89. Witz, "'Los Suns' Join Protest of Arizona's New Law," B13. Also: "Los Suns."

90. Davey and Schmidt, "Immigration Activists Take Arizona Protest Out to the Ballgame," A12.

91. In addition, the players' union pointedly noted that half the 30 major ball clubs usually held their spring training in Arizona. Schmidt, "Ballplayers Join Protest of New Law," A9.

92. Preston, "Latino Groups Urge Arizona Boycott Over Immigration Law," A14.

93. Archibold, "In Wake of Immigration Law, Calls for an Economic Boycott of Arizona," A13.

94. Lacey, "Taking Their Fight on Illegal Immigrants To The Arizona Border," A9.

95. "Mexico Warns Citizens."

96. McKinley and Wollan, "New Border Fear: Violence by a Rogue Militia," A1.

97. Archibold, "Ranchers Alarmed By Killing," A9.

98. Medina, "The Sheriff of Tucson."

99. Steinhauer, "A Harsh Spotlight on a State's Unique Politics," A13; and Archibold, "Arizona's Attempt to Bolster Local Immigration Authority."

100. McKinley, "An Arizona Morgue Grows Crowded," A14.

101. Dever, "Abandoned on the Border," A25.

102. Ibid.

103. Kobach, "Why Arizona Drew a Line," A31.

104. Hulse and Herszenhorn, "Democrats Detail Immigration Plan In Plea to G.O.P," A12.

105. Preston, "Democrats Reframe the Debate on Immigration," A1.

106. Hulse and Herszenhorn, "Democrats Detail Immigration Plan In Plea to G.O.P.," A12.

107. Carr, "A Star Turn for a Sheriff On Fox TV," B1.

108. "Immigration, Outsourced," A26.

109. Carr, "A Star Turn for a Sheriff On Fox TV," B1.

110. Finnegan, "Sheriff Joe," 47.

111. Archibold, "Challenges To a Sheriff Both Popular and Reviled," 14.

112. Archibold, "Immigration Hard-Liner Has His Wings Clipped," A13; and Friedman, "Nativism vs. Security."

113. Finnegan, "Sheriff Joe," 45.

114. Robbins, "'America's Toughest Sheriff' Takes on Immigration."

115. Archibold, "Challenges to a Sheriff Both Popular and Reviled."

116. Stelzer, "The Selma of Immigration Rights," 35–38; also Giblin, "Arizona Sheriff Conducts Immigration Raid."

117. Riccardi, "Sheriff riding out of town," A8.

118. Finnegan, "Sheriff Joe," 45.

119. These problems were uncovered by two local journalists who won a 2009 Pulitzer prize for their reporting on the Maricopa County sheriff's department; Ibid., 49. Also see "Journalists who Revealed."

120. Downes, "In Arapaio's Arizona, They Fought Back," SR10; Archibold, "Challenges To a Sheriff Both Popular and Reviled."; Finnegan, "Sheriff Joe"; "Crackdown on Immigrants Draws Protests in Phoenix," A17.

121. As president of the Arizona legislature, Pearce continued to stuff its agenda with nativist bills. He promoted laws that would deny citizenship to babies born in Arizona whose parents could not prove their legal status (so-called "anchor babies"), "Another Bad Idea From Arizona," WK7; Lacey, "On Immigration Birthright Right"; and Templeton, "Baby Baiting." Arizona also moved to bar presidential candidates from appearing on ballots unless they first proved they were native-born Americans, a spin-off from an absurdist campaign to question President Obama's citizenship, "Memo to Arizona Republicans: Papers, Please," A20. In January 2011, a new state law banned school classes that "promote resentment toward a race or class of people," or "advocate ethnic solidarity instead of treatment of pupils as individuals." Newly-elected State Attorney General Tom Horne, the law's author, promptly declared illegal the Tucson Unified School District's Mexican-American program; "Arizona, in the Classroom," A20. The District's programs for black, Asian, and American Indians were left in place ostensibly because no complaints had been received about them; Lacey, "Citing 'Brainwashing' Arizona Declares a Latino Class Illegal," A1.

122. "Arizona Flinches," A22; Oppel Jr., "Arizona, Bowing to Business, Softens Stand on Immigration," A1.

123. "Angry Arizona, Again," WK7.

124. "Arizona Flinches," A22.

125. Other Arizona recall targets included Governor Jan Brewer, who had transformed herself into a defender of SB1070. Lacey, "Immigration Law Backer Faces Recall," A16.

126. Lacey, "Justice Dept. Sues Sheriff Over Bias Investigation," A11.

127. "Arizona: County Says Its Sheriff Spent $99 Million Inappropriately," A16.

128. Sanneh, "Raging Arizona:" and Santos, "Arizona Sheriff's Trial Begins," A11.

129. Preston, "Justices' Decision a Narrow Opening," A12.

130. The differences between the two cities are discussed in Barry, "Border Towns across Rio."

131. Martinez-Cabrera, "Flight Brings Plight," 1A; McKinley, "Fleeing Extreme Drug Violence, Mexican Families Pour into U.S.," 1.

132. Martinez-Cabrera, "Flight Brings Plight," 1A. The city's population grew by 21 percent between 1990 and 1995, but only by 7 percent between 2000 and 2005. In 2005, there were just over 70,000 unoccupied buildings in Juárez; but by 2011, that number reached over 110,000 (or 24 percent of all private homes in the city).

133. Archibold, "Despite Violence, Mexico Plants Hum at Border," A1.

134. Schladen, "Mayor Lauds Development," 1B.

135. Malkin and Thompson, "In Mexico, Official Promises Do Little to Ease a Stricken City's Pain," A6.

136. Martinez-Cabrera, "Juárez to add 'heroic' to name," 1A; Martinez-Cabrera, "Calderon highlights successes in Juárez," 1A.
137. Martinez-Cabrera, "Calderon highlights successes in Juárez."
138. One example of the kind of "victory" governments hope for is an ambitious residential development, planned for San Augustin, just a few miles southeast of Juárez. San Augustin is located along the Juárez–El Porvenir highway that connects Juárez to a string of riverside communities. Its population fluctuates between 1,500 and 2,000. It is an agricultural settlement known for its charming regional museum and community cohesiveness. A Mexican company (Industrial Global Solutions) is spearheading the project with funding through Prudential Real Estate Investors. The megaproject (planned for 100,000 new residents) is located 6 miles from the new port of entry (PoE) at the Tomillo–Guadalupe international bridge project. Longtime San Augustin residents are fearful of the impact of the new development on their way of life, but equally concerned that they may end up with a failed or unfinished housing project on their doorstep. See Valdez, "$400M development planned for area around San Agustin," 1A.
139. Cave, "A Crime Fighter draws Plaudits, and Scrutiny," A10.
140. McKinley, "Fleeing Extreme Drug Violence, Mexican Families Pour into U.S.," 1.
141. Roberts, "Turmoil in Hudspeth," 1A.
142. McKinley, "Fleeing Extreme Drug Violence, Mexican Families Pour into U.S."
143. Schladen, "Mayor Lauds Development," 1B.
144. Pullen, "Rubin Center exhibits look at border in very different ways," 3F.
145. Zabludovsky, "Slivers of Hope amid the Melancholy," A7.
146. Cave, "Angels Rushing In Where Others Fear to Tread," A8.
147. Zabludovsky, "Slivers of Hope amid the Melancholy," A7.
148. Powell, "Team of Hope, Gone in City of Violence," B15.
149. Kun, "Death Rattle."

Bibliography

"A Sensible Path in California: New laws uphold immigrants' rights and sound governing." October 17, 2011. *New York Times*, A22.

Adams, William L., and Anthony K. Knopp. *Portrait of a Border City: Brownsville, Texas*. Austin: Eakin Press, 1997.

Adelman, Jeremy, and Stephan Aron. "From Borderlands to Borders: Empires, Nation–States, and the Peoples in between in North American History." *The American Historical Review* 104/3 (1999): 814–841.

Adler, Rudy, Victoria Criado and Brett Huneycutt, eds. *Border Film Project: Photos by Migrants & Minutemen on the U.S.–Mexico Border*. New York: Harry N. Abrams, 2007.

Adovasio, James M., and Jake Page. *The First Americans: In Pursuit of Archaeology's Greatest Mystery*. New York: The Modern Library, 2003.

Aguayo Quezada, Sergio. *La transición en México: una historia documental 1910–2010*. México D.F.: El Colegio de México/Fondo de Cultura Económica, 2010.

Aguayo Quezada, Sergio. *Vuelta en U: Guía para entender y reactivar la democracia estancada*. México D.F.: Taurus, 2010.

Aguilar Camín, Héctor, and Jorge G. Castañeda. *Un futuro para Mexico*. Mexico, D. F.: Punto de Lectura, 2009.

Aguilar Camín, Héctor, and Lorenzo Meyer. *In the Shadow of the Mexican Revolution: Contemporary Mexican History, 1910–1989*. Austin: University of Texas Press, 1993.

Aguilar V., Rubén, and Jorge G. Castañeda. *El Narco: La Guerra Fallida*. Mexico, D.F.: Punto de Lectura, 2009.

Alegría, Tito. "The Cross-border Metropolis Fallacy." PhD Dissertation. University of Southern California, 2006.

Alexander, Michelle. *The New Jim Crow: Mass Incarceration in the Age of Colorblindness*. New York: The New Press, 2012.

Alonzo-Zaldivar, Ricardo. "U.S., Mexico OK Deportation by Air." June 9, 2004. *Los Angeles Times*, A11.

Alvarez de Williams, Anita. *Primeros Pobladores de la Baja California: Introducción a la Antropología de la Península*. Mexicali: Centro INAH de Baja California, 2004.

Alvarez Jr., Robert R. "The Mexican–U.S. Border: The Making of an Anthropology of Borderlands." *Annual Review of Anthropology* **24** (1995): 447–470.

Amón, Benny. "Life After Death in Tecate, Baja California: Re-Humanizing Criminal Deportees." University of California, Berkeley. Department of City & Regional Planning. December 7, 2010.

Anaya, Rudolfo A., and Francisco A. Lomeli, eds. *Aztlán: Essays on the Chicano Homeland.* Albuquerque: El Norte Publications, 1989.

Anaya, Rudolfo A., and Francisco A. Lomeli, eds. *Aztlán: Essays on the Chicano Homeland.* Albuquerque: University of New Mexico Press, 1991.

Anderson, Benedict. *Imagined Communities: Reflections on the Origin of Nationalism.* Brooklyn: Verso Books, 1993.

Anderson, Gary Clayton. *The Conquest of Texas: Ethnic Cleansing in the Promised Land, 1820–1875.* Norman: University of Oklahoma Press, 2005.

Anderson, Joan B., and James Gerber. *Fifty Years of Change on the U.S.—Mexico Border: Growth, Development, and Quality of Life.* Austin: University of Texas Press, 2008.

Andreas, Peter. *Border Games: Policing the U.S.–Mexico Divide.* Ithaca: Cornell University Press, 2000.

"Another Bad Idea From Arizona," June 20, 2010. New York Times, WK–7.

Anzaldúa, Gloria. *Borderlands: La Frontera: The New Mestiza.* San Francisco: Aunt Lute Books, 1987.

Appendini, Manuel. "Promuven neonazis exterminio de cholos." *Reforma* **22** (April 2005): 14A.

Applebaum, Binyamin. "U.S. and Mexico Sign Trucking Deal." July 7, 2011. *New York Times*, B1.

Arana, Gabriel. "The Border Violence Myth." May 27, 2009. *The Nation.* Available: http://www.thenation.com/article/border-violence-myth. January 13, 2012.

Archibold, Randal C. "Arizona Seeing Signs of Flight by Immigrants." February 12, 2008. *New York Times*, A13.

Archibold, Randal C. "Challenges To a Sheriff Both Popular and Reviled." September 28, 2008. *New York Times*, 14.

Archibold, Randal C. "Border Counties Shortchanged in Immigrant Costs, Study Says." March 6, 2009. *New York Times*, A14.

Archibold, Randal C. "Immigration Hard-Liner Has His Wings Clipped." October 7, 2009. *New York Times*, A13.

Archibold, Randal C. "Immigration Officials Arrest 300 in California." December 12, 2009. *New York Times*, A10.

Archibold, Randal C. "Report Questions Immigration Program that Uses Local Police." March 4, 2009. *New York Times*, A12.

Archibold, Randal C. "U.S. Alters Disputed Program Letting Local Officers Enforce Immigration Law." October 17, 2009. *New York Times*, A9.

Archibold, Randal C. "Arizona's Effort to Bolster Local Immigration Authority Divides Law Enforcement." April 22, 2010. *New York Times*, A16.

Archibold, Randal C. "Arizona Enacts Stringent Law on Immigration." April 24, 2010. *New York Times*, A1.

Archibold, Randal C. "In Border Violence, Perception Is Greater Than Crime Statistics." June 20, 2010. *New York Times*, 16.

Archibold, Randal C. "In Wake of Immigration Law, Calls for an Economic Boycott of Arizona." April 27, 2010. *New York Times*, A13.

Archibold, Randal C. "Mexico Seeking Unified Police." October 2, 2010. *New York Times*, A1, A6.

Archibold, Randal C. "Ranchers Alarmed By Killing." April 5, 2010. *New York Times*, A9.

Archibold, Randal C. "Tijuana Killings Erode Image of a City Recovering From Past Woes." October 26, 2010. *New York Times*, A11.

Archibold, Randal C. "Bit by Bit, a Mexican Police Force Is Eradicated." January 12, 2011. *New York Times*, A1, A8.

Archibold, Randal C. "Despite Violence, Mexico Plants Hum at Border." July 11, 2011. *New York Times*, A1.

"Another Bad Idea From Arizona," June 20, 2010. *New York Times*, WK7.

"Arizona: County Says Its Sheriff Spent $99 Million Inappropriately." April 14, 2011. *New York Times*, A16.

"Arizona Flinches." March 21, 2011. *New York Times*, A22.

"Arizona, in the Classroom." January 17, 2011. *New York Times*, A20.

Armendariz, Jacqueline. "Border Influences Brownsville Economics." *The Brownsville Herald*. July 2, 2011. Available: http://www.brownsvilleherald.com/news/border-128407-brownsville-expensive.html. January 13, 2012.

Armendariz, Jacqueline. "Parade wraps up Charro Days in style." *The Brownsville Herald*. February 26, 2011. Available: http://www.brownsvilleherald.com/articles/days-123296-charro-style.html. January 13, 2012.

"Army Crosses into Mexico," *Santa Fe New Mexican*. March 15, 1916. Facsimile.

Arreola, Daniel D., and James R Curtis. *The Mexican Border Cities: Landscape Anatomy and Place Personality*. Tucson: The University of Arizona Press, 1993.

Associated Press. "Feds Ready to Build Virtual Fence along Arizona–Mexico Border." May 7, 2009. *AZCentral*. Available: http://www.azcentral.com/news/articles/2009/05/07/20090507virtual-fence0507-ON.html. December 26, 2011.

Associated Press. "Mexico's Net Migration Down 50%." February 20, 2009. *Los Angeles Times*, A9.

Astorga, Luis. *Seguridad, Traficantes y Militares: El poder y la sombra*. Mexico, D. F.: Tusquets Editores, 2007.

Audley, John J. et al., "NAFTA's Promise and Reality: Lessons from Mexico for the Hemisphere." Carnegie Endowment for International Peace. 2004. Available. www.carnegieendowment.org/files/nafta1.pdf. December 8, 2011.

Bacon, David. *The Children of Nafta: Labor Wars on the U.S. Mexico Border*. Berkeley: University of California Press, 2004.

Bajak, Frank. "Prepaid Cards Are Magnets for Drug-Money Laundering." May 23, 2011. *El Paso Times*, 6A.

Baker, Raymond, and Eva Joly. "Illicit Money: Can It Be Stopped?" December 3, 2009. *The New York Review of Books*, 61–64.

Balderrama Francisco E. and Raymond Rodríguez. *Decade of Betrayal: Mexican Repatriation in the 1930s*. Albuquerque: University of New Mexico Press, 1995.

Baldwin, Neil. *Legends of the Plumed Serpent: Biography of a Mexican God*. New York: PublicAffairs, 1998.

Ballinas, Victor, and Andrea Becerril. "Establece el Senado protección para niños indocumentados deportados." April 22, 2005. *La Journada*, 49.

Barry, Dan. "A Natural Treasure That May End Up Without a Country." April 7, 2008. *New York Times*, A14.

Barry, Dan. "Border Towns Across Rio, Worlds Apart in Drug War." February 14, 2010. *New York Times*, 17.

Barry, Tom. "Operation Stonegarden's 'Friendly Forces' on the Border." April 21, 2009. *Border Lines*. Available: http://borderlinesblog.blogspot.com/2009/04/operation-stonegardens-friendly-forces.html. December 26, 2011.

Barry, Tom. "The Failed Border Security Initiative." April 21, 2009. *Americas Program*. Available: http://www.cipamericas.org/archives/1682. December 26, 2011.

Barry, Tom. *Border Wars*. Cambridge: MIT Press, 2011.

Bartlett, John R. *Personal Narrative of Explorations and Incidents in Texas, New Mexico, California, Sonora, and Chihuahua*. 2 vols. 1854. Reprint. Chicago: The Rio Grande Press, 1965.

Batalova, Jeanne, Marlene Lee, Mark Mather, and Michelle Mittelstadt. *Immigration: Data Matters*. Washington, DC: Migration Policy Institute and Population Reference Bureau, 2008.

Baum, Dan. "The Man Who Says Keep Out." March 17, 2004. *Los Angeles Times Magazine*, 9–17.

Beaubien, Jason. "As The Drug War Rages On, Will Mexico Surrender?" August 6, 2010. National Public Radio. Available: http://www.npr.org/templates/story/story.php?storyId=129009629. October 25, 2011.

Beebe, Rose M. and Robert M. Senkewicz, eds. *Lands of Promise and Despair: Chronicles of Early California, 1535–1846*. Berkeley: Heyday Books, 2001.

Beezley, William H. *Mexico in World History*. Oxford: Oxford University Press, 2011.

Beith, Malcolm. "Generals in Their Labyrinths." June 25, 2012. *Newsweek* 27–29.

Bell, Horace. *Reminiscences of a Ranger, or Early Times in California*. Santa Barbara: Wallace Hebberd, 1927.

Benavides, Jude et al. "Obstructing Human Rights: The Texas–Mexico Border Wall." Submission to the Inter-American Commission on Human Rights by The Working Group on Human Rights and the Border Wall. The Rapoport Center for Human Rights and Justice, University of Texas School of Law, University of Texas at Austin. June 2008.

Berelowitz, Jo-Anne. "Border Art since 1965." In *Postborder City: Cultural Spaces of Bajalta California*, eds. Michael Dear and Gustavo Leclerc, 143–182. New York: Routledge, 2003.

Berelowitz, Jo-Anne. "The spaces of home in Chicano and Latino representations of the San Diego–Tijuana borderlands (1968–2002)." *Environment and Planning D: Society and Space* **23** (2005): 323–350.

Berger, Joseph. "An Undocumented Princetonian." January 3, 2010. *New York Times*, 28.

Bernstein, Nina. "Effort on U.S. Immigrant Raids Cast Wider Net." February 4, 2009. *New York Times*, A1 and A18.

Bernstein, Nina. "U.S. To Overhaul Detention Policy for Immigrants." August 6, 2009. *New York Times*, A1 and A4.

Bernstein, Nina. "Ideas for Immigrant Detention Include Converting Hotels and Building Models." October 6, 2009. *New York Times*, A16.

Bernstein, Nina. "Immigrant Jail Tests U.S. View of Legal Access." November 2, 2009. *New York Times*, A1 and A4.

Bernstein, Nina. "Report Critical of Scope and Cost of Immigration Detention." October 7, 2009. *New York Times*, A17.

Bernstein, Nina. "Two Groups Find Faults in Immigration Detentions." December 3, 2009. *New York Times*, A23 and A27.

Bernstein, Nina. "Lawsuits Renew Questions on Immigrant Detention." March 4, 2010. *New York Times*, A20.

Bernstein, Nina. "Officials Obscured Truth of Migrant Deaths in Jail." January 9, 2010. *New York Times*, 1 and 22.

Berrin, Kathleen and Virginia M. Fields, eds. *Olmec: Colossal Masterworks Works of Ancient Mexico*. New Haven: Yale University Press, 2010.

Blake, Tupper A., and Peter Steinhart. *Two Eagles / Dos Aguilas: A Natural History of the United States–Mexico Borderlands*. Berkeley: University of California Press, 1994.

"Blazing Arizona." December 18, 2007. *New York Times*, A30.

Blow, Charles M. "Plantations, Prisons and Profits." May 26, 2012. *New York Times*, A17.

Bolaño, Roberto. *2066*. New York: Picador, 2008.

Bonfil Batalla, Guillermo. *México Profundo: Reclaiming a Civilization*. Austin: University of Texas Press, 1996.

"Border Crossing/Entry Date: Query Detailed Statistics." *Research and Innovative Technology Administration*. Available: http://www.bts.gov/programs/international/ transborder/.

"Border News." September 5, 2010. *New York Times*, WK7.

"Border Trade Vehicle Crossings." *Texas Center for Border Economic and Enterprise Development. Texas Center*. Available: http://texascenter.tamiu.edu/texcen_ser-vices/vehicle_crossings.asp?framepg=datavehicle.

Borneman, Walter. *Polk: The Man Who Transformed the Presidency and America*. New York: Random House, 2008.

Bourbon, Fabio. *The Lost Cities of the Maya: The life, art, and discoveries of Frederick Catherwood*. New York: Abbeville Press, 1999.

Bowden, Charles. *Murder City: Ciudad Juárez and the Global Economy's New Killing Fields*. New York: Nation Books, 2010.

Briscoe, Daren. "Marchers Want Changes in U.S.–Mexico Extradition Pact." May 9, 2004. *Los Angeles Times*, B3.

Brookings Institution. *A Report on the Media and the Immigration Debate*. University of Southern California, Norman Lear Center. 2008.

Brown, Lenard E. "Survey of the United States Mexico Boundary, 1849–1855: Background Study." US Department of the Interior, National Park Service, Division of History, Office of Archeology and Historic Preservation. May 1, 1969.

Broyles, Bill, and Haynes, Mark. *Desert Duty: On the line with the U.S. Border Patrol*. Austin, University of Texas Press: 2010.

Burke, Peter. *Cultural Hybridity*. Cambridge: Polity Press, 2009.

Burridge, Andrew. "Differential Criminalization under Operation Streamline: Challenges to Freedom of Movement and Humanitarian Aid Provision in the Mexico–US Borderlands." *Refuge* **26/2** (2011): 78–91.

Bustamante Redondo, Joaquín. *La Comisión Internacional de Límites y Aguas entre México y los Estados Unidos: Sus Orígines y su actuación hasta 1996*. Ciudad Juárez: Universidad Autónoma de Ciudad Juárez, 1999.

Bustamante, Jorge. *Report of the Special Rapporteur on the human rights of migrants: Promotion and Protection of All Human Rights, Civil, Political, Economic, Social and Cultural Rights, Including the Right to Development*. United Nations. Human Rights Council, Seventh Session, Agenda item 3. March 5, 2008.

Bustillo, Miguel. "Border Pollution Fight Gets New U.S.–Mexico Commitment." April 5, 2003. *Los Angeles Times*, A24.

Bustillo, Miguel, and Richard Fausset. "Immigrant Raid Splits Miss. Town." August 31, 2008. *Los Angeles Times*, A15.

Cabeza de Vaca, Alvar N. *The Account: Alvar Núñez Cabeza de Vaca's* Relación. Trans. M. A. Favata and J. B. Fernández. 1542. Reprint, Houston: Arte Público Press, 1993.

Calloway, Colin G. *One Vast Winter Count: The Native American West before Lewis and Clark*. Lincoln: University of Nebraska Press, 2003.

Camarota, Steven A., and Karen Jensenius. "A Shifting Tide: Recent Trends in the Illegal Immigrant Population." *Center for Immigration Studies*. July 2009. Available: http://www.cis.org/IllegalImmigration-ShiftingTide. January 13, 2012. United Nations.

Campbell, Howard. *Drug War Zone: Frontline Dispatches from the Streets of El Paso and Juárez*. Austin: University of Texas Press, 2009.

Campo-Flores, Arian, and Andrew Murr. "Brownsville's Bad Lie." May 5, 2008. *Newsweek*, 40.

Capps, Randy, Muzaffar Chishti, Christina Rodriguez, and Marc R. Rosenblum. *Delegation and Divergence: A Study of 287(g) State and Local Immigration*

Enforcement. Washington DC: Migration Policy Institute, 2011. Available: http://migrationpolicy.org/pubs/287g-divergence.pdf.

Cárdenas, Cuauhtémoc. "The Promise and Legacy of the Mexican Revolution." Spring–Summer 2010. *Berkeley Review of Latin American Studies*, 30–55.

Carr, David. "A Star Turn For a Sheriff On Fox TV." January 5, 2009. *New York Times*, B1.

Carrasco, David. *The Oxford Encyclopedia of Mesoamerican Cultures*. 3 vols. Oxford: Oxford University Press, 2001.

Carrera, Magali M. *Traveling from New Spain to Mexico: Mapping Practices of Nineteenth-Century Mexico*. Durham: Duke University Press, 2011.

Casares, Oscar. "Crossing the Border Without Losing Your Past." September 16, 2003. *New York Times*, A29.

Castañeda, Jorge G., and Douglas S. Massey. "Do-It-Yourself Immigration Reform." June 2, 2012. *New York Times*, A19.

Cathcart, Rebecca. "Los Angeles Archbishop to Lead a Rally Against the Arizona Measure." May 1, 2010. *New York Times*, A9.

Cave, Damien. "A Crime Fighter Draws Plaudits, and Scrutiny." December 24, 2011. *New York Times*, A10.

Cave, Damien. "A Mexican City's Troubles Reshape Its Families." February 9, 2011. *New York Times*, A1, A6.

Cave, Damien. "Angels Rushing In Where Others Fear to Tread." November 10, 2011. *New York Times*, A8.

Cave, Damien. "Better Lives for Mexicans Cut Allure of Going North." July 6, 2011. *New York Times*, A1.

Cave, Damien. "Former General to Face A Runoff in Guatemala." September 13, 2011. *New York Times*, A6.

Cave, Damien. "Mexican Church Looks Closer at Its Benefactors." April 7, 2011. *New York Times*, A1.

Cave, Damien. "Wave of Violence Swallows more Women in Juárez." June 24, 2012. *New York Times*, Y6.

Chacón, Justin Akers, and Mike Davis. *No One is Illegal: Fighting Racism and Violence on the U.S.–Mexico Border*. Chicago: Haymarket Books, 2006.

Chamberlin, Eugene. "Nicholas Trist and Baja California." *Pacific Historical Review* 32/1 (1963): 49–63.

Chatfield, Walter H. "The Twin Cities of the Border and the Country of the Lower Rio Grande: Brownsville, Texas; Matamoros, Mexico." New Orleans: E.P. Brandao, 1893. Reprint. Brownsville: The Harbert Davenport Memorial Fund, The Brownsville Historical Saldaña Association, and the Lower Rio Grande Valley Historical Society, 1959.

Chávez, John R. "Aztlán, Cíbola, and Frontier New Spain." In *Aztlán: Essays on the Chicano Homeland*, eds. Rudolfo A. Anaya and Francisco Lomeli, 49–71. Albuquerque: El Norte Publications, 1989.

Chávez, Leo R. *Covering Immigration: Popular Images and the Politics of the Nation.* Berkeley: University of California Press, 2001.

Chávez, Leo R. *The Latino Threat: Constructing Immigrants, Citizens, and the Nation.* Stanford: Stanford University Press, 2009.

Childs, Craig. *House of Rain: Tracking A Vanished Civilization Across the American Southwest.* New York: Little, Brown & Co., 2007.

Chu, Henry. "Journey into U.S. Turns Deadly for Brazilians." July 1, 2005. *Los Angeles Times*, A5.

Coe, Michael D. *The Maya.* London: Thames & Hudson, 1966.

Coe, Michael D. and Rex Koontz. *Mexico: From the Olmecs to the Aztecs.* London: Thames & Hudson, 2002.

Comisión Latinoamericana sobre Drogas y Democracia. "Drogas y democracia: hacia un cambio de paradigma." 2009. Available: http://www.drogasedemocracia.org/Arquivos/livro_espanhol_04.pdf. October 24, 2011.

"Confusion Over Secure Communities." October 5, 2010. *New York Times*, A26.

Cooper, Mark. "On the Border of Hypocrisy." December 5, 2003. *LA Weekly*, 27–33.

"Corruption Perceptions Index 2010." *Transparency International.* 2010. Available: http://www.transparency.org/policy_research/surveys_indices/cpi/2010. May 6, 2011.

Cortez, Constance. "The New Aztlan: *Nepantla* (and Other Sites of Transmogrification)." In *The Road to Aztlan: Art from a Mythic Homeland*, eds. V. M. Fields and V. Zamudio-Taylor, 358–373. Los Angeles: Los Angeles County Museum of Art, 2001.

"Crackdown on Immigrants Draws Protests in Phoenix." April 14, 2008. *New York Times*, A17.

Craib, Raymond B. *Cartographic Mexico: A History of State Fixations and Fugitive Landscapes.* Durham: University of Duke Press, 2004.

Cravey, Altha. *Women and Work in Mexico's Maquiladoras.* Lanham: Rowman and Littlefield, 1998.

Crosby, Harry W. *The Cave Paintings of Baja California: Discovering the Great Murals of an Unknown People.* San Diego: Sunbelt Publications, 1997.

Crouch, Dora P., Daniel J. Garr, and Axel I. Mundingo. *Spanish City Planning in North America* Cambridge: MIT Press, 1982.

Cruz, Gilbert R. *Let there be Towns: Spanish Municipal Origins in the American Southwest, 1610–1810.* College Station: Texas A&M University Press, 1988.

Cruz, Teddy. "Border Tours: Strategies of Surveillance, Tactics of Encroachment." In *Indefensible Space: The Architecture of the National Insecurity State*, ed. Michael Sorkin, 111–140. New York: Routledge, 2008.

Cull, Nicholas J. and David Carrasco, eds. *Alhambrista and the U.S.–Mexico Border: Film, Music, and Stories of Undocumented Immigrants.* Albuquerque: University of New Mexico Press, 2004.

Dana, Jr., Richard Henry. *Two Years Before the Mast.* New York: Penguin Books, 1981.

Davey, Monica, and Michael S. Schmidt, "Immigration Activists Take Arizona Protest Out to the Ballgame." April 30, 2010. *New York Times*, A12.

Davidow, Jeffrey. *The Bear and the Porcupine: The U.S. and Mexico*. Princeton: Markus Wiener Publishers, 2007.

Davidson, Miriam. *Lives on the Line: Dispatches from the U.S.–Mexico Border*. Tucson: The University of Arizona Press, 2000.

De las Casas, Bartolomé. *A Short Account of the Destruction of The Indies*. 1552. Reprint. London: Penguin Books, 1992.

De León, Arnoldo. *They Called Them Greasers: Anglo Attitudes toward Mexicans in Texas, 1821–1900*. Austin: University of Texas Press, 1983.

de Oñate, Juan. "Letter written by Don Juan de Oñate from New Mexico to the Viceroy, the Count of Monterrey, on March 2, 1599." In *The Norton Anthology of Latino Literature*, ed. Ilan Stavans, 82. New York: Norton, 2011.

Dear, Michael. "In the City, Time Becomes Visible." In *Los Angeles and Urban Theory at the End of the Twentieth Century*, eds. Allen J. Scott and Edward W. Soja, 76–105. Berkeley and Los Angeles: University of California Press, 1996.

Dear, Michael. "Peopling California." In *Made in California: Art, Image, Identity, 1900–2000*, eds. Stephanie Baron, Sheri Bernstein, and Ilene S. Fort, 48–63. Los Angeles County Museum of Art & University of California Press, 2000.

Dear, Michael. *The Postmodern Urban Condition*. Oxford: Wiley-Blackwell, 2000.

Dear, Michael, ed. *From Chicago to LA: Making Sense of Urban Theory*. Thousand Oaks: Sage Publications, 2002.

Dear, Michael. "Los Angeles and the Democratization of History." *Planning Theory & Practice* 4.4 (2003): 321–328.

Dear, Michael. "Photography's Geography." In *Robbert Flick* exhibition catalogue, Los Angeles County Museum of Art. (2004): 25–31.

Dear, Michael. "Monuments, Manifest Destiny and Mexico." *Prologue* **37/2** (2005): 32–41.

Dear, Michael. "Rediscovering Reyner Banham's Los Angeles." *Architecture California* **06.2** (2006): 18–21.

Dear, Michael. "La tercera nación." May 2007. *National Geographic en español*, xiv–xx.

Dear, Michael. "Es una frontera, no es una barrera / It's a border not a barrier." *Society and Space, Environment and Planning D* 29 (2011): 209–211.

Dear, Michael, and Andrew Burridge. "Cultural Integration and Hybridization at the U.S.–Mexico Borderlands." *Cahiers de Géographie du Québec* **49/138** (2005): 301–318.

Dear, Michael, and Jacqueline Holzer. "Altered States: The U.S.–Mexico Borderlands as a Third Nation." In Graham Dawson, Jim Aulich, and Louise Purbrick, 74–93. *Contested Spaces: Representations and Histories of Conflict*. Basingstoke: Palgrave Macmillan, 2007.

Dear, Michael, and Gustavo Leclerc. "Introduction: The Postborder Condition." In *Postborder City: Cultural Spaces of Bajalta California*, eds. Michael Dear and Gustavo Leclerc, 1–30. New York: Routledge, 2003.

Dear, Michael, and Gustavo Leclerc, eds. *Postborder City: Cultural Spaces of Bajalta California*. New York: Routledge, 2003.

Dear, Michael, and Gustavo Leclerc. "Tijuana Desenmascarada." *Wide Angle: Cityscapes II* **20.3** (2009): 210–221.

Dear, Michael, and Marolijn Dijkman. "Here Be Dragons: the Art of Place." *Theatrum Orbis Terrarum*, Matrix 234. Berkeley Art Museum, (2010): 7–12.

Dear, Michael, Jim Ketchum, Sarah Luria, and Douglas Richardson, eds. *Geohumanities: Art, History & Text at the Edge of Place*. New York: Routledge, 2011.

Dear, Michael, Eric Schockman, Greg Hise, eds. *Rethinking Los Angeles*. Thousand Oaks: Sage Publications, 1996

DeBuys, William, and Joan Myers. *Salt Dreams: Land and Water in Low-down California*. Albuquerque: University of New Mexico Press, 1999.

DeLay, Brian. *War of a Thousand Deserts: Indian Raids and the U.S.–Mexico War*. New Haven: Yale University Press, 2008.

DeLay, Brian. "Forgotten Foes." *Berkeley Review of Latin American Studies* (Fall 2010): 14–19.

"Democracy Index 2010: A report from the Economist Intelligence Unit." 2010. Available: http://graphics.eiu.com/PDF/Democracy_Index_2010_web.pdf. October 24, 2011.

DeSoucy, M. David. *Arizona Rangers*. Charleston: Arcadia Publishing, 2008.

Dever, Larry A. "Abandoned on the Border." May 13, 2011. *New York Times*, A25.

Dickerson, Marla. "Funds Sent to Mexico Hit Record." July 30, 2003. *Los Angeles Times*, C1.

Diehl, Richard A. *The Olmecs: America's First Civilization*. London: Thames and Hudson, 2004.

Diguet, León. *Territorio de la Baja California; reseña geográfica y estadística*. París y México: Librería de la Vda. de C. Bouret. 1912.

Dobyns, Henry F., ed. *Hepah, California! The Journal of Cave Johnson Couts, from Monterey, Nuevo Leon, Mexico to Los Angeles, California during the years 1848–1849*. Tucson: Arizona Pioneers' Historical Society, 1961.

Doty, Roxanne L. *The Law into their own hands: Immigration and the Politics of Exceptionalism*. Tucson: University of Arizona Press, 2009.

Dougherty, J. "Crossings From Mexico, Legally, With Money." December 24, 2008. *New York Times*, B1.

Downes, Lawrence. "American Stories, From Mexican Roots." December 9, 2009. *New York Times*, A36.

Downes, Lawrence. "Don't Deport Benita Veliz." March 28, 2009. *New York Times*, A16.

Downes, Lawrence. "The Hunt for American Decency in the Arizona Quicksand." August 4, 2010. *New York Times*, A18.

Downes, Lawrence. "In Arpaio's Arizona, They Fought Back." July 22, 2012. *New York Times*, SR10.

Draper, Robert. "Shattered Somalia." September 2009. *National Geographic*, 70–99.

"Dreaming of Reform." November 30, 2010. *New York Times*, A16.

Dresser, Denise. "Carta abierta a Carlos Slim." February 15, 2009. Available: http://las-tresyuncuarto.wordpress.com/2009/02/15/denise-dresser-carta-abierta-a-carlos-slim/. October 24, 2011.

Dresser, Denise. "Why Mexico Is Sick." May 11, 2009. *Project Syndicate*. Available: http://www.project-syndicate.org/commentary/dresser6/English. October 13, 2011.

"Drugs: Virtually Legal." November 14, 2009. *The Economist*, 70–71.

Dunn, Timothy. *The Militarization of the U.S.–Mexico Border: 1978–1992: Low-Intensity Conflict Doctrine Comes Home.* Austin: University of Texas Press, 1995.

Dunn, Timothy. *Blockading the Border and Human Rights: The El Paso Operation that Remade Immigration Enforcement.* Austin: University of Texas Press, 2010.

Durand, Jorge, and Douglas S. Massey, eds. *Crossing the Border: Research from the Mexican Migration Project.* New York: Russell Sage Foundation, 2006.

Dusard, Jay, and Alan Weisman. *La Frontera: The United States Border with Mexico.* New York: Houghton Mifflin Harcourt Publishing, 1986.

Eckholm, Erik. "In Drug War, Tribe Feels Invaded by Both Sides." January 25, 2010. *New York Times*, A1.

Editorial Santillana, *Tijuana, la tercera nación.* México D.F.: Editorial Santillana, 2005.

Edwards, Jr., James R., and Jessica M. Vaughan. "The 287(g) Program: Protecting Hometowns and Homeland." October 2009. *Center for Immigration Studies.* Available: http://www.cis.org/articles/2009/287g.pdf. December 26, 2011. December 26, 2011.

Edwards, Sebastian. *Left Behind: Latin America and the False Promise of Populism.* Chicago: University of Chicago Press, 2010.

Egan, Linda. *Carlos Monsiváis: Culture and Chronicle in Contemporary Mexico.* Tucson: University of Arizona Press, 2001.

Ehrenreich, Ben. "A Lucrative War." October 21, 2010. *London Review of Books*, 15–18.

Eisenhower, John S. D. *So Far from God: The U.S. War with Mexico, 1846–1848.* New York: Random House, 1989.

Elizondo Elizondo, Ricardo. "Monterrey's Habit." October 17, 2010. *New York Times*, WK9.

Ellingwood, Ken. "U.S. Mail Delivers—for Tijuana Residents." December 10, 2001. *Los Angeles Times*, B6.

Ellis, Arthur M. "Introduction." *Reminiscences of a Ranger*, Horace Bell. Santa Barbara: Wallace Hebberd, 1927.

Emory, William H. *Notes of a Military Reconnaissance from Fort Leavenworth, in Missouri, to San Diego, in California.* Washington, DC: US Senate, 30th Congress, 1848.

Emory, William H. *Report on the United States and Mexico Boundary Survey.* 3 vols. 1857. Reprint, Texas State Historical Association, Washington, D.C.: US House of Representatives, 34th Congress, 1987.

Engardio, Pete and Geri Smith. "Business Is Standing Its Ground." April 20, 2009. *Businessweek*, 34–39.

Erickson, Winston P. *Sharing the Desert: The Tohono O'odham in History*. Tucson: University of Arizona Press, 1994.

Eriksson, Lindsay and Melinda Taylor. "The Environmental Impacts of the Border Wall between Texas and Mexico." Submission to the Inter-American Commission on Human Rights by The Working Group on Human Rights and the Border Wall. The Rapoport Center for Human Rights and Justice, University of Texas School of Law, University of Texas at Austin. June 2008.

Erlandson, Jon M., et al. "Paleoindian Seafaring, Maritime Technologies, and Coastal Foraging on California's Channel Islands," *Science* 331 (March 4, 2011): 1181–1185.

"Europe falls from its pedestal, no respite in the dictatorships." *Reporters Without Borders*. May 6, 2011. Available: http://en.rsf.org/press-freedom-index-2010,1034. html. October 24, 2011.

Evans, R. Tripp. *Romancing the Maya: Mexican Antiquity in the American Imagination, 1820–1915*. Austin: University of Texas Press, 2004.

Fagan, Brian. *Before California: An Archaeologist Looks at Our Earliest Inhabitants*. Lanham: Rowman & Littlefield Publishers, 2003.

Fagan, Brian. *Chaco Canyon: Archaeologists Explore the Lives of an Ancient Society*. Oxford: Oxford University Press, 2005.

Fagan, Brian. *The First North Americans*. London: Thames and Hudson, 2011.

Farer, Tom. *Transnational Crime in the Americas*. New York: Routledge, 1999.

Ferguson, William M., Arthur H. Rohn, and John Q. Royce. *Mesoamerica's Ancient Cities*. Niwot: University Press of Colorado, 1990.

Fernández-Kelly, Patricia and Jon Shefner, special eds. *Annals of the American Academy of Physical and Social Science* 610. "NAFTA and Beyond." (March: 2007).

Fields, Virginia and Victor Zamudio-Taylor. *The Road to Aztlan: Art from a Mythic Homeland*. Los Angeles: Los Angeles County Museum of Art, 2001.

Finnegan, William. "In the Name of the Law." October 18, 2010. *The New Yorker*, 60–71.

Finnegan, William. "Letter From Mexico: The Kingpins." July 2, 2012. *The New Yorker*, 40–53.

Finnegan, William. "Sheriff Joe." September 20, 2009. *The New Yorker*, 42–53.

Finnegan, William. "Silver or Lead." May 31, 2010. *The New Yorker*, 39–51.

Florescano, Enrique. *National Narratives in Mexico: A History*. Trans. N. T. Hancock. Norman: University of Oklahoma Press, 2006.

Flusty, Steven. "Miscege-Nation." In *De-Coca-Colonisation: Making the Globe from the Inside Out*, 105–131. New York: Routledge, 2004.

Ford, Anabel et al. "Modeling Settlement Patterns of the Late Classical Maya Civilization with Bayesian Methods and Geographic Information Systems." *Annals of the Association of American Geographers* 99.3 (Jul. 2009): 496.

Foster, Michael S. "The Aztatlán Tradition of West and Northwest Mexico and Casas Grandes." In *The Casas Grandes World*, eds. Curtis F. Schaafsma and Carroll L. Riley, 149–163. Salt Lake City: The University of Utah Press, 1999.

Foster, Michael S. and Shirley Gorenstein, eds. *Greater Mesoamerica: The Archaeology of West and Northwest Mexico*. Salt Lake City: The University of Utah Press, 2000.

Fox, Claire F. *The Fence and the River: Culture and Politics at the U.S.–Mexico Border*. Minneapolis: University of Minnesota Press, 1999.

Fox, Vicente, and Rob Allyn. *Revolution of Hope: The Life, Faith, and Dreams of a Mexican President*. New York: Plume, 2008.

Fredrickson, George M. *Racism: A Short History*. Princeton: Princeton University Press, 2002.

Freedman, Samuel. "Latino Parents Decry Bilingual Programs." July 14, 2004. *New York Times*, A21.

Friedman, Ann. "Nativism Versus Security." *The American Prospect*. September 11, 2009. Online: Available: http://prospect.org/cs/articles?article=nativism_versus_security. January 13, 2012.

Friedman, Thomas L. "Narcos, No's, and Nafta." May 1, 2010. *New York Times*, WK10.

Frosch, Dan. "In Colorado, Debate over Program to Check Immigration History of the Arrested." July 29, 2010. *New York Times*, A12.

Fuentes, Carlos. *Destiny and Desire*. Trans. Edith Grossman. New York: Random House, 2011.

Fuentes-Berain, Rossana. "Where Roma Soap Meets Dove." January 13, 2004. *New York Times*, A27.

Ganster, Paul and David E. Lorey. *The U.S.–Mexico Border into the Twenty-first Century*. Lanham: Rowman & Littlefield, 2007.

García Canclini, Nestor. *Hybrid Cultures: Strategies for Entering and Leaving Modernity*. Minneapolis: University of Minnesota Press, 1995.

García Canclini, Nestor. "Rewriting Cultural Studies in the Borderlands." In *Postborder City: Cultural Spaces of Bajalta California*, eds. Michael Dear and Gustavo Leclerc, 277–286. New York: Routledge, 2003.

Gardner, Erle S. *The Hidden Heart of Baja*. New York: William Morrow, 1962.

Garland, David. "Unequal Protection." June 1, 2012. *The Times Literary Supplement*, 7.

Garza, Osvaldo, and Cecilia Garza. *Parajes Fugitivos/ Fugitive Sites: New Contemporary Art Projects for San Diego–Tijuana*. San Diego: Installation Gallery, 2002.

Gasca Zamora, José. *Espacios transnacionales: interacción, integración y fragmentación en la frontera México—Estados Unidos*. México DF: Universidad Nacional Autónoma de México, 2002.

Gebeloff, Robert, and Julia Preston. "Unlicensed Drivers Who Risk More Than a Fine." December 10, 2010. *New York Times*, A1 and A21.

"Getting Away With Murder." *Committee to Protect Journalists*. April 20, 2010. Available: http://www.cpj.org/reports/2010/04/cpj-2010-impunity-index-getting-away-with-murder.php. May 6, 2011.

Giblin, Paul. "Arizona Sheriff Conducts Immigration Raid at City Hall, Angering Officials." October 18, 2008. *New York Times*, A10.

Gilman, Denise. "Background and Context." *Obstructing Human Rights: The Texas–Mexico Border Wall*. The Working Group on Human Rights and the Border Wall. The Rapoport Center for Human Rights and Justice. University of Texas School of Law, University of Texas at Austin. June 2008.

"Gini Coefficient: An Indicator of Income Inequality." *Sustainable Middle Class*. Available: http://www.sustainablemiddleclass.com/Gini-Coefficient.html. May 6, 2011.

Glendinning, Jim. *Mexico: Unofficial Border Crossings*. Alpine, Texas: Alpine Company Press, 2000.

Goetzmann, William H. "Introduction." In *Report on the United States and Mexican Boundary Survey made under the direction of the Secretary of the Interior*, William H. Emory, vii and ix-xxx. Reprint, Texas State Historical Association, Washington, DC: US House of Representatives, 34th Congress, 1987.

Gomez-Peña, Guillermo. *The New World Border: Prophecies, Poems & Loqueras For the End of the Century*. San Francisco: City Lights Books, 1996.

González Rodríguez, Sergio. *The Femicide Machine*. Published by Semiotext(e), Intervention Series 11. Distributed by Cambridge: MIT Press.

Gopnik, Adam. "The Caging of America: Why do we lock up so many people?" January 30, 2012. *The New Yorker*, 72–77.

Gorman, Anna. "Mexico Cuts Gas to Regain Sales Lost to U.S." December 9, 2002. *Los Angeles Times*, B5.

Gorman, Anna. "A life divided by borders." February 29, 2008. *Los Angeles Times*, A1 and A16.

Gorman, Anna. "Fed sues over detention conditions." April 3, 2009. *Los Angeles Times*, A4.

Gorman, Anna. "Immigrant detention facility is considered." February 3, 2009. *Los Angeles Times*, B5.

Gorman, Anna. "Immigrant focus of police is questioned." February 26, 2009. *Los Angeles Times*, B5.

Gorman, Anna. "No longer rounding up just fugitive immigrants." February 5, 2009. *Los Angeles Times*, A12.

Gorman, Anna. "New edict on immigrant arrests." July 11, 2009. *Los Angeles Times*, A14.

Gorman, A., and J. Meyer. "U.S. agents will target bosses over immigrants." March 31, 2009. *Los Angeles Times*, A1 and A10.

Gorney, Cynthia. "How do you say 'Got Milk' en Español?." September 23, 2007. *New York Times Magazine*, 58.

Grant, Ulysses S. *Personal Memoirs of U.S. Grant*. 1865. Reprinted in *Ulysses S. Grant: Memoirs and Selected Letters*. New York: Library of America, 1990.

Grayson, George W. "Mexico's Southern Flank: The 'Third' U.S. Border." *Orbis* (2006): 53–69.

Grayson, George W. *Mexico: Narco-Violence and a Failed State?* New Brunswick: Transaction Publishers, 2010.

Grey, Mark, Michele Devlin, and Aaron Goldsmith. *Postville, U.S.A.: Surviving Diversity in Small-town America*. Boston: GemmaMedia, 2009.

Griswold del Castillo, Richard. *The Treaty of Guadalupe Hidalgo: A Legacy of Conflict*. Norman: University of Oklahoma Press, 1990.

Grosby, Steve. *Nationalism: A Very Short Introduction*. New York: Oxford University Press, 2005.

Gugliotta, Guy. "The Maya Glory and Ruin." August 2007. *National Geographic*, 68–109.

Guillermoprieto, Alma. "Days of the Dead." November 10, 2008. *The New Yorker*, 44–51.

Guillermoprieto, Alma. "The Narcovirus." Spring 2009. *Berkeley Review of Latin American Studies*, 3–9.

Guillermoprieto, Alma. "Troubled Spirits." May 2010. *National Geographic*, 54–73.

Guillermoprieto, Alma. "The Murders of Mexico." October 28, 2010. *The New York Review*, 46–48.

Guillermoprieto, Alma. "Mexico's Widening War." January 2, 2011. *New York Times*, WK9.

Gutiérrez, Ramón A. and Richard J. Orsi, eds. *Contested Eden: California Before the Gold Rush*. Berkeley: University of California Press, 1998.

Guzman, Michelle, and Zachary Hurwitz. "Violations on the Part of the United States Government of Indigenous Rights Held by Members of the Lipan Apache, Kickapoo, and Ysleta del Sur Tigua Tribes of the Texas–Mexico Border." Submission to the Inter-American Commission on Human Rights by The Working Group on Human Rights and the Border Wall. The Rapoport Center for Human Rights and Justice, University of Texas School of Law. University of Texas at Austin: 2008.

Haas, Lisbeth. *Conquests and Historical Identities in California, 1769–1936*. Berkeley: University of California Press, 1995.

Hackel, Steven W., ed. *Alta California: Peoples in Motion, Identities in Formation, 1769–1850*. Berkeley: University of California Press, 2010.

Haddal, Chad. *Unaccompanied Alien Children: Policies and Issues*. CRS Report for Congress. March 1, 2007. Available: http://trac.syr.edu/immigration/library/P1642.pdf. December 26, 2011.

Haederle, Michael. "Mysteries of Ancient Puebloan Jars Solved." February 4, 2009. *New York Times*, A14.

Hall, Dawn, ed. *Drawing the Borderline: Artist-Explorers of the U.S.–Mexico Boundary Survey*. Albuquerque: The Albuquerque Museum, 1996.

Hämäläinen, Pekka. *The Comanche Empire*. New Haven: Yale University Press, 2008.

"Hands across borders ceremony unite sister cities." *The Brownsville Herald*. February 24, 2011. Available: http://www.brownsvilleherald.com/articles/sister-123221-ceremony-unite.html.

Hawley, Chris. "The richest man you've never heard of." *USA Today*. May 30, 2007. Available: http://www.usatoday.com/money/world/2007-05-30-carlos-slim-usat_ N.htm?csp=34. October 24, 2011.

Hendricks, Tyche. *The Wind Doesn't Need a Passport: Stories from the U.S.–Mexico Borderlands*. Berkeley: University of California Press, 2010.

Hernández, Anabel. *Los señores del narco*. Grijalbo: Mexico, 2010.

Hernandez, Daniel. "A Hybrid Tongue or Slanguage?" December 23, 2004. *Los Angeles Times*, A29–31.

Hernández, Kelly L. *Migra!: A History of the U.S. Border Patrol*. Berkeley: University of California Press, 2010.

Herzog, Lawrence A. *Shared Space: Rethinking the U.S.–Mexico Border Environment*. San Diego: Center for U.S.–Mexican Studies, University of California, San Diego, 2000.

Herzog, Lawrence A. "Global Tijuana: The Seven Ecologies of the Border." In *Postborder City: Cultural Spaces of Bajalta California*, eds. Michael Dear and Gustavo Leclerc, 119–142. New York: Routledge, 2003.

Hewitt, Harry. "The Mexican Boundary Survey Team: Pedro Garcia Conde in California." *The Western Historical Quarterly* **21/2** (1990): 171–196.

Hine, Robert. *Bartlett's West: Drawing the Mexican Boundary*. New Haven: Yale University Press, 1968.

Hine, Robert V., and John Mack Faragher. *The American West: A New Interpretive History*. New Haven: Yale University Press, 2000.

Hine, Robert V., and John Mack Faragher. *Frontiers: a Short History of the American West*. New Haven: Yale University Press, 2007

Hodges, Glenn. "Cahokia: America's Forgotten City." January 2011. *National Geographic*, 127–145.

Hondagneu-Sotelo, Pierrette. *God's Heart has no Borders: How religious activists are working for immigrant rights*. Berkeley: University of California Press, 2008.

Howley, Kerry. "The One-Man Wall." *Reason Magazine* 40/5 (2008): 34–44.

Hsu, Spencer S. "Border Deaths Are Increasing." *Washington Post*. September 20, 2009. Available: http://www.washingtonpost.com/wp-dyn/content/article/2009/09/ 29/AR2009092903212.html. January 13, 2012.

Hsu, Tiffany. "Speaking the shopping language of immigrants." December 24, 2008. *Los Angeles Times*, C1.

Hughes, Charles W. "'La Mojonera' and the Making of California's U.S.–Mexico Boundary Line, 1849–1851." *Journal of San Diego History* **53/3** (2007): 126–147.

Hulse, Carl and David M. Herszenhorn. "Democrats Detail Immigration Plan In Plea to G.O.P." April 30, 2010. *New York Times*, A12.

Hurtado, Albert L. *Indian Survival on the California Frontier*. New Haven: Yale University Press, 1988.

Hyland, Justin R. "The Central Sierras." In *The Prehistory of Baja California*, eds. Don Laylander and Jerry D. and Moore, 117–134. Gainesville: University Press of Florida, 2006.

Iglesias, Norma. *Entre hierba, polvo y plomo: lo fronterizo visto por el cine Mexicano*. 2 vols. Tijuana: El Colegio de la Frontera Norte, 1991.

Iglesias Prieto, Norma. *Beautiful Flowers of the Maquiladora: Life Histories of Women Workers in Tijuana*. Austin: University of Texas Press, 1997.

Iglesias Prieto, Norma. *Emergencias: Las artes visuales en Tijuana*. Tijuana: Centro Cultural Tijuana, 2008.

"Immigration Bait and Switch." August 18, 2010. *New York Times*, A20.

"Immigration Case Backlog Still Growing in FY 2011." *TRAC*, Syracuse University. Available: http://trac.syr.edu/whatsnew/email.110207.html. December 26, 2011.

"Immigration Ground Zero." December 26, 2007. *Washington Post*, A20.

"Immigration, Outsourced." May 9, 2008. *New York Times*, A26.

Informe General de la Comisión Pesquisidora. "Depredaciones de los bárbaros en Nuevo Léon." México: Imprente de Diaz de Leon y White, 1875. Reprint, Brownsville: Edición de El Porvenir, 1915.

Iritani, Evelyn. "U.S. Reaps Bittersweet Fruit of Merger." January 19, 2004. *Los Angeles Times*, A1.

Jackson, Robert H. *Indian Population Decline: The Missions of Northwestern New Spain, 1687–1840*. Albuquerque: University of New Mexico Press, 1994.

Jackson, Robert H., and Edward Castillo. *Indians, Franciscans, and Spanish Colonization: The Impact of the Mission System on California Indians*. Albuquerque: University of New Mexico Press, 1996.

Jacoby, Karl. *Shadows at Dawn: A Borderlands Massacre and the Violence of History*. New York: The Penguin Press, 2008.

James, Scott. "Aware of Its Dependence, Napa Takes Care of Migrant Workers." May 27, 2011. *New York Times*, A23.

Jameson, John. *The Story of Big Bend National Park*. Austin: University of Texas Press, 1996.

Janofsky, Michael. "Burden Grows for Southwest Hospitals." April 14, 2003. *New York Times*, A14.

Jimenez, Maria. "Humanitarian Crisis: Migrant Deaths at the U.S.–Mexico Border." American Civil Liberties Union Report. October 1, 2009. Available: http://www.aclu.org/immigrants-rights/humanitarian-crisis-migrant-deaths-us-mexico-border. January 13, 2012.

Joaquin, Linton, Ranjana Natarajan, and Karen Tumlin. *A Broken System: Confidential Reports Reveal Failures in U.S. Immigrant Detention Centers*. ACLU of Southern California, National Immigration Law Center, Hollam & Knight. 2009. Available: http://www.aclu-sc.org/documents/view/197. December 26, 2011.

Johnson, Bradley. "Political Culture and Public Governance in the Third Nation," Department of City and Regional Planning, University of California, Berkeley, 2010. www.latinobarómetro.org.

Johnson, Kenneth M. "Baja California and the Treaty of Guadalupe Hidalgo." *Journal of the West* 11/2 (1972): 328–347.

Johnson, Reed. "A 'Saint' of last Resort." March 19, 2004. *Los Angeles Times*, E21.

Johnson, Reed. "A new direction south of the border." February 23, 2006. *Los Angeles Times*, E28.

Johnson, Reed. "Unreal Ordeal: A Simulation in Mexico Offers a Taste of Migration, Sans the Suffering." May 24, 2008. *Los Angeles Times*, A1.

Jones, Maggie. "Coming Out Illegal." October 24, 2010. *New York Times Magazine*, 37.

Jones, Maggie. "Our Town Could be Yours," July 15, 2012, *New York Times* Magazine, 34–39.

Jordan, Bill. *Tales of the Rio Grande*. El Paso: National Border Patrol Museum, 1995.

"Journalists Who Revealed Sheriff Arpaio's Activities Win Pulitzer Prize: Series Reveals Negative Impact of Local Police Taking on Immigration Enforcement." April 30, 2009. Immigration Policy Center. Available: http://www.immigrationpolicy.org/sites/default/files/docs/CongratsEValleyTribune4-20-09_2.pdf.

Kapchan, Deborah A., and Pauline T. Strong. "Theorizing the Hybrid." *The Journal of American Folklore* **112/445** (1999): 239–253.

Katzew, Ilona. *Casta Painting: Images of Race in Eighteenth-Century Mexico*. New Haven: Yale, 2004.

Katzew, Ilona, and Susan Deans-Smith. *Race and Classification: The Case of Mexican America*. Stanford: Stanford University Press, 2009.

Kearney, Milo and Anthony Knopp. *Boom and Bust: The Historical Cycles of Matamoros and Brownsville*. Austin: Eakin Press, 1991.

Kearney, Milo and Anthony Knopp. *Border Cuates: A History of the U.S.–Mexican Twin Cities*. Austin: Eakin Press, 1995.

Kelley, J. C. "The Aztalán Mercantile System: Mobile Traders and the Northwestward Expansion of Mesoamerican Civilization." In *Greater Mesoamerica: The Archaeology of West and Northwest Mexico*, eds. Michael S. Foster and Shirley Gorenstein, 137–154. Salt Lake City: The University of Utah Press, 2000.

Kelly, David. "Fight for Human Freight." December 14, 2003. *Los Angeles Times*, A1.

Kephart, Janice. "Secure Border Initiative Proves Itself Again." March 8, 2011. *Center for Immigration Studies*. Available: http://www.cis.org/kephart/SBInet-proves-itself-again. December 26, 2011.

Kephart, Janice. "USA Today Op-ed: Keep SBInet." January 26, 2011. *Center for Immigration Studies*. Available: http://www.cis.org/Kephart/USATodayOped. December 26, 2011.

Kerwin, Donald, and Doris Meissner. *DHS and Immigration: Taking Stock and Correcting Course*. Washington, DC: Migration Policy Institute, 2009.

Kessell, John L. *Spain in the Southwest*. Norman: University of Oklahoma Press, 2002.

Kitchens, John W. "Some Considerations on the Rurales of Porfirian Mexico." *Journal of Inter-American Studies* 9.3 (July 1967): 441–455.

Knight, Alan. *Mexico: From the Beginning to the Spanish Conquest*. Cambridge: Cambridge University Press, 2002.

Knight, Alan. *Mexico: The Colonial Era.* Cambridge: Cambridge University Press, 2002.

Kobach, Kris W. "Why Arizona Drew a Line." April 29, 2010. *New York Times*, A25.

Kohler, Timothy A., et al. "Simulating Ancient Societies." *Scientific American* (Jul. 2005): 77–84.

Kraul, Chris. "Illegal Immigrants Receive a One-Way Ticket to Mexico." July 13, 2004. *Los Angeles Times*, A1.

Kraul, Chris, Robert Lopez, and Rich Connell. "L.A. Violence Crosses the Line." May 15, 2005. *Los Angeles Times*, A28.

Kraul, Chris, and Sam Quinones. "Mexican Voting May Extend into U.S." June 29, 2005. *Los Angeles Times*, A1.

Krauze, Enrique. "The Mexican Evolution." March 24, 2009. *New York Times*, A25.

Krauze, Enrique. "In Mexico, a War Every Century." September 15, 2010. *New York Times*, A25.

Krauze, Enrique. "Can this poet save Mexico?" October 2, 2011. *New York Times*, SR-6.

Kun, Josh. "The New Border Aesthetic." January 18, 2004. *Los Angeles Times Magazine*, **18**, 20–34.

Kun, Josh. "Born in America, Heart in Mexico." July 20, 2008. *New York Times*, Music 20.

Kun, Josh. "Minstrels in the Court of the Kingpin." March 7, 2010. *New York Times*, 22.

Kun, Josh. "Master of a New Tijuana." March 9, 2011. *New York Times*, D6.

Kun, Josh. "Death Rattle." January 5, 2012. *The American Prospect.* Available: http://prospect.org/article/death-rattle. February 20, 2012.

Lacey, Marc. "For Some Taxi Drivers, A Different Kind of Traffic." March 2, 2009. *New York Times*, A10.

Lacey, Marc. "Justice Dept. Sues Sheriff Over Bias Investigation." September 31, 2010. *New York Times*, A11.

Lacey, Marc. "Lost at the Border." August 1, 2010. *New York Times*, 1.

Lacey, Marc. "National Briefing." August 31, 2010. *New York Times*, A14.

Lacey, Marc. "Taking Their Fight On Illegal Immigrants To The Arizona Border." August 16, 2010. *New York Times*, A9.

Lacey, Marc. "On Immigration, Birthright Right in U.S. is Looming: Citizenship is at Issue." January 5, 2011. *New York Times*, A1.

Lacey, Marc. "Citing 'Brainwashing,' Arizona Declares a Latino Class Illegal." January 8, 2011. *New York Times*, A1.

Lacey, Marc. "Injunction On Arizona is Upheld." April 12, 2011. *New York Times*, A12.

Lacey, Marc. "Immigration Law Backer Faces Recall." June 19, 2011. *New York Times*, A16.

Lacey, Marc. "In Echo of Pancho Villa: modern raid shakes town on the verge of extinction." August 26, 2011. *New York Times*, A14.

Lacey, Marc, and Elisabeth Malkin. "Mexican Arrested in Killing of U.S. Consular Employee." July 3, 2010. *New York Times*, A6.

Lacey, Marc, and Ginger Thompson. "Obama Says Immigration Changes Remain on his Agenda, but for 2010 Enactment." August 11, 2009. *New York Times*, A6.

Laglagaron, Laureen. *Protection through Integration: The Mexican Government's Effort to Aid Migrants in the United States*. Migration Policy Institute, National Center on Immigrant Integration Policy, 2010.

Lamar, Howard R. *The New Encyclopedia of the American West*. New Haven: Yale University Press, 1998.

Latin American Commission on Drugs and Democracy. "Drugs and Democracy: Toward a Paradigm Shift." Available: http://www.drogasedemocracia.org/Arquivos/ declaracao_ingles_site.pdf. October 24, 2011.

The Latinobarómetro Poll. "The discontents of progress." October 29, 2011. *The Economist*, 48.

Lavender, David. *De Soto, Coronado, Cabrillo: Explorers of the Northern Mystery*. Washington, DC: US Department of the Interior, 1992.

Lawson, Guy. "The Making of a Narco State." March 19, 2009. *Rolling Stone*, 59–65, 88.

Lawson, Guy. "The War Next Door: As Drug Cartels Battle the Government, Mexico Descends into Chaos." November 13, 2008. *Rolling Stone*, 75–111.

Laylander, Don. "Issues in Baja California Prehistory." In *The Prehistory of Baja California*, eds. D. Laylander and J. D. Moore, 1–13. Gainesville: University Press of Florida, 2006.

Laylander, Don. "Toward a More Complex Understanding of Baja California's Past." In *The Prehistory of Baja California*, eds. D. Laylander and J. D. Moore, 202–206. Gainesville: University Press of Florida, 2006.

Laylander, Don, and Jerry D. Moore, eds. *The Prehistory of Baja California: advances in the archeology of the forgotten peninsula*. Gainesville: University Press of Florida, 2006.

Leclerc, Gustavo, Michael Dear, and Raul Villa, eds. *Urban Latino Cultures: La vida latina en LA*. Thousand Oaks: Sage Publications, 1999.

Leclerc, Gustavo, and Michael Dear. "Introduction." In *Urban Latino Cultures—La vida latina en LA*, eds. Gustavo Leclerc, Michael Dear and Raul Villa, 1–6. Thousand Oaks: Sage Publications, 1999.

Leclerc, Gustavo, and Michael Dear. "Hitting Soft and Looking South/Golpes suaves cara al sur." In *Mixed Feelings/Sentimientos Contradictorios*, Exhibition Catalogue, 14–31. University of Southern California, Fisher Gallery, 2002.

Lekson, Stephen H. *A History of the Ancient Southwest*. Santa Fe: School for Advanced Research Press, 2008.

León-Portilla, Miguel. "Aztlan: From Myth to Reality." In *The Road to Aztlan: Art from a Mythic Homeland*, eds. Virginia M. Fields and Victor Zamudio-Taylor, 20–33. Los Angeles: Los Angeles County Museum of Art, 2001.

Lesley, Lewis B. "The International Boundary Survey from San Diego to the Gila River, 1849–50." *California Historical Society Quarterly* **4** (1930): 3–18.

Liptak, Adam. "Court splits immigration law verdicts." June 26, 2012. *New York Times*, A1, A13.

"List of countries by income equality." *Wikipedia*. Available: http://en.wikipedia.org/wiki/List_of_countries_by_income_equality. May 6, 2011.

Lister, Robert H. and Florence Lister. *Those Who Came Before*. Tucson: Southwest Parks and Monuments Association, 1983.

Lomnitz, Claudio. "Modes of Citizenship in Mexico." *Public Culture*, **11** (1999): 269–293.

Longmire, Sylvia. "Legalization Won't Kill The Cartels." June 19, 2011. *New York Times*, WK10.

López Austin, Alfredo and Leonardo López Luján. *Mexico's Indigenous Past*. Trans. Bernard R. Ortiz de Montellano. Norman: University of Oklahoma Press, 2001.

"Los Suns." May 8, 2010. *New York Times*, A18.

Lovato, Roberto. "Fear of A Brown Planet." June 28, 2004. *The Nation*, 278(25): 17–22.

Lowenthal, Abraham. *Global California: Rising to the Cosmopolitan Challenge*. Stanford: Stanford University Press, 2009.

Lucero Velasco, Héctor M. *Mexicali Cien Años*. México DF: Grupo Patria, 2002.

Lucero Velasco, Héctor M. "Peopling Baja California." In *Postborder City: Cultural Spaces of Bajalta California*, eds. Michael Dear and Gustavo Leclerc, 83–150. New York: Routledge, 2003.

Lyall, James D. "Vigilante State: Reframing the Minutemen Project in American Politics and Culture." *Georgetown Immigration Law Journal* **23** (2009): 257–291.

Lydersen, Kari. "Breaking the ICE Record." November 2008. *In These Times*, 8.

Lydgate, Joanna. "Assembly Line Justice: A Review of Operation Streamline." Policy Brief, UC Berkeley School of Law. January 2010. Available: http://www.law.berkeley.edu/files/Operation_Streamline_Policy_Brief.pdf. December 26, 2011.

Lynch, John. *Bourbon Spain 1700–1808*. Oxford: Oxford University Press, 1989.

Lyons, Claire L. and John M. D. Pohl. *The Aztec Pantheon and the Art of Empire*. Los Angeles: Getty Publications, 2010.

Maciel, David R. *El Norte: the U.S.–Mexican Border in Contemporary Cinema*. San Diego State University, Institute for Regional Studies of the Californias. 1990.

Magaña, Lisa. *Straddling the Border: Immigration Policy and the INS*. Austin: University of Texas Press, 2003.

Malkin, Elisabeth. "Mexicans Miss Money from Relatives Up North." October 26, 2007. *New York Times*, A1.

Malkin, Elisabeth, and Ginger Thompson. "In Mexico, Official Promises Do Little to Ease a Stricken City's Pain." March 17, 2010. *New York Times*, A6.

Mangan, Katherine. "Texas Colleges Argue That a Border Fence Would Divide a Community." December 7, 2007. *New York Times*, A24.

Mann, Charles C. *1491: New Revelations of the Americas before Columbus.* New York: Knopf, 2005.

Mann, Charles C. *1493: Uncovering the New World Columbus Created.* New York: Knopf, 2011.

Marosi, Richard. "Deported immigration activist is toast of Tijuana." August 22, 2007. *Los Angeles Times*, B9.

Marosi, Richard. "U.S. to extend border fence 300 feet into Pacific." November 25, 2011. *Los Angeles Times.* Available: http://articles.latimes.com/2011/nov/25/local/la-me-border-fence-20111124. December 5, 2011.

Marosi, Richard and John Meyer, J. "Border czar to try to repeat success." April 14, 2009. *Los Angeles Times*, 20.

Martínez, Maria E. *Genealogical Fictions: Limpieza de Sangre, Religion, and Gender in Colonial Mexico.* Stanford: Stanford University Press, 2008.

Martínez, Oscar J. *Troublesome Border.* Tucson: University of Arizona Press, 1988.

Martínez, Oscar J. "Surveying & Marking the U.S.–Mexico Boundary: The Mexican Perspective." In *Drawing the Borderline: Artist-Explorers of the U.S.-Mexico Boundary Survey*, ed. Dawn Hall, 13–22. Albuquerque: The Albuquerque Museum, 1997.

Martínez, Reuben. *Crossing Over: A Mexican Family on the Migrant Trail.* New York: Henry Holt and Company, 2001.

Martínez, Reuben. "Don't fence them in." October 17, 2007. *Los Angeles Times*, A17.

Martinez-Cabrera, Alejandro. "Calderon highlights successes in Juárez." May 21, 2011. *El Paso Times*, 1A.

Martinez-Cabrera, Alejandro. "Flight Brings Plight." May 23, 2011. *El Paso Times*, 1A.

Martinez-Cabrera, Alejandro. "Juárez to add 'heroic' to name." May 19, 2011. *El Paso Times*, 1A.

Massey, Douglas S., Jorge Durand and Nolan J. Malone. *Beyond Smoke and Mirrors: Immigration in an Era of Economic Integration.* New York: Russell Sage Foundation Publications, 2003.

Maugh II, Thomas H. "Earlier Traces of Cacao Use Found in Southwest." February 3, 2009. *Los Angeles Times*, A12.

Mazzetti, Mark and Ginger Thompson. "U.S. Drones Fly Deep in Mexico To Fight Drugs." March 16, 2011. *New York Times*, A1 and A12.

Mazzetti, Mark and Ginger Thompson. "U.S. Widens Role in Mexican Fight." August 26, 2011. *New York Times*, A1.

McCarthy, Cormac. *Blood Meridian.* New York: Vintage Books, 1985.

McCarthy, Cormac. *All the Pretty Horses.* New York: Vintage Books, 1992.

McCarthy, Cormac. *The Crossing.* New York: Vintage Books, 1994.

McCarthy, Cormac. *Cities of the Plain.* New York: Vintage Books, 1998.

McCawley, William. *The First Angelinos: The Gabrielino Indians of Los Angeles.* Banning: Malki Museum Press, 1996.

McCombs, Brady. "'Deadliest Migrant Trail in U.S.' Is Right on Tucson's Doorstep." *Arizona Daily Star*. December 9, 2007. Available: http://azstarnet.com/news/local/border/article_d536fd04–0718–56ad-af32-d3480b8b46a6.html. January 13, 2012.

McCombs, Brady. "O'odham Increasingly Drawn to Drug Smuggling for Money." *Arizona Daily Star*. July 12, 2009. Available: http://azstarnet.com/news/local/border/article_551d2f0d-939c-51dc-9275-b9e7f8406758.html. January 13, 2012.

McCombs, Brady. "$7.2M Added for AZ cops' Border Efforts." *Arizona Daily Star*. August 12, 2009. Available: http://mobile.azstarnet.com/site/more/915541/15. January 13, 2012.

McCombs, Brady. "No Sign of Letup in Border Deaths," *Arizona Daily Star*. December 27, 2009. Available: http://azstarnet.com/news/local/border/no-signs-of-letup-in-entrant-deaths/article_faf5b437-b728–527b-9eb8–77977d0cdf84.html

McCombs, Brady. "Pot Smugglers with Smaller Loads being Prosecuted Now." March 28, 2010. Online, Arizona Daily Star. Available: http://azstarnet.com/news/local/border/article_e85c410c-bc34–53b6–9f08-e8ac419984c9.html

McCombs, Brady. "US to Revisit Glitch-Prone 'Virtual Fence' Set for Border." January 13, 2010. *Arizona Daily Star*. Available: http://azstarnet.com/sn/printDS/325016.

McCombs, Brady, and Stephen Ceasar. "Border Program Has Vague Goals, Little Oversight." November 15, 2009. *Arizona Daily Star*. Available: http://azstarnet.com/news/local/border/border-program-has-vague-goals-little-oversight/article_1d28018f-800d-5610-a34d-d8a430c14192.html.

McDougall, Christopher. *Born to Run: A Hidden Tribe, Superathletes, and the Greatest Race the World Has Never Seen*. New York: Knopf, 2009.

McGuire, Randall H., Maria Elisa Villalpando C., Victoria D. Vargas, and Emiliano Gallaga M. "Cerro de Trincheras and the Casas Grandes World." In *The Casas Grandes World*, eds. Curtis F. Schaafsma and Carroll L. Riley. 134–146. Salt Lake City: The University of Utah Press, 1999.

McKeever, Michael. *A Short History of San Diego*. San Francisco: Léxicos, 1985.

McKinley, Jr., James C. "Napolitano Focuses on Immigration Enforcement, not Overhaul." August 12, 2009. *New York Times*, A11.

McKinley, Jr., James C. "San Francisco Changes When Police Must Report Immigrants." October 21, 2009. *New York Times*, A19.

McKinley, Jr., James C. "U.S. Stymied as Guns Flow to Mexican Cartels." April 15, 2009. *New York Times*, A1, A14.

McKinley, Jr., James C. "An Arizona Morgue Grows Crowded." July 29, 2010. *New York Times*, A14.

McKinley, Jr., James C. "Fleeing Extreme Drug Violence, Mexican Families Pour into U.S." April 18, 2010. *New York Times*, 1.

McKinley, Jr., James C. "On the Border, a Fishing Paradise Gains a Deadly Reputation." October 8, 2010. *New York Times*, A14.

McKinley, Jr., James C. "Killing of Missionary Rattles Texas Border." February 7, 2011. *New York Times*, A11.

McKinley, Jesse, and Malia Wollan. "New Border Fear: Violence by a Rogue Militia." June 27, 2009. *New York Times*, A1.

McMurtry, Larry. "Texas: The Death of the Natives." September 21, 2006. *The New York Review*, 63–65.

McMurtry, Larry. "Indian Terror on Our New Frontier." July 2, 2009. *The New York Review*, 51–52.

McWilliams, Carey. *North from Mexico: The Spanish-Speaking People of the United States*. New York: Praeger, 1990.

Medina, Jennifer. "The Sheriff of Tucson Expresses His Views." January 10, 2010. *New York Times*, A1.

Medina, Jennifer. "Economic Downturn Holds Fierce Grip on Border Town." March 17, 2011. *New York Times*, A20.

Meed, Douglas V. *Bloody Border: Riots, Battles and Adventures Along the Turbulent U.S.–Mexican Borderlands*. Tucson: Westernlore Press, 1992.

Meeks, Eric V. *Border Citizens: The Making of Indians, Mexicans, and Anglos in Arizona*. Austin: University of Texas Press, 2007.

Meighan, Clement W. "Prehistoric Rock Paintings in Baja California." *American Antiquity* **3.3.1** (1966): 372–392.

"Memo to Arizona Republicans: Papers, Please." April 15, 2011. *New York Times*, A20.

Memoria de la Sección Mexicana de la Comisión Internacional de Limites entre México y los Estados Unidos que restableció los monumentos de El Paso al Pacífico. New York: John Polhemus y compañia, 1901.

Mena, Jennifer. "A Great Familial Divide." June 23, 2004. *Los Angeles Times*, A14.

Menand, Louis. "Patriot Games." May 17, 2004. *The New Yorker*.

Mendelson, Margot, Shayna Strom, and Michael Wishnie. *Collateral Damage: An Examination of ICE's Fugitive Operations Program*. Washington, DC: Migration Policy Institute, 2009. Available: http://www.migrationpolicy.org/pubs/NFOP_Feb09.pdf.

Mendoza, Martha. "US businesses reluctant to open in Mexico." May 15, 2012, El Paso Times. Available: http://www.elpasotimes.com/juarez/cI_18068684.

Merry, Robert. *A Country of Vast Designs: James K. Polk, the Mexican War and the Conquest of the American Continent*. New York: Simon & Schuster, 2009.

Metz, Leon. *Border: The U.S.–Mexico Line*. Fort Worth: Texas Christian University Press, 2008.

"Mexico warns citizens, " Available: nytimes.com/gst/fullpage.html?res=9B01EEDC1 63BF93BA15757C0A9669D8B63&ref=harry_reid

Meyer, Josh. "Cartels snatch coyote trade." March 23, 2009. *Los Angeles Times*, A1.

Meyer, Lorenzo "Petroestado, narcoestado y estado fallido." August 20, 2009. *El Siglo de Durango*, 2.

Meyer, Michael C., William L. Sherman and Susan M. Deeds. *The Course of Mexican History*. New York: Oxford University Press, 1999.

Miranda, Carolina. "Fifteen Candles." July 19, 2004. *Time*, 70.

Monsiváis, Carlos. *Mexican Postcards*. Trans. John Kraniauskas. 1997. New York: Verso, 1997.

Montejano, David. *Anglos and Mexicans in the Making of Texas, 1836–1986*. Austin: University of Texas Press, 1987.

Moore, Alvin E. *Border Patrol*. Santa Fe: Sunstone Press, 1988.

Moore, Solomon. "Focus on Immigration Crimes is said to Overtax U.S. Prosecutors." January 12, 2009. *New York Times*, A1 and A15.

Moore, Solomon, and Hector Becerra. "House Crammed With Illegal Immigrants Raided in Watts." April 22, 2004. *Los Angeles Times*, A1.

Morales, Rebecca, and Jesús Tamayo-Sánchez. "Urbanization and Development of the United States–Mexico Border." In *Changing Boundaries in the Americas*, ed. Lawrence Herzog, 49–68. San Diego: Center for US–Mexican Studies, 1992.

"More Immigration Non-Solutions." July 13, 2009. *New York Times*, A16.

Morris, Stephen D. "Exploring Mexican Images of the United States." *Mexican Studies / Estudios Mexicanos* 16/1. Berkeley: University of California Press, (2000): 105–139.

Morris, Stephen D. *Gringolandia: Mexican Identity and Perceptions of the United States*. Lanham: Rowman & Littlefield Publishers, 2005.

Mraz, John. *Looking for Mexico: Modern Visual Culture and National Identity*. Durham and London: Duke University Press, 2009.

Mundy, Barbara E. *The Mapping of New Spain: Indigenous Cartography and the Maps of the Relaciones Geográficas*. Chicago: University of Chicago Press, 1996.

Murphy, Dean E. "New California Identity Predicted by Researchers." February 7, 2003. *New York Times*, A13.

Myers, Dowell. "Demographic Dynamism and Metropolitan Change: Comparing Los Angeles, New York, Chicago, and Washington DC." In *From Chicago to L.A.: Making Sense of Urban Theory*, ed. Michael J. Dear, 17–53 Thousand Oaks: Sage Publications, 2002.

Navalón, Antonio. "La Frontera." In *Tijuana, la tercera nación*, Editorial Santillana, 10–17 México D.F.: Editorial Santillana, 2005.

Nedderman, Leah, Ariel Dulitzky, and Denise Gilman. "Violations on the Part of the United States Government of the Right to Property and Non-Discrimination Held by Residents of the Texas Rio Grande Valley." Submission to the Inter-American Commission on Human Rights by The Working Group on Human Rights and the Border Wall. The Rapoport Center for Human Rights and Justice, University of Texas School of Law, University of Texas at Austin. June 2008.

Neiwert, David. "The Fence to Nowhere." October 2008. *The American Prospect*, 16–19.

Nevins, Joseph. "How High Must Operation Gatekeeper's Death Count Go?" November 16, 2000. *Los Angeles Times*, M2.

Nevins, Joseph. "The Remaking of the California–Mexico Boundary in the Age of NAFTA." In *The Wall around the West*, eds. Peter Andreas and Timothy Snyder, 99–114. Lanham: Rowman & Littlefield, 2000.

Nevins, Joseph. *Operation Gatekeeper: The Rise of the "Illegal Alien" and the Making of the U.S.–Mexico Boundary.* New York: Routledge, 2002.

Nevins, Joseph. "Security First: The Obama Administration and Immigration 'Reform.'" January 9, 2010. *ZNET.* Available: http://www.zcommunications.org/security-first-the-obama-administration-and-immigration-reform-by-joseph-nevins. December 26, 2011.

Nexos en línea, "Sueños y aspiraciones de l@s Mexican@s." México D.F., 2001.

Nieto, Enrique Peña. "Mexico's Next Chapter." July 3, 2012. *New York Times*, A19.

Noble, David G. *New Light on Chaco Canyon.* Santa Fe: School of American Research Press, 1984.

Noriega, Chon, ed. Special issue on "Border Crossings: Mexican and Chicano Cinema." *Spectator, University of Southern California, Journal of Film and Television Criticism,* **13(1)**, 1992, entire issue.

Norris, L. David, James C. Milligan, and Odie B. Faulk, *William H. Emory: Soldier–Scientist.* Tucson: University of Arizona Press, 1998.

Novaes, Lucas and Sinaia Urrusti Frenk. "Limited Independence, Limited Democracy." Spring–Summer 2010. *Berkeley Review of Latin American Studies,* 56–61.

Nuñez-Neto, Blas, and Yule Kim. "CRS Report for Congress, Border Security: Barriers Along the U.S. International Border." May 13, 2008. Available: http://opencrs.com/document/RL33659/.

Ochoa Palacio, Pedro. "Notas sobre el desarollo cultural de Tijuana." In *Extraño Nuevo Mundo: arte y diseño desde Tijuana / Strange New World: Art and Design from Tijuana*, ed. Rachel Reagle, ed., 236–245. San Diego: Museum of Contemporary Art San Diego, 2006.

Ohrt, Wallace. *Defiant Peacemaker: Nicholas Trist in the Mexican War.* College Station: Texas A&M University Press, 1997.

O'Neal, Bill. *The Arizona Rangers.* Austin: Eakin Press, 1987.

Olivo, Antonio. "Raid Leaves Town Worn, Torn." May 12, 2009. *Los Angeles Times*, A9.

"Operation Stonegarden Fact Sheet." February 2010. *National Immigration Forum.* Available: http://www.immigrationforum.org/images/uploads/2010/Operation Stonegarden FactSheet.pdf. December 26, 2011.

"Operation Streamline Fact Sheet." July 21, 2009. *National Immigration Forum.* American Civil Liberties Union. Available: http://www.immigrationforum.org/images/uploads/OperationStreamlineFactsheet.pdf. December 26, 2011.

Oppel, Jr., Richard A. "Arizona, Bowing to Business, Softens Stand on Immigration." March 19, 2011. *New York Times*, A1.

Ortiz-Gonzalez, Victor M. *El Paso: Local Frontiers at a Global Crossroads.* Minneapolis: University of Minnesota Press, 2004.

Osio, Antonio M. *The History of Alta California: A Memoir of Mexican California.* Madison: University of Wisconsin Press, 1996.

Pace, Robert F., and Frazier, Donald S. *Frontier Texas: History of a Borderland to 1880*. Abilene: State House Press, 2004.

Padgett, Tim, and Ioan Grillo. "Mexico's Meth Warriors." June 28, 2010. *TIME*, 30–33.

Palacio, Raymundo Riva. "Mission to Mexico." March 25, 2009. *Los Angeles Times*, A31.

Parker, Allison. "Locked Up Far Away: The Transfer of Immigrants to Remote Detention Centers in the United States." December 2, 2009. *Human Rights Watch*. Available: http://www.hrw.org/en/node/86760/section/14.

Parker, Allison and Brian Root. "Forced Apart (By the Numbers): Non-Citizens Deported Mostly for Non-Violent Offenses." April 15, 2009. *Human Rights Watch*. Available: http://www.hrw.org/en/reports/2009/04/15/forced-apart-numbers. December 26, 2011.

Parker, T. Jefferson. *Iron River*. New York: Dutton, 2010.

Pavlakovich-Kochi, Vera. " Cross-border Cooperation and Regional Responses to NAFTA and Globalization." In *The Ashgate Research Companion to Border Studies*, ed. Doris Wastl-Walter, 481–503. Farnham: Ashgate, 2011.

Payan, Tony. *The Three U.S.–Mexico Border Wars: Drugs, Immigration, and Homeland Security*. Westport: Praeger Security International, 2006.

Pedersen, Brian J. "O'odham hope to build prison near Sahuarita." *Arizona Daily Star*. April 18, 2009. Available: http://mobile.azstarnet.com/site/more/748573/460.

Perera, David. "DHS cancels SBInet." January 14, 2011. *Fierce Government IT*. Available: http://www.fiercegovernmentit.com/story/dhs-cancels-sbinet/2011-01-14. December 26, 2011.

Perkinson, Robert. "Drug of Choice." August 1, 2010. *New York Times Book Review*, 21.

Perlmann, Joel. *Italians Then, Mexicans Now: Immigrant Origins and Second-Generation Progress, 1690–2000*. New York: Russell Sage Foundation, 2005.

Phelan, Sarah. "Crossing the line." November 11–17, 2009. *The San Francisco Bay Guardian*, 45(06), 10.

Pitt, Leonard. *The Decline of the Californios: A Social History of the Spanish-Speaking Californians, 1846–1890*. Berkeley: University of California Press, 1998.

Pohl, John M. "Chichimecatlalli: Strategies for Cultural and Commercial Exchange Between Mexico and the American Southwest, 1100–1521." In *The Road to Aztlan: Art from a Mythic Homeland*, eds. Virginia M. Fields and Victor Zamudio-Taylor, 86–101. Los Angeles: Los Angeles County Museum of Art, 2001.

Pohl, John M., and Claire L. Lyons. *The Aztec Pantheon and the Art of Empire*. Los Angeles: Getty Publications, 2010.

Polaski, Sandra. "The Employment Consequences of NAFTA." Carnegie Endowment for International Peace. 2006. Available: http://finance.senate.gov/imo/media/doc/091106sptest.pdf. December 8, 2011.

Powell, Robert Andrew. "Team of Hope, Gone in City of Violence." April 10, 2012. *New York Times*, B11.

Pratten, David, and Atreyee Sen. *Global Vigilantes*. New York: Columbia University Press, 2008.

Preston, Caroline. "Carlos Slim Is Skeptical About Philanthropy." *The Chronicle of Philanthropy*. June 14, 2011. Available: http://philanthropy.com/blogs/the-give-away/carlos-slim-is-skeptical-about-philanthropys-potential/33. October 24, 2011.

Preston, Julia. "Officials Split on Viability of Border-Fence Project." February 29, 2008. *New York Times*, A20.

Preston, Julia. "Study Finds Immigration Courtrooms Backlogged." June 18, 2009. *New York Times*, A20.

Preston, Julia. "Staying Tough in Crackdown on Immigrants." August 4, 2009. *New York Times*, A1 and A14.

Preston, Julia. "Opposing Immigration Program." August 28, 2009. *New York Times*, A13.

Preston, Julia. "Immigrants Are Matched to Crimes." November 13, 2009. *New York Times*, A13.

Preston, Julia. "Democrats Reframe the Debate on Immigration." May 1, 2010. *New York Times*, A1.

Preston, Julia. "Fueled by Anger Over Arizona Law, Immigration Advocated Rally for Change." May 2, 2010. *New York Times*, 13.

Preston, Julia. "Latino Groups Urge Arizona Boycott Over Immigration Law." May 7, 2010. *New York Times*, A14.

Preston, Julia. "Former Manager of Kosher Slaughterhouse Is Acquitted of Labor Charges." June 8, 2010. *New York Times*, A13.

Preston, Julia. "27-Year Sentence for Slaughterhouse Manager in Financial Fraud Case." June 22, 2010. *New York Times*, A18.

Preston, Julia. "Illegal Workers Swept From Jobs in 'Silent Raids.'" July 10, 2010. *New York Times*, A1 and A12.

Preston, Julia. "Obama Signs Border Bill to Increase Surveillance." August 14, 2010. *New York Times*, A8.

Preston, Julia. "Immigration Agency Ends Some Deportations." August 27, 2010. *New York Times*, A14.

Preston, Julia. "After a False Dawn, Anxiety for Illegal Immigrant Students." February 9, 2011. *New York Times*, A15.

Preston, Julia. "In Test of Deportation Policy, 1 in 6 Get a Fresh Look and Reprieve." January 20, 2012. *New York Times*, A11.

Preston, Julia. "Mixed Reviews On Program For Immigrants With Records." April 7, 2012. *New York Times*, A10, A12.

Preston, Julia. "Despite Opposition, Immigration Agency to Expand Fingerprint Program." May 12, 2012. *New York Times*, A10.

Preston, Julia. "Justices' Decision A Narrow Opening For Other States." June 26, 2012. *New York Times*, A12.

Preston, Julia, and Samuel Dillon. *Opening Mexico: The Making of a Democracy*. New York: Farrar, Straus and Giroux, 2004.

Pringle, Heather. "The First Americans." *Scientific American*, **305**(5) (November 2011): 36–41.

Pullen, Doug. "Rubin Center exhibits look at border in very different ways." May 22, 2011. *El Paso Times*, 3F.

Rebert, Paula. "Mapping the United States–Mexico Boundary: Cooperation and Controversy." *Terrae Incognitae* **28** (1996): 58–71.

Rebert, Paula. *La Gran Línea: Mapping the United States–Mexico Boundary, 1849–1857*. Austin: University of Texas Press, 2001.

Rebert, Paula. "*Trabajos Desconocidos, Ingenieros Olvidados:* Unknown Works and Forgotten Engineers of the Mexican Boundary Commission." In *Mapping and Empire: Soldier-Engineers on the Southwestern Frontier*, eds. D. Reinhartz and G. Saxon, 156–184. Austin: University of Texas Press, 2005.

Rebert, Paula. "Views of the Borderlands: The Report on the United States and Mexican Boundary Survey, 1857–1859." *Terrae Incognitae* **37** (2005): 75–90.

Recinos, Adrian, Delia Goetz, and Sylvanus Morley. *Popul Vuh: The Sacred Book of the Ancient Quiché Maya*. Norman: University of Oklahoma Press, 1950.

Reséndez, Andrés. *Changing National Identities at the Frontier: Texas and New Mexico, 1800–1850*. Cambridge: Cambridge University Press, 2005.

Reséndez, Andrés. *A Land So Strange: The Epic Journey of Cabeza de Vaca*. New York: Basic Books, 2007.

Riccardi, Nicholas. "Sheriff riding out of town." October 13, 2008. *Los Angeles Times*, A8.

Richardson, Lisa, and Patrick McDonnell. "Immigration Crackdown Ineffective, Study Finds." July 17, 2002. *Los Angeles Times*, B8.

Rico, Johnny. "The Prisoner of Patriot Point." April 2008. *Penthouse*, 60–67.

Riding, Alan. *Distant Neighbors: A Portrait of the Mexicans*. New York: Knopf, 1984.

Rieger, Shannon. "Re-imagining Urban Structure in the Mexican Cities of the Mexican–American Border." Undergraduate thesis, University of California, Berkeley, 2012.

Ritter, Eric W. "South-Central Baja California," In *The Prehistory of Baja California*, eds. D. Laylander and J. D. Moore, 99–116. Gainesville: University Press of Florida, 2006.

Rivera Saldaña, Oscar. *Diccionario biográfico de la heroica Matamoros*. Matamoros: Librería Española, 2001.

Robbins, Ted. "'America's Toughest Sheriff' Takes on Immigration." April 1, 2008. National Public Radio.

Roberts, Crystal. "Turmoil in Hudspeth." May 22, 2011. *El Paso Times*, 1A.

Rodriguez, Gregory. *Mongrels, Bastards, Orphans, and vagabonds: Mexican Immigration and the Future of race in America*. New York: Pantheon Books, 2007

Rodriguez, Teresa and Diana Montané with Lisa Pulitzer. *The Daughters of Juárez*. New York: Atria Books, 2007.

Roebuck, Jeremy. "Mayors decry 'culture of fear' on border." *The Brownsville Herald*. March 9, 2009. Available: http://www.brownsvilleherald.com/news/border-95645-violence-mayor.html. January 13, 2012.

Rohter, Larry. "The Crisis Came. Mexico Didn't Fail. Surprised?" May 10, 2009. *New York Times*, WK3.

Romero, Simon. "Mexican Wealth Gives Texas City A New Vitality." June 14, 2003. *New York Times*, B1.

Romo, David D. *Ringside Seat to a Revolution: An underground cultural history of El Paso and Ciudad Juárez: 1893–1923*. El Paso: Cinco Punto Press, 2005.

Rotella, Sebastian. "Joint effort targets border crime." February 17, 2010. *Los Angeles Times*. Available: http://articles.latimes.com/2010/feb/17/nation/la-na-border18-2010feb18/2. December 26, 2011.

Rouse, Roger. "Mexican Migration and the Space of Postmodernism." In *Between Two Worlds: Mexican Immigrants in the United States*, ed. David G. Gutiérrez, 247–263. Wilmington: Jaguar Books, 1996.

Ruiz, Ramón Eduardo. *Mexico: Why a Few Are Rich and the People Poor*. Berkeley: University of California Press, 2010.

Salazar Ylarregiu, José. *Datos de los trabajos astronómicos y topográficos, dispuestos en forma de diario*. Mexico: Imprenta de Juan R. Navarro, 1850.

"Salvaging Immigration Detention." October 6, 2009. *New York Times*, A26.

Sánchez, George. *Becoming Mexican American*. New York: Oxford University Press, 1993.

Sánchez, Mario L., ed. *A Shared Experience: The History, Architecture and Historic Designations of the Lower Rio Grande Heritage Corridor*. Austin: Los Caminos Del Rio Heritage Project and the Texas Historical Commission, 1994.

Sánchez, Osvaldo, and Cecilia Garza, eds. *InSite 2000–2001/Fugitive Sites*. San Diego: Installation Gallery, 2002.

Sanders, William T., Jeffery R. Parson, and Robert S. Santley. *The Basin of Mexico: Ecological Processes in the Evolution of a Civilization*. New York: Academic Press, 1979.

Sanneh, Kelefa. "Raging Arizona: How a Border State Became a Battleground." May 28, 2012. *The New Yorker*, 28–37.

Santos, Fernanda. "Arizona Sheriff's Trial Begins With Focus on Complaints About Illegal Immigrants." July 20, 2012. *New York Times*, A11.

Sauer, Carl. *The Road to Cíbola, Ibero-Americana: 3*. Berkeley: University of California Press, 1932.

Sauer, Carl, and Donald Brand. *Aztatlán: Prehistoric Mexican Frontier on the Pacific Coast, Ibero-Americana: 1*. Berkeley, University of California Press, 1932.

Savage, Charlie. "New Reporting Rules on Multiple Sales of Guns Near Border." July 12, 2011. *New York Times*, A13.

Savage, Charlie. "N.R.A. Sues Over Rule That Arms Dealers at Mexico Border Report Bulk Rifle Sales." August 4, 2011. *New York Times*, A15.

Scarpinato, Daniel. "Problems of Border: The Focus Is Shifting." March 2, 2009. *Arizona Daily Star*. Available: http://azstarnet.com/news/local/govt-and-politics/problems-of-border-the-focus-is-shifting/article_12a93311–4ff4–541e-83ca-50eba907c128.html.

Schaafsma, Curtis F. and Carroll L. Riley. *The Casas Grandes World*. Salt Lake City: The University of Utah Press, 1999.

Schladen, Marty. "Mayor Lauds Development." May 19, 2011. *El Paso Times*, 1B.

Schmidt, Michael S. "Ballplayers Join Protest of New Law." May 1, 2010. *New York Times*, A9.

Schrag, Peter. "Blowback at the Border." May 4, 2009. *The Nation*, 288 (17): 23–24.

Schulz, George W. "Texas counties claiming exclusion from security grants cashed in." May 14, 2010. *Center for Investigative Reporting*. Available: http://centerfor-investigativereporting.org/blogpost/exascountiesclaimingexclusionfromsecuri-tygrantscashedin. December 26, 2011.

"Secure Communities." *National Immigration Forum*. Available: http://www.immigrationforum.org/images/uploads/Secure_Communities.pdf. December 26, 2011.

"Secure Communities: A Fact Sheet." November 4, 2010. *Immigration Policy Center*. Available: http://www.immigrationpolicy.org/just-facts/secure-communities-fact-sheet. December 26, 2011.

Seigenthaler, John. *James K. Polk*. New York: Henry Holt and Company, 2004.

Serrano, Richard A. "Delays, Failures Trip up High-Tech Border Fence." February 22, 2010. *Los Angeles Times*, A1 and A9.

Serrano, Richard A., and Sam Quinones. "No Longer 'Next Door.'" November 16, 2008. *Los Angeles Times*, A1, A30.

Shatz, Howard, and Luis-Felipe Lopez-Calva. "The Emerging Integration of the California–Mexico Economies." 2004. Public Policy Institute of California.

Sicilla, Javier. "Carta abierta a políticos y criminales" April 3, 2011. *Proceso*. Available: http://www.proceso.com.mx/?p=266990. October 24, 2011.

Simmons, Marc. *The Last Conquistador: Juan de Oñate and the Settling of the Far Southwest*. Norman: University of Oklahoma Press, 1991.

Simmons, Merle E. "Attitudes toward the United States Revealed in Mexican Corridos." *Hispania* **36.1** (1953): 34–42.

Sontag, Deborah. "Deported, by U.S. Hospitals." August 3, 2008. *New York Times*, 1 and 12.

Sorkin, Andrew R. "Dealbook; The Mystery of Jobs's Giving." *New York Times*. August 30, 2011. Available: http://dealbook.nytimes.com/2011/08/29/the-mystery-of-steve-jobss-public-giving/. October 24, 2011.

Spence, Michael W. "From Tzintzuntzan to Paquimé: Peers or Peripheries in Greater Mesoamerica?" In *Greater Mesoamerica: The Archaeology of West and Northwest Mexico*, eds. Michael S. Foster and Shirley Gorenstein, 255–261. Salt Lake City: The University of Utah Press, 2000.

Spicer, Edward H. *Cycles of Conquest: The Impact of Spain, Mexico, and the United States on the Indians of the Southwest, 1553–1960*. Tucson: University of Arizona Press, 1962.

St. John, Rachel. *Line in the Sand*. Princeton: Princeton University Press, 2011.

Stanish, Charles, and Abigail Levine. "War and Early State Formation in the northern Titica Basin, Peru." *Proceedings of the National Academy of Sciences* (June 23, 2011). Available: www.pnas.org/cgi/doi/10.1073/pnas.1110176108. December 6, 2011.

Stavans, Ilan. "The Gravitas of Spanglish." October 13, 2000. *The Chronicle of Higher Education*, B7.

Stavans, Ilan. *Spanglish: The Making of a New American Language*. New York: Rayo, 2003.

Stavans, Ilan, general editor. *The Norton Anthology of Latino Literature*. New York: W.W. Norton, 2011.

Stavans Ilan and Lalo Alcaraz. *Latino U.S.A.: A Cartoon History*. New York: Basic Books, 2000.

Steinberg, Nik. "The Monster and Monterrey," June 13, 2011. *The Nation*, 27–33.

Steinhauer, Jennifer. "A Harsh Spotlight on a State's Unique Politics." January 10, 2010. *New York Times*, A13.

Steller, Tim. "Disputes Splinter Border Watchers." August 30, 2009. *Arizona Daily Star*. Available: http://azstarnet.com/news/local/border/disputes-splinter-border-watchers/article_670e66ef-a0c2-50fc-a283-b3bf678cc210.html.

Stelzer, Andrew. "The Selma of Immigration Rights." November 2008. *In These Times*, 35–38.

Stephens, John L. *Incidents of Travel in Yucatán*. 2 Vols. 1843. Reprint, New York: Dover Publications, 1963.

Stephens, John L. *Incidents of Travel in Central America, Chiapas and Yucatán*. 2 Vols. 1854. Reprint, New York: Dover Publications, 1969.

Stevens, Jacqueline. "America's Secret ICE Castles." January 4, 2010. *The Nation*, 13.

Stevens, Jacqueline. "Lawless Courts." November 8, 2010. *The Nation*, 18.

Stoddard, Ellwyn. "Frontiers, Borders and Border Segmentation: Toward a Conceptual Clarification." *Journal of Borderlands Studies* **6/1**, (Spring 1990): 1–22.

Stuntz, William J. *The Collapse of American Criminal Justice*. Cambridge: Harvard University Press, 2011.

"Suenos y aspiraciones de las Mexicanas." *Nexos en línea*. February 1, 2011. Online: Available: http://www.nexos.com.mx/?P=leerarticulov2print&Article=2047019. February 25, 2011.

Suro, Roberto. "Breadwinners Who Know No Borders." November 10, 2003. *Los Angeles Times*, B11.

Talbot, Margaret. "The Lost Children." March 3, 2008. *The New Yorker*, 57.

Tamayo Perez, Luz María O., and José O. Moncada Maya. "José Salazar Ilarregui, 1832–1892." In *Geographers: Bibliographic Studies* 23, eds. Patrick H. Armstrong and Geoffrey J. Martin. New York: Continuum, 2004, 116–125.

Teagle, Rachel and Fernando Feliu-Moggi, eds. *Strange New World: Art and Design from Tijuana / Extraño Nuevo Mundo: Arte y diseño desde Tijuana*. La Jolla: Museum of Contemporary Art San Diego, 2006.

Tedlock, Dennis, trans. *Popol Vuh: The Mayan Book of the Dawn of Life*. New York: Simon & Schuster, 1985.

Templeton, Robin. "Baby Baiting." August 16–23, 2010. *The Nation*, 20.

"Testimony of Denise Dresser." United States Senate, Committee on the Judiciary. March 17, 2009. Available: http://www.judiciary.senate.gov/hearings/testimony. cfm?id=e655f9e28 09e5476862f735da1457041&wit_id=e655f9e2809e5476862f73 5da1457041-2-1 October 24, 2011.

"That's 8 Out of 457,000." August 25, 2008. *New York Times*, A20.

"The Constitution Trumps Arizona," July 7, 2010. *New York Times*, A20.

"The Failed States Index 2010." *Foreign Policy*. 2010. Available: http://www.foreign-policy.com/failedstates. May 6, 2011.

"The History of Charro Days." *75th Annual Charro Days Fiesta*. Available: http://www. charrodaysfiesta.com/media_11.htm. January 13, 2012.

"The Reach of Mexico's Drug Cartels." *New York Times*. March 29, 2009. Available: http://www.nytimes.com/interactive/2009/03/22/us/BORDER.htm. May 6, 2011.

Thompson, Ginger. "Littlest Immigrants, Left in Hands of Smugglers." November 3, 2003. *New York Times*, A1.

Thompson, Ginger. "Money Sent Home by Mexicans is Booming." October 28, 2003. *New York Times*, A12.

Thompson, Ginger. "'Tomato King' Seeks a New Title." July 5, 2005. *New York Times*, A4.

Thompson, Ginger. "A Shift to Make the Border Safe, From the Inside Out." April 6, 2009. *New York Times*, A12.

Thompson, Ginger. "U.S. Widens Its Role in Battle." August 7, 2011. *New York Times*, 7 Aug. 2011, 1.

Thrower, Norman J. W. "William H. Emory and the Mapping of the American Southwest Borderlands." *Terrae Incognitae* **22** (1990): 41–91.

Timmons, Wilbert H. *El Paso: A Borderlands History*. El Paso: Texas Western Press, 2004.

Tobar, Hector. "Mexico's immigrant sanctuary: The mayor of Ecatepec says those on their way north illegally are safe and welcome in his city." January 31, 2008. *Los Angeles Times*, A5.

Torres, Elías L. *Twenty Episodes in the Life of Pancho Villa*. Trans. Sheila M. Ohlendorf. Austin: Encino Press, 1973.

Torres, Rebecca M., and Janet D. Momsen. "Gringolandia: The Construction of a New Tourist Space in Mexico." *Annals, Association of American Geographers*, **95/2** (2005): 314–335.

TRAC. "Federal Criminal Enforcement and Staffing: How Do the Obama and Bush Administrations Compare?" February 2, 2011. TRAC, Syracuse University. Available: http://trac.syr.edu/tracreports/crim/245. December 26, 2011.

"U.S. Says Refineries Bought Oil Smuggled From Mexico." August 11, 2009. *New York Times*, B7.

Umali, Lenine. "The Devil to Pay: the relationship between Arizona and the CCA." Department of City and Regional Planning. University of California, Berkeley. 2010.

Uriarte, Maria T., ed. *Pre-Columbian Architecture in Mesoamerica.* Trans. T. Harrington. New York: Abbeville Press, 2010.

Uriarte, Maria T. and Ilán Vit Suzan. "The Central Altiplano." In *Pre-Columbian Architecture in Mesoamerica,* ed. M. T. Uriarte, ch. 5, 83–119. Trans. T. Harrington. New York: Abbeville Press, 2010.

Uribe, Ana B. *Mi México imaginado: Telenovelas, television y migrantes.* Tijuana: El Colegio de la Frontera Norte, 2009.

US Customs and Border Protection. "SBInet: Securing U.S. Borders." Available: http://www.dhs.gov/xlibrary/assets/sbinetfactsheet.pdf. December 26, 2011.

US Department of Health and Human Services. "Unaccompanied Children's Services." February 17, 2011. Administration for Children and Families. Available: http://www.acf.hhs.gov/programs/orr/programs/unaccompanied_alien_children.htm#press/08/UnaccompaniedAlienChildrenApr08.htm. December 26, 2011.

US Department of Homeland Security. "Fact Sheet: Secure Border Initiative." November 2, 2005. Available: http://www.dhs.gov/xnews/releases/press_release_0794.shtm. December 26, 2011.

US Department of Homeland Security. *An Assessment of United States Immigration and Customs Enforcement's Fugitive Operations Teams.* March 2007. Available: http://www.dhs.gov/xoig/assets/mgmtrpts/OIG_07-34_Mar07.pdf. December 26, 2011.

US Department of Homeland Security. "Fact Sheet: Southwest Border: The Way Ahead." April 15, 2009. Available: http://www.dhs.gov/ynews/releases/pr_1239821496723.shtm. December 26, 2011.

US Department of Homeland Security. "Communication Regarding Participation in Secure Communities." March 27, 2012.

US Department of Homeland Security. "Operations of United States Immigration and Customs Enforcement's Secure Communities." April 5, 2012.

US Department of Justice. "Unaccompanied Alien Children in Immigration Proceedings." April 22, 2008. Executive Office for Immigration Review. Available: http://www.justice.gov/eoir/

US Department of State, International Boundary Commission, United States and Mexico. "Placing of additional monuments to more perfectly mark the international boundary line through the town of Naco, Arizona–Sonora." 1900.

US Department of State, International Boundary Commission, United States and Mexico. "Placing of an Additional Monument to More Perfectly Mark the International Boundary Line through the Towns of Calexico, California, and Mexicali, Baja California." 1909.

US Department of State, International Boundary Commission, United States and Mexico. "Monumentation of the Railroad Bridges between Brownsville and Matamoros, and Laredo and Nuevo Laredo." 1910, 1912.

US Government Accountability Office. "SBInet Expenditure Plan Needs to Better Support Oversight and Accountability." February 2007. Available: http://www.gao.gov/new.items/d07309.pdf. December 26, 2011.

US Immigration and Customs Enforcement. "Fugitive Operations." Available: http://www.ice.gov/fugitive-operations/. December 26, 2011.

US Immigration and Customs Enforcement. "Delegation of Immigration Authority Section 287(g) Immigration and Nationality Act." Available: http://www.ice.gov/287g/. December 26, 2011.

US Immigration and Customs Enforcement. "Fact Sheet: Updated Facts on ICE's 287(g) Program." Available: http://www.ice.gov/news/library/factsheets/287g-reform.htm. December 26, 2011.

US International Boundary and Water Commission, United Sates and Mexico. *Report of the Boundary Commission upon the survey and re-marking of the boundary between the United States and Mexico west of the Rio Grande, 1891–1896.* Washington, DC: US Government Printing Office, 1898.

US International Boundary and Water Commission, United Sates and Mexico. Report of the Boundary Commission upon the survey and re-marking of the boundary between the United States and Mexico west of the Rio Grande, 1891–1896. ALBUM. Washington D.C.: US Government Printing Office, 1898.

Utley, Robert M. *Changing Course: The International Boundary, United States and Mexico, 1848–1963.* Tucson: Southwest Parks and Management Association, 1996.

Valdez, Diana W. "$400M Development Planned for Area around San Agustin." May 23, 2011. *El Paso Times*, 1A.

Valenzuela, José M. *Paso del Norte: This is Tijuana!.* México D.F.: Trilce Ediciones, 2004.

Valenzuela, José M. "Tijuana, ¿la tercera nación?… pastiches y palimpsestos," In *Tijuana, la tercera nación*, Editorial Santillana, 18–25 México D.F.: Editorial Santillana, 2005.

Vanderpool, Tim. "Border Brush." April 24, 2008. *Tucson Weekly*. Available: http://www.tucsonweekly.com/tucson/border-brush/Content?oid=1091112. January 13, 2012.

Vanderpool, Tim. "Eye of the Storm." May 14, 2009. *Tucson Weekly*. Available: http://www.tucsonweekly.com/tucson/eye-of-the-storm/Content?oid=1184712. January 13, 2012.

Vanderpool, Tim. "The Activist Question." July 9, 2009. *Tucson Weekly*. Available: http://www.tucsonweekly.com/tucson/the-activist-question/Content?oid=1230781. January 13, 2012.

Vanderwood, Paul J. "Genesis of the Rurales: Mexico's Early Struggle for Public Security." *The Hispanic American Historical Review* **50.2** (May 1970): 323–344.

Vanderwood, Paul J. "Los Rurales: Producto de una necesidad social." *Historia Mexicana* **22.1** (Jul.–Sep. 1972): 34–51.

Vanderwood, Paul J. "Mexico's Rurales: Reputation versus Reality." *The Americas* **34.1** (Jul. 1977): 102–112.

Vanderwood, Paul J. "Mexico's Rurales: Image of a Society in Transition." *Hispanic American Historical Review* **61.1** (Feb. 1981): 52–83.

Vanderwood, Paul J. *Disorder and Progress: Bandits, Police, and Mexican Development.* Lanham: SR Books, 1992.

Vargas, Jose A. "Outlaw: My life in America as an undocumented immigrant." June 26, 2011. *New York Times Magazine*, 22.

Vaughan, Jessica. "New Report: 287(g) Works." February 1, 2011. *Center for Immigration Studies.* Available: http://www.cis.org/vaughan/287g-works. December 26, 2011.

Velasco Ortiz, Laura. *Mixtec Transnational Identity.* Tucson: The University of Arizona Press, 2005.

Vila, Pablo. *Crossing Borders, Reinforcing Borders: Social Categories, Metaphors, and Narrative Identities on the U.S.–Mexico Frontier.* Austin: University of Texas Press, 2000.

Vila, Pablo, ed. *Ethnography at the Border.* Minneapolis: University of Minnesota Press, 2003.

Vila, Pablo. *Border Identification: Narratives of Religion, Gender, and Class on the US–Mexico Border.* Austin: University of Texas Press, 2005.

"Villa Invades the U.S.: Bandits Burn and Kill in Columbus." March 9, 1916. *Santa Fe New Mexican.* Facsimile.

Villalpando, Maria E. "The Archaeological Traditions of Sonora." In *Greater Mesoamerica: The Archaeology of West and Northwest Mexico*, eds. Michael S. Foster and Shirley Gorenstein, 241–254. Salt Lake City: The University of Utah Press, 2000.

Vistas de los monumentos, a lo largo de la línea divisoria entre México y los Estados Unidos de El Pase al Pacífico. New York: John Polhemus y compañia, 1901.

Vulliamy, Ed. *Amexica: War Along the Borderline.* New York: FSG, 2010.

Vulliamy. "As Juárez Falls." December 27, 2010. *The Nation*, 39–44.

Wald, Elijah. *Narcocorrido: A Journey into the Music of Drugs, Guns, and Guerrillas.* New York: Harper Collins Publishers, 2001.

Waldinger, Roger, and Mehdi Bozrgmehr, eds. *Ethnic Los Angeles.* New York: Russell Sage Foundation, 1996.

Walker, Margath A. "The Cultural Economy of a Border Renaissance: Politics and Practices in the City." *Space and Polity* **11/2** (2007): 185–200.

Warnock, John. The Other Mexico: The North American Triangle Completed. Montreal: Black Rose Books, 1995.

Waters, Michael R. et al. "The Buttermilk Creek Complex and the Origins of Clovis at the Debra L. Friedkin Site, Texas." *Science,* **331** (25 Mar. 2011): 1599–1603.

Weber, David J. *The Spanish Frontier in North America.* New Haven: Yale University Press, 1992.

Weber, David J., ed. *Foreigners in their Native Land: Historical Roots of the Mexican Americans.* Albuquerque: University of New Mexico Press, 2003.

Weber, David J. *Barbaros: Spaniards and Their Savages in the Age of Enlightenment.* New Haven: Yale University Press, 2005.

"Who's Running Immigration?" March 4, 2009. *New York Times*, A20.

Weigand, Phil C., and Acelia García de Weigand. "A Macroeconomic Study of the Relationships Between the Ancient Cultures of the American Southwest and Mesoamerica." In *The Road to Aztlan: Art from a Mythic Homeland*, eds. Virginia M. Fields and Victor Zamudio-Taylor, 184–195. Los Angeles: Los Angeles County Museum of Art, 2001.

Weiner, Tim. "Border Custom Agents Are Pushed to the Limit." July 25, 2002. *New York Times*, A14.

Weiner, Tim. "McTaco vs. Fried Crickets: A Duel in the Oaxaca Sun." August 24, 2002. *New York Times*, A2.

Weiner, Tim. "Water Crisis Grows Into a Test of U.S.–Mexico Relations." May 24, 2002. *New York Times*, A3.

Weiner, Tim. "Americans Stake Claims in a Baja Land Rush." November 16, 2003. *New York Times*, A1.

Weiner, Tim. "Of Gringos and Old Grudges: This Land is Their Land." January 9, 2004. *New York Times*, A4.

Werne, Joseph R. "Major Emory and Captain Jiménez: Running the Gadsden Line." *Journal of the Southwest* **29/2** (1987): 203–221.

Werne, Joseph R. *The Imaginary Line: A History of the United States and Mexican Boundary Survey, 1848–1857*. Fort Worth: Texas Christian University Press, 2007.

Whalen, Michael E. and Paul E. Minnis. *Casas Grandes and its Hinterland: Prehistoric Regional Organization in Northwest Mexico*. Tucson: The University of Arizona Press, 2001.

Wheat, Carl I. *Mapping the Transmississippi West, 1540–1861*. vol. 3, *From the Mexican War to the Boundary Surveys, 1846–1854*. San Francisco: Institute of Historical Cartography, 1959.

White, Richard. "Race Relations in the American West." *American Quarterly* **38.3** (1986): 396–416.

Wilford, John N. "Stone Said to Contain Earliest Writing in Western Hemisphere." September 15, 2006. *New York Times*, A8.

Wilford, John N. "Arrowheads Found in Texas Dial Back Arrival of Humans in America." March 25, 2011. *New York Times*, A14.

Wilson, Janet and Sandra Murillo. "Inland Latinos Alarmed by New Border Patrol Sweeps." June 10, 2004. *Los Angeles Times*, A1.

Wilson, Janet, H.G. Reza and Sandra Murillo. "Immigration Arrests Not Policy Shift." June 11, 2004. *Los Angeles Times*, B1.

Wilson, Jeff G. et al. "An analysis of demographic disparities associated with the proposed U.S.–Mexico border fence in Cameron County, Texas." Submission to the Inter-American Commission on Human Rights by The Working Group on Human Rights and the Border Wall. The Rapoport Center for Human Rights and Justice, University of Texas School of Law, University of Texas at Austin. June 2008.

Wise, Carol, ed. *The Post-NAFTA Political Economy: Mexico and the Western Hemisphere*. University Park: Penn State University Press, 1998.

Witt, Howard. "Immigration debate a new symptom." April 30, 2009. *Los Angeles Times*, A21.

Witz, Billy. "'Los Suns' Join Protest of Arizona's New Law." May 6, 2010. *New York Times*, B13.

Wood, Gordon S. *The American Revolution: A History*. New York: Modern Library, 2002.

Wood, Stephanie. *Transcending Conquest: Nahua Views of the Colonial Conquest*. Norman: University of Oklahoma Press. 2003.

Wood, Tony. "Silver and Lead." July–August 2011. *New Left Review*, 70, 127–138.

Wright, Lawrence. "Slim's Time." June 1, 2009. *The New Yorker*, 52–67.

Yardley, Jim. "A River That United Lives Is Now A Barrier." August 1, 2004. *New York Times*, A12.

Ybarra-Frausto, Tomás. "El Movimiento: The Chicano Cultural Project since the 1960s /Interview by Michael Dear." In *Urban Latino Cultures: La vida latina en LA*, eds. Gustavo Leclerc, Raúl Villa and Michael Dear, 23–34. Thousand Oaks: Sage Publications, 1999.

Zabludovsky, Karla. "Slivers of Hope Amid the Melancholy in a Mexican Border Town." May 10, 2012. *New York Times*, A7.

Zeller, Tom. "Migrants Take Their Chances on a Harsh Path of Hope." March 18, 2001. *New York Times*, 14.

Zorrilla, Luis G. *Monumentación de la frontera norte en el siglo XIX*. México D.F.: Secretaría de Relaciones Exteriores, 1981.

Zucchino, David. "Immigration Arrests Roil Small Town." August 24, 2008. *Los Angeles Times*, A18.

Zúñiga, Victor and Ruben Hernández-León, eds. *New Destinations: Mexican Immigration in the United States*. New York: Russell Sage Foundation, 2006.

Index